P9-ARG-179

THE ORIGINS OF DETENTE

*The Genoa Conference and Soviet–Western
Relations, 1921–1922*

SOVIET AND EAST EUROPEAN STUDIES

Editorial Board

JULIAN COOPER, RON HILL,
MICHAEL KASER, PAUL LEWIS,
MARTIN McCAULEY, FRED SINGLETON, STEPHEN WHITE

The National Association for Soviet and East European Studies exists for the purpose of promoting study and research on the social sciences as they relate to the Soviet Union and the countries of Eastern Europe. The Monograph Series is intended to promote the publication of works presenting substantial and original research in the economics, politics, sociology and modern history of the USSR and Eastern Europe.

SOVIET AND EAST EUROPEAN STUDIES

THE ORIGINS OF DETENTE

The Genoa Conference and Soviet–Western Relations, 1921–1922

STEPHEN WHITE

Department of Politics, University of Glasgow

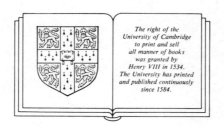

The right of the
University of Cambridge
to print and sell
all manner of books
was granted by
Henry VIII in 1534.
The University has printed
and published continuously
since 1584.

CAMBRIDGE UNIVERSITY PRESS

CAMBRIDGE

LONDON   NEW YORK   NEW ROCHELLE
MELBOURNE   SYDNEY

378852

Published by the Press Syndicate of the University of Cambridge
The Pitt Building, Trumpington Street, Cambridge CB2 1RP
32 East 57th Street, New York, NY 10022, USA
10 Stamford Road, Oakleigh, Melbourne 3166, Australia

© Cambridge University Press 1985

First published 1985

Printed in Great Britain at the University Press, Cambridge

British Library cataloguing in publication data
White, Stephen, 1945–
The origins of detente: the Genoa Conference and Soviet–Western
relations, 1921–1922. – (Soviet and East European Studies)
1. Detente   2. Soviet Union – Foreign relations – 1917–1945
I. Title   II. series
327.470171′3   JX1393.D46

Library of Congress cataloguing in publication data
White, Stephen, 1945–
The origins of detente.
(Soviet and East European studies)
Bibliography: p.
Includes index.
1. Genoa Conference (1922). 2. Reconstruction (1914–1939).
3. Europe – Politics and government – 1918–1945. 4. Soviet Union –
Foreign relations – 1917–1945. 5. Detente. I. Title. II. Series.
D727.W48   1986   940.5′1   85–12749

ISBN 0 521 30876 3

CE

Contents

Preface

The Genoa Conference of April–May 1922 was the largest and most representative international gathering that had taken place since the Paris Peace Conference, and in some respects since the Congress of Vienna or even earlier. The British prime minister, David Lloyd George, called it the 'greatest gathering of European nations which has ever been assembled'; the *Manchester Guardian*, more cautiously, described it as the 'largest since the Crusades'. It met to consider the economic reconstruction of the continent of Europe after the devastation of the First World War; and it was particularly concerned to re-establish a mutually advantageous relationship between the major western powers and the Soviet government in Moscow, where a revolution had brought the Bolsheviks to power five years earlier. Some thirty-four nations took part in the conference's deliberations, and no fewer than forty-two prime ministers were in attendance; it met for a month and a half, consuming five carriage-loads of duplicating paper in an attempt to deal with a set of issues that have remained at the centre of international affairs from that time up to the present. An early example of 'instant history', J. Saxon Mills's *The Genoa Conference*, appeared a few months after the conference had concluded, and subsequent scholarship has devoted considerable attention to various aspects of the diplomatic history of this period, particularly the relations between the Soviet Union and individual western powers. No modern study, however, has attempted to deal with the international diplomacy of this period as a whole, at least so far as the development of Soviet–Western relations is concerned;[1] the

[1] This deficiency is remarked upon by Sally Marks, *The Illusion of Peace: International Relations in Europe 1918–1933* (London 1976), p. 165 n.22, and in respect of the Soviet literature by A. O. Chubar'yan, *V. I. Lenin i formirovanie sovetskoi vneshnei politiki* (Moscow 1972), p. 10. Carole Fink's impressive *The Genoa Conference* (Chapel Hill,

Preface

present study is intended both to repair that deficiency and more generally to provide the basis for a re-examination of a period of history in which Soviet–Western relations arguably acquired their modern form.

The relative neglect of the Genoa Conference is presumably attributable, at least in part, to the fact that its immediate results were limited if not entirely negligible. The conventional verdict that the conference simply 'failed', however, is I believe a simplistic and unduly hasty one. Measured against the imposing tasks by which it was confronted, certainly, it would be difficult to argue that the conference achieved a great deal of practical significance. Those tasks, however, were of unprecedented scope and complexity: no less than the reconstruction of the international economic order, the establishment of a secure peace and the negotiation of a viable basis for future Soviet–Western relations. It would be difficult to argue that subsequent generations of diplomats have grappled with these problems with a significantly greater degree of success. More generally, the conference provided an occasion for the first sustained attempt to regenerate the European economy by joint political action, a development of some intrinsic importance with many lessons for our own time; it was the first conference to bring together the defeated belligerents of the First World War and the victorious Allied powers upon a footing of formal equality; and above all, from the point of view of this study, it was the first major international conference at which the newly formed Soviet government was in attendance and at which the first serious attempt was made to construct a more stable and satisfactory basis for East–West relations in the future. The attempt to find a Soviet–Western *modus vivendi* provides both the focus and the title of this study, and in the final chapter it has prompted some observations about the place of the conference within the evolution of East–West relations in general as well as an assessment of the achievements and significance of the conference itself.

This study is based for the most part upon public archival sources, particularly the archives of governments and foreign ministries, supplemented by the private papers of individual statesmen, published documentary collections, parliamentary proceedings, the

N.C. 1984), which was published after this study had been completed, deals extensively with the European diplomatic background but is less directly concerned with the development of Soviet–Western relations, which is the primary focus of the present study. Details of other secondary works consulted may be found in the bibliography.

contemporary press and other sources. On the western side the relevant archival collections were consulted in Great Britain, where the holdings of the Public Record Office at Kew are both extremely full and well catalogued; in France, where the holdings of the Ministère des Affaires Étrangères, although seriously damaged during the Second World War, were of the greatest importance; and in Italy, particularly the voluminous but still incompletely catalogued holdings of the Archivio Storico Diplomatico at the Ministero degli Affari Esteri in Rome. The corresponding but less substantial archives of the Belgian and Dutch foreign ministries were also examined, in Brussels and The Hague respectively. In Germany, the foreign ministry archives at the Politisches Archiv of the Auswärtiges Amt in Bonn were consulted, together with government records in the Bundesarchiv in Koblenz; and in the United States, which was involved in the pre-conference diplomacy although not represented at Genoa as such, the relevant records in the Diplomatic Branch of the National Archives at Washington DC were examined. Japan, although one of the five 'inviting powers', played a marginal role at the conference and no attempt appeared necessary to trace the development of policy by that power beyond memoir and secondary sources. On the whole the western archives, despite occasional gaps due to war damage or other causes, are fully open to scholars for the period in question and provide a detailed picture of the development of policies by the governments concerned over the same period.

So far as Soviet sources are concerned the position is a good deal less straightforward. Within the USSR itself no public or private archives of a kind relevant to this study are made available to western (or even to all but a very few Soviet) researchers. There is, on the other hand, a very extensive range of documentary sources in existence, including not only the official foreign policy documents series *Dokumenty vneshnei politiki SSSR* but also related collections of documents on Soviet–German, Soviet–Polish and Soviet–Czechoslovak relations as well as the records of bodies such as the presidium of Gosplan (the State Planning Committee), all of which contain a good deal of previously unpublished primary material relating to this period. The proceedings of party and state bodies, which at this time still permitted an element of genuine debate, contained much of interest, as did the contemporary press and the extensive memoir and ephemeral literature. These sources may be supplemented by archives of Soviet origin available in the West, such as the Krasin and

Trotsky papers and Chicherin's correspondence with Louis Fischer, and by the contemporary emigre press, which was unusually extensive during this period and frequently in sufficiently close touch with developments in Moscow to allow party and state officials to discuss policy options, in interviews or elsewhere, in fuller and franker form than would have been possible at the same time within the USSR itself. Western archives also contain occasional items of interest obtained by their intelligence services, such as intercepted telegrams between the Soviet delegation at Genoa and the political leadership in Moscow, although obviously uncorroborated sources of this kind must be used with particular care. Taking all these sources together, a picture of Soviet policy-making during this period may be composed which, if not in every respect beyond dispute, is nonetheless considerably fuller and much richer than any that is available for Soviet interactions with the western powers at perhaps any other period.

The study that follows, which is basically chronological in approach, reflects my debts to a variety of individuals and institutions. My first and most immediate debt is to the supervisor at Oxford of the thesis on which this work is based, Richard Kindersley, and to Archie Brown, who deputised for him for two terms, for their close and sympathetic interest in my progress. Elsewhere in Oxford, Jonathan Wright and Hartmut Pogge von Strandmann were kind enough to advise me on the German aspects of my work, and Denis Mack Smith and Alan Cassels (on leave from McMaster University) were very helpful in regard to Italy. Wolfson College, through Dr Cranstoun, made a number of contributions towards my research expenses within the United Kingdom, and the University's Committee for Graduate Studies made a contribution towards my expenses in Belgium and the Netherlands. The Social Science Research Council, through its exchange agreement with the CNRS, made possible a month's research in Paris, and the Carnegie Trust for the Universities of Scotland financed my research in Italy and Germany. At Glasgow, my greatest debts are to Bill Wallace and James Kellas, for their continuing interest and support, and to the University itself, for financial assistance which made possible my visits to Sweden (to consult Soviet and emigre newspapers at Uppsala) and to the United States. The British Academy made possible a month's visit to the Institute of History of the USSR Academy of Sciences, where Dr Vilnis Sipols, director of the department of the history of Soviet foreign policy, received me with the greatest courtesy and did everything possible to ensure that my visit was academically productive. Christopher Barnes, Douglas Johnson and Ian Brownlie very kindly answered specific queries. The departmental secretaries at Glasgow, Barbara Fisher, Avril Johnstone and Elspeth Shaw, coped with my various drafts with skill, efficiency and good humour. My greatest debt is once again to my wife Ishbel, without whose support this study could not have been undertaken and without whom it would not have been worthwhile to attempt to do so.

Glasgow   S.L.W.

Abbreviations

ACS	Archivio Centrale dello Stato, Rome
AN	Archives Nationales, Paris
ASD	Archivio storico diplomatico, Ministero degli Affari Esteri, Rome
BFM	Belgian foreign ministry archives, Brussels
Cab	Cabinet papers in the Public Record Office, London
DBFP	*Documents on British Foreign Policy, 1919–1939*, ed. E. L. Woodward and Rohan Butler, 1st ser., vols. 1– (London 1947–)
DVP	*Dokumenty vneshnei politiki SSSR*, ed. A. A. Gromyko et al., vols. 1– (Moscow 1957–)
FO	Foreign Office papers in the Public Record Office, London
FRUS	*Papers relating to the Foreign Relations of the United States, 1918–* (Washington DC 1931–)
FRUS: PPC	*Papers relating to the Foreign Relations of the United States: The Paris Peace Conference, 1919*, 13 vols. (Washington DC 1942–7)
M.	Moscow
MAE	Ministère des Affaires Étrangères archives, Paris
PA	Politisches Archiv des Auswärtiges Amtes, Bonn
PSS	V. I. Lenin, *Polnoe sobranie sochinenii*, 55 vols. (Moscow 1958–65)
SGO	*Sovetsko-germanskie otnosheniya ot peregovorov v Brest–Litovske do podpisaniya Rapall'skogo dogovora. Sbornik dokumentov*, ed. S. Dërnberg et al., 2 vols. (Moscow 1968–71)
SGO 1922–25	*Sovetsko-germanskie otnosheniya 1922–25 gg. Dokumenty i*

materialy, ed. S. Dërnberg et al., 2 vols. (Moscow 1977)

USNA   National Archives of the United States, Washington DC.

Technical note

The system of transliteration from Russian employed by this study is based upon that of the journal *Soviet Studies*, except where other forms have become familiar in English (thus Zinoviev rather than Zinov′ev, Moscow rather than Moskva). 'Russian' and 'Soviet' have been used almost interchangeably, as in the contemporary sources, although the RSFSR did not formally become part of a federal Soviet state until December 1922; similarly the wartime term 'Allies' has sometimes been used to describe the post-war 'Entente' powers, both to avoid reputation and to reflect contemporary usage. In 1914, one U.S. dollar was worth approximately 1.94 roubles, and one pound sterling was worth approximately 9.46 roubles.

I

Europe and Russia after the war

The Genoa Conference of April–May 1922 was the twentieth in a series of inter-Allied gatherings which took place after the end of the First World War and which has subsequently become known to historians as the period of 'conference diplomacy'.[1] The meetings generally took place in Mediterranean seaside resorts – the French prime minister, Raymond Poincaré, dubbed them 'la politique des casinos'[2] – and they generally dealt with matters that the Versailles peace settlement had left unresolved, or in which subsequent complications had occurred. Gatherings of diplomats to rearrange the international system in this way had of course taken place before, most obviously during the Congress of Vienna and the 'Congress system' of 1815–22, and precedents could be found in the Treaty of Westphalia of 1648 and perhaps earlier.[3] Traditional in its form, the Genoa Conference was at the same time a gathering whose proceedings had a distinctively modern tone. Its leading figures were politicians, rather than career diplomats, and its proceedings concerned the reconstruction of the European economy, rather than traditional matters such as the settlement of the terms of peace and the renegotiation of state boundaries. Above all, from the point of view of this study, it was the first conference at which political leaders from both East and West met together and attempted to resolve the nature of the relationship between them, a relationship which has lain at the centre of international politics from the October revolution of 1917 up to the present.

The need for European reconstruction was certainly not in doubt, for the war just concluded had left the continent devastated. Population losses, for instance, are estimated to have amounted to between 22 and 24 million, adding together military and civilian deaths as well as births that failed to take place because of wartime conditions. This was equivalent to some 7 per cent of the population of the continent before the war had begun. A further 7 million were disabled and 15 million were seriously wounded.[4] War losses and injuries affected the combatant nations more than the non-combatants, and some of the combatant nations were affected more severely than others. Germany, France and Russia all lost between 1 and 2 million of their respective populations in military casualties alone; France, in particular, lost some 3.3 per cent of her population and, because losses were disproportionately concentrated among adult males of working age, about 10 per cent of her total workforce. The war was followed by an influenza epidemic which took more lives – an estimated 20 million – than all the wartime hostilities had done, and left a weakened population susceptible to further outbreaks. Apart from this, there were further losses of population due to famine in eastern Europe and the Balkans, and due to border conflicts and pogroms, particularly in south-eastern Europe. Total population losses over the period 1914–21 may have amounted to as much as 50 to 60 million; military casualties alone were more than twice as great as all those that had been suffered over the previous century put together.[5]

Losses of productive potential had also been enormous. About one-thirtieth of income-yielding property is estimated to have been destroyed by the war, together with about the same proportion of fixed assets such as roads, railways and housing. There were further losses of foreign investments and losses of property and territory, particularly for the defeated nations under the terms of the peace treaties. Again, the incidence of destruction and loss varied considerably from country to country. The neutral nations were almost entirely unaffected; some belligerent countries suffered relatively little; but in the main theatres of war, particularly in France and Belgium, damage was very substantial indeed. In Belgium, for instance, about 6 per cent of the total housing stock was destroyed or damaged beyond repair, together with half of the steel mills and three-quarters of the railway rolling stock, and thousands of acres of agricultural land were rendered unfit for cultivation. In France the severest losses were in the north-east of the country, the richest and most advanced area before the war. In 1919 these areas produced no more than 34 per cent of what they had produced in 1913, and total French losses were estimated to have amounted to about fifteen months' pre-war national income or about eleven years' investment.[6] The loss of productive potential in some other countries was even greater: Poland, for instance, was devastated, and Serbia, Austria and some other areas also suffered heavily. Germany suffered less material damage but most of her foreign assets were sold or seized, and Britain lost much of her shipping and a substantial proportion of her overseas investments.[7]

The financial consequences of the war were equally serious. The war had for the most part been financed by borrowing, rather than by taxation, and much of the borrowing represented bank credit rather than savings or other assets. On average 80 per cent of the total war expenditure of the belligerents had been raised in this way, and in Germany and France almost the entire total. The outcome was that public debts rose rapidly in all countries, short-term debts rose still more rapidly, the money supply increased considerably, and the banks' metallic reserves in relation to liabilities fell sharply.[8] Nearly all the European countries were forced to abandon fixed parities against gold for their currencies, and prices rose rapidly. Most countries experienced a doubling or trebling of prices over the course of the war; wholesale prices in Germany at the end of the war were in fact five times higher than their pre-war level, and the mark had declined to half of its former value. Austria and Hungary suffered a still greater depreciation in their currency values, and the French, Belgian and other currencies also lost considerably in value. Attempts to deal with the problem by severe cuts in public spending had serious consequences for output and employment in countries like Great Britain after the war; where the problem was evaded, however, as in Germany, the results were even worse. More generally the instability of currencies which was a legacy of the war hindered the development of trade and the recovery of prosperity, and the intergovernmental debts which had been contracted during the war imposed an additional burden and seriously complicated the reform of international finances.[9]

The Versailles peace treaty, signed on 28 June 1919, provided no solution to these deep-seated problems and indeed made no attempt to do so. Loosely based upon the 'fourteen points' that President Wilson had enunciated on 8 January 1918, the treaty, and those that followed it, sought rather to demonstrate that it had indeed been a 'war for democracy' and for the principle of national self-determination in particular. Quite apart from the difficulty of implementing

such principles in complicated situations such as central and eastern
Europe and of reconciling them with economic and other realities,
the peace conference was hampered by poor organisation and a fatal
lack of agreement among the major powers.[10] The Americans, who
had joined the war only in 1917 and were separated by an ocean from
European concerns, tended on the whole to place most emphasis
upon the conclusion of a just peace which would be consistent with
the fourteen points. The British representatives at the conference
were rather more concerned to ensure that German colonies and the
German navy should pose no future threat to their interests in these
areas, and were already reverting to the traditional British view that
no single power, France just as much as Germany, should be allowed
to dominate the European continent. A German recovery was also
important for the revival of British trade. Georges Clemenceau, the
French prime minister, had seen two German invasions of France in
his lifetime and was determined to make sure that no future German
government was allowed to do likewise. He tended accordingly to
press for the harshest possible treatment of Germany in the peace
settlement, though he was also aware of France's need for economic
recovery and sought so far as possible to avoid antagonising his
British and American counterparts. The Italians, who played a less
prominent role in the negotiations than the other victorious powers,
were more concerned to satisfy their territorial ambitions in the
Adriatic area than to influence the terms of peace more generally.

The Versailles treaty, accordingly, dealt severely with Germany,
as with the other defeated belligerents, but not as severely as
Clemenceau and many sections of the press and public opinion in the
Allied countries would have wished. The German colonies were
confiscated and distributed under mandate to the powers that had
occupied them; and a number of border areas were lost, most notably
Alsace–Lorraine to France, a part of upper Silesia (after a plebiscite)
to Poland and Czechoslovakia, and a strip of territory, the 'Polish
corridor', to Poland in order to provide that country with access to
the sea as the fourteen points had promised. The Saar coalmines were
ceded to France and the whole area was placed under League of
Nations trusteeship for a fifteen-year period, after which a plebiscite
was to be held to determine under whose sovereignty the local
population wished to be placed; and the Rhineland was to be
demilitarised and temporarily occupied, although not, as the French
had wished, transferred to France or established as an independent

buffer state. In all, Germany lost about 14 per cent of her pre-war territory, about the same proportion of her economic potential, and some 10 per cent of her pre-war population.[11] Apart from this, Germany was allowed to have no air force, the army was reduced to a 100,000-man peace-keeping force, Kaiser Wilhelm II was to be handed over for trial as a war criminal (in the event the Dutch, among whom he had taken refuge, refused to extradite him), and a number of other alleged war criminals were to be sent for trial to Allied military courts (in the end only twelve were brought to justice in this way, the majority of whom were acquitted).[12]

Above all, the treaty required the Germans to pay a substantial though as yet undetermined sum to the Allies in the form of reparations. The legal basis for this exaction was article 231 of the treaty, which bound the Germans to accept responsibility for the losses and damage suffered by the Allied and associated governments 'as a consequence of the war imposed upon them by the aggression of Germany and her allies'.[13] The treaty did not specifically mention 'war guilt', and analogous clauses were incorporated without much controversy into the treaty settlements with Austria and Hungary respectively. There had nonetheless been strong pressure in both Britain and France for the recovery of the entire cost of the war from Germany, and, although American resistance prevented the adoption of this view as Allied policy, it was agreed that Belgium should receive an indemnity (as the ocupation of that country had been a violation of international law as well as an act of aggression) and that German liability should include pensions and separation allowances for the Allied armies. A reparations commission was to determine the total sum payable by 1 May 1921; in the meantime the Germans were required to make a payment of 20 milliard gold marks in cash and in kind. A total liability of 132 milliard gold marks was eventually agreed and announced on 27 April 1921. The new German authorities accepted the schedule which was agreed the following month and made a first cash payment in the summer of 1921, but the issue, together with that of international indebtedness more generally, proved a potent source of inter-Allied friction and complicated the task of economic recovery for at least the first half of the decade.[14]

The treaty settlement was a source of other international complications as well. The attempt to institutionalise the principle of national self-determination, for instance, led – perhaps inevitably – to the establishment of a fragile network of states in eastern and central Europe whose boundaries coincided far from perfectly with those of the national groups they purportedly represented. Poland, for example, with a population of 27 million, contained 18 million Poles by Polish estimates but far fewer in the view of others. Czechoslovakia's population of over 14 million included more than 3 million Germans and three-quarters of a million Magyars, and more than 3 million Magyars were left outside the borders of Hungary. There were substantial German minorities of half a million or more in Romania, Hungary and Yugoslavia, a Magyar minority of approaching 2 million in Romania and of half a million in Yugoslavia, and minorities of Ukrainians, Slovaks, Albanians and others elsewhere in the same area.[15] Italy subsequently acquired the substantially German area of South Tyrol, while Greece (under the stillborn Treaty of Sèvres) was allocated a number of Turkish islands in the Aegean and a part of the Turkish mainland. All of this left ample scope for irredentist and other movements throughout the inter-war period. Nor were the states which had lost rather than gained territory necessarily more viable. Austria, for instance, lost territory and population to Italy, Czechoslovakia, Poland, Romania and Yugoslavia. The rump state that was left retained an imperial superstructure in Vienna, the city in which a third of its population resided, but it had lost the productive hinterland by which it had previously been sustained and was to prove chronically insolvent throughout the 1920s.[16]

Still more serious were the implications of these new arrangements for the economic recovery of the continent. The Versailles treaty settlement had been the most extensive redrawing of the political map of Europe that had ever been undertaken. Seven entirely new states came into existence with the collapse of the German, Austro-Hungarian and Russian empires; some 12,500 miles of new frontiers were created, more than twenty new customs unions, and many new currencies and legal systems. Communications networks were naturally disturbed and traditional trading relationships were severely disrupted. Indeed even within the newly established states the problems of economic integration were often formidable. Yugoslavia, for instance, inherited five railway systems with four different gauges, each of which served a different centre, so that together they failed to form an integrated national system.[17] In states which had lost territory the situation was hardly better. The Austrian textile industry, for instance, was broken up; the spindles were

located in Bohemia and Moravia, which became part of Czechoslovakia, while the weaving looms remained in the vicinity of Vienna.
An Austrian reunion with Germany, which would have left that
country more populous than in 1914 but would have accorded with
the principle of national self-determination, was specifically ruled out
under the peace treaties with both countries. Elsewhere Hungary
retained about half of its industrial undertakings but lost most of the
supplies of timber, iron ore, water power and other resources on
which they largely depended; Silesia was broken into three separate
parts; and the coal of the Ruhr was separated from the iron ore of
Lorraine, which was now in France.[18]

The main constructive element in the treaty settlement was the
establishment of the League of Nations, which was incorporated as
Part I in each of the peace treaties. Its establishment was the
principal concern of President Wilson, and at his insistence its
Covenant was the first major document to be agreed upon at the
peace conference. The Covenant provided for an Assembly, within
which decisions had to be unanimous on matters of substance, and
for a Council, permanent membership in which was accorded to the
five major Allies (Britain, France, Italy, the United States and
Japan). The central obligation of the Covenant was contained in
article 10, which bound the members of the League to 'respect and
preserve as against external aggression the territorial integrity and
existing political independence of all Members of the League'.[19]
Every war or threat of war was declared a matter of concern to the
League; every member agreed to submit all disputes to arbitration,
legal settlement or inquiry by the Council of the League; and under
the provisions of article 16, if any member resorted to war in defiance
of its obligations to the League it would be deemed to have committed an act of war against all other members and would be
sanctioned accordingly. Other provisions related to matters such as
the reduction of armaments and the peaceful revision of boundaries.[20] The League, however, lacked the means of imposing its will
when countries chose to disregard its moral authority, and its influence in the early 1920s was further reduced by the somewhat arbitrary exclusion from membership of the major defeated belligerent,
Germany, and of Soviet Russia. In general it was not a significant
factor in the international politics of the period.[21]

The failure of the Allies to deal systematically with the economic
reconstruction of the continent was perhaps an even more serious

shortcoming in the treaty settlement. The immediate crisis in central Europe did lead to some measures of famine relief, particularly through the American Relief Administration, which was established early in 1919 by the Allied Supreme Council to deal with matters of this kind. Under its auspices a steady stream of food deliveries began to take place, and by the late summer of 1919 a substantial quantity of produce had been supplied, most of it on a cash or credit basis, to the defeated countries and to the Allies respectively. No more than 10 per cent consisted of outright gifts, however, and the programme was in any case curtailed by the latter part of the year, with responsibility for relief operations passing mainly to private and semi-official organisations. By this time it had scarcely begun to make an impression upon the problem, particularly in central and eastern Europe.[22] Apart from food, capital and raw materials were also in very short supply; but no serious attempt was made to deal with these matters either, and in the early post-war years many central and eastern European countries either went short or else paid for imports at high prices by borrowing, which ultimately made matters worse. Recovery was in turn delayed, and unemployment benefits and relief payments, in addition to high levels of military spending, kept government expenditure at record levels at a time when the taxable capacity of the population had been reduced to an exceptionally low ebb. Budgets failed to balance, inflation accelerated, and currencies depreciated still further as a result.[23]

The treaties were not lacking in critics at the time, the most influential of whom was a young Cambridge economist, John Maynard Keynes, who had been attached to the Treasury and then to the British delegation at the Paris peace conference. Keynes's book, *The Economic Consequences of the Peace*, was published in December 1919; in six months it had sold 100,000 copies, and it was swiftly translated into all the major European languages, including Russian.[24] The book began with an unflattering examination of the organisation of the peace conference and of the leading personalities involved, and then went on to consider the practicability of the peace settlement that had been produced. Whatever the moral arguments might be, Keynes argued, a Carthaginian peace was not '*practically right or possible*'. The coal deliveries that Germany had been required to make as a contribution towards reparations, for instance, could not in practice be made, not at least without making it still more difficult for that country to produce the goods that would have to be produced if reparations were to be paid. The claims for damages that had been made were also exaggerated and excessive, partly because of political pressures in the Allied countries, and partly also because of the deficit financing that had been indulged in during the war, particularly by France and Italy, on the assumption that a defeated Germany would meet the bill. Germany, Keynes pointed out, would simply be unable to provide the sums concerned, as neither a reduction in imports nor an increase in exports on the scale required was feasible.[25]

More seriously, Keynes charged, the treaties made no provision for the economic rehabilitation of a continent still devastated by the consequences of war. There was nothing to persuade the defeated belligerents to become good neighbours; there was nothing to stabilise the new states that had been established, particularly in eastern Europe; there was nothing to reintegrate Russia into the economic life of the outside world; and there was nothing to place economic relations among the Allies themselves upon a more satisfactory footing, or more particularly to regulate the disordered finances of France and Italy or to deal with financial relations between the European powers and the USA. It was an 'extraordinary fact', wrote Keynes, that the 'fundamental economic problem of a Europe starving and disintegrating before their eyes was the one question in which it was impossible to arouse the interest of the Four'.[26] There were three key problems, in Keynes's view: levels of productivity in Europe had fallen significantly, for a variety of reasons; the system of transport and exchange had broken down; and currency difficulties made it impossible for the continent to obtain the supplies it had previously obtained from overseas. His own solution contained four elements: a revision of the treaty, particularly in respect of reparations; the settlement of inter-Allied debts, for the most part by cancellation; an international loan, provided for the most part by the United States, combined with currency reform; and the restoration of economic relations between central Europe and Russia, for the benefit of Allied traders as well as of those countries themselves. The alternative, Keynes concluded, was the 'bankruptcy and decay of Europe'.[27]

Cogent though this was as a critique of the post-war settlement, it perhaps assumed too great a freedom of manoeuvre on the part of those who had framed it. In the first place, the Allies had few means of enforcing their will once the war had ended. The great armies that had been built up during the war were rapidly demobilised once the peace settlement had been concluded; in Britain's case, for instance, a total strength of 3.8 million in October 1918 had dropped to barely 1 million a year later,[28] and in the case of France, an active army of over 8 million in January 1918 had been reduced to barely 800,000 by the end of 1919. Both totals continued to decline rapidly thereafter.[29] Beyond this again, the very nature of the diplomatic process had changed over the wartime period. The outbreak of war, followed by the publication of the inter-Allied secret treaties, appeared to confirm the view of many radicals that conflicts of this kind sprang not from human wickedness but from the 'old diplomacy', conducted by governments and diplomats beyond the scrutiny of the public. After the war there were very strong pressures to conduct external policy in a manner more in keeping with the democratic spirit of the times; the Soviet government formally abandoned secret diplomacy altogether, and even the Allies were compelled to defer to the 'new diplomacy' by establishing the League of Nations and later by conducting their affairs in conferences rather than by diplomatic correspondence. The influence of popular feeling on matters of this kind was strengthened by the extension of the franchise in most European countries after the war to the whole adult population, and by a series of general elections which brought public and parliamentary opinion more closely into correspondence than they had been since the outbreak of the war.[30]

Not simply were the means of enforcing the settlement lacking, or at least subject to constraints; perhaps more important, the political will was also absent. The treaty, indeed, had scarcely been concluded before the Allied front began to collapse. In the United States, whose president had been the treaty's intellectual architect, the Senate had to approve its signature by a two-thirds majority for it to be ratified. The Republican party, which had secured a majority in the Senate in the elections of November 1918, was naturally reluctant to add to the standing of a Democratic president by approving the negotiations in which he had engaged abroad. Opponents of the treaty in the Senate took advantage of a popular mood which was hostile to the notion that the United States should become a party to further conflict in Europe, and which was increasingly disposed, now that the war had ended, to see the Allies as ungrateful and selfish, the peoples of central Europe as insatiable in their demands for aid, and the defeated Germans, in their misery, as worthy of sympathy rather than further punishment. Wilson, returning from the peace conference, undertook a vigorous campaign to persuade the American people of the merits of the settlement; but his health gave way, and on 2 October 1919 he suffered a stroke. Unable to promote the treaty as effectively as before, he nonetheless remained determined to resist what he regarded as damaging amendments moved in the Senate by his Republican opponents. On 19 November 1919 most of the Democratic senators, under orders from Wilson, voted against ratifying the treaty with the reservations that its opponents had attached to it; finally, on 19 March 1920, a majority voted for the treaty as amended, but the total vote in favour fell short of the two-thirds majority necessary for ratification.[31]

Wilson remained confident that the treaty would be approved after the presidential elections of November 1920; but popular opinion had become increasingly hostile to the treaty and to the League of Nations framework generally, and a Republican president, Warren G. Harding, was returned by a large majority on a slogan of 'return to normalcy'. In August 1921 his administration signed a separate treaty ending the state of war with Germany, and analogous treaties were signed with Austria and Hungary, confirming America's privileges but not responsibilities under the treaties of Versailles, Saint-Germain and Trianon. Senate approval was contingent upon the reservation that the United States would not participate in any treaty commissions without Congressional approval.[32] The United States, accordingly, which had played a central role in the negotiation of the treaty and especially in the establishment of the League, ended up a non-party to the Versailles settlement and a non-member of the League. American troops remained in the Rhineland until January 1923, but thereafter American dealings with the other Allies were limited essentially to demands for the repayment of the substantial debts that the other Allies had accumulated during the war, which successive American presidents refused to associate in any way with the question of German reparations ('They hired the money, didn't they?', as President Coolidge is reported to have remarked), and to negotiations on naval matters, where an active American programme of construction appeared to threaten that country's traditionally good relations with the United Kingdom.[33]

America's withdrawal from the peace settlement was of particular concern to France, the Allied country most severely affected by the war and the one most fully committed to a harsh settlement with Germany. Clemenceau had fought hard to have the Rhineland

separated from Germany, and had given way only when Lloyd
George and Wilson gave a formal guarantee that in the event of
another German invasion France would not fight alone. Two treaties
of guarantee, signed on 28 June 1919 at the same time as the
Versailles treaty itself, bound both Britain and the Unites States to
come to the assistance of France in the event of any 'unprovoked
movement of aggression against her being made by Germany'.[34] The
treaty with Britain, however, was to come into force only when the
corresponding treaty with the United States had been ratified, and
when the United States Senate rejected the Versailles treaty Wilson
lost interest in it and the treaty of guarantee was not put to a vote.
The British as well as the American treaty of guarantee lapsed as a
result. The French naturally felt they had been duped, and
Clemenceau, who had accepted the guarantee in place of the material
guarantees of security urged by Marshal Foch and President Poincaré, paid the penalty himself. At an election in January 1920 he was
defeated for the post of president; the next day he resigned as premier
and his long career in French politics came to an abrupt end. The
major French preoccupations in the year that followed were to secure
the full implementations of the Versailles treaty, to strengthen
French security by developing relations with the 'Little Entente'
(Czechoslovakia, Romania and Yugoslavia) as a counterweight to
Germany in the East, to build up a strong and independent Poland,
and to negotiate a bilateral treaty with Britain which might take the
place of the lapsed treaty of guarantee.[35]

French domestic politics in the early 1920s conveyed an 'mpression
to many outside observers of intransigence and even vengefulness.[36]
The unilateral occupation of Darmstadt and Frankfurt in April 1920,
when the German government sent troops into the demilitarised zone
in order to suppress a left-wing rising, certainly gave grounds for such
a view. French concerns, however, rested on a solid foundation.
France had accumulated enormous debts to the United States and
Britain, on whose repayment the United States authorities in particular were insisting and which could be repaid only if France's full
share of reparations were forthcoming from Germany. Beyond this
again lay the reality of a long Franco-German border, and appre-
hensions not unreasonably engendered by the dominance that
Germany had come to exercise upon the continent generally. In the
1860s French population numbers had been comparable with those
of Germany, at just over 38 million in 1866 as compared with

Germany's 37.8 million in 1864. The German population, however, increased much more rapidly than that of France, and by the early 1920s, even after the return of Alsace–Lorraine, France's population had reached no more than 38.8 million as compared with Germany's 60 million or more. In industry a similar process had occurred. In 1870, for instance, France produced about half as much coal as Germany, but by the early 1920s the proportion had dropped to about a quarter; and French steel production had fallen from about two-thirds to no more than a third of that of Germany over the same period.[37] In agricultural terms French performance was relatively more creditable, but from a French perspective there was every reason in the early 1920s to fear that Germany would acquire the political and perhaps military role for which her population, area and resources appeared to equip her, and every reason to insist upon the full implementation of a peace treaty which appeared to offer at least some prospect of security in this connection.

Britain, the other member of the 'Big Three', had suffered relatively little in the war, and with the onset of peace more traditional preoccupations began to reassert themselves. David Lloyd George, prime minister since December 1916, headed a coalition government whose mandate had been massively renewed at the 1918 'Khaki' general election. He headed the British delegation at the Paris peace conference, and began, with the assistance of a personal secretariat, to develop a role in the making of British foreign policy which threatened to eclipse that of the Foreign Office and of his foreign secretaries, Arthur Balfour and (from October 1919) Lord Curzon. The prime minister had a number of personal prejudices, such as a hostility towards Poland and a sympathy towards Greece, which made a substantial independent contribution to the making of British foreign policy on a number of occasions during the early 1920s. Yet there was little serious disagreement, among politicians or among the public more generally, about the broad lines of British policy. After the jingoism of the 1918 elections had faded, it began to be felt that Germany had been treated rather too harshly and that France, by insisting on the full execution of the treaty, was threatening the future peace of the continent. British public as well as official opinion, moreover, tended to favour a balance of power in Europe rather than the dominance of a single power, and particular importance was attached to the development of opportunities for trade and commerce upon which Britain, much more than its continental neighbours, depended for its prosperity. As Germany's share of British exports began to drop, from 8.3 per cent before the war to only 1.5 per cent in 1920, it began to appear less than the height of wisdom to insist upon a peace settlement which impoverished the defeated powers.[38]

Britain, moreover, had differences with France over a wide range of issues, from the construction of submarines to the status of Tangier and the position of both powers in the Middle East, as well as a variety of extra-European commitments which made it appear even less wise to bind British policy too closely to that of France. Most obviously, there was the empire or, as it was shortly to become, the British Commonwealth of Nations. Still the largest empire the world had ever seen, it was threatened at many points by a rising tide of nationalist sentiment, which the Wilsonian doctrine of the rights of small nations and the experience of the war itself had helped to encourage. Nationalist pressures were increasing in the immediate post-war period in India and in Egypt; but it was Ireland which posed the most serious political danger in the early 1920s. The 1918 elections in that country had produced a sweeping victory for the nationalists; the elected members refused to take their seats in Westminster and declared the country's independence. An increasingly bloody military conflict followed. In July 1921 a truce was declared, and by the end of the year a treaty had been concluded which brought into being an Irish Free State exercising authority over most of the island. Apart from all this, Lloyd George and his colleagues faced a vigorous resumption of pre-war industrial conflicts upon the British mainland itself. The miners, railwaymen and transport workers resurrected their earlier 'triple alliance'; the railwaymen went on strike in September 1919, the miners in October 1920 and again the following year. Yet powerful as these domestic and extra-European preoccupations might be, Britain remained a trading nation; and when the post-war boom collapsed at the end of 1920 it was clear that the economic recovery of the continent was a necessity for Great Britain just as much as it was for the countries most immediately concerned.[39]

Of the other Allies, Italy had entered the war rather late, in May 1915, and played a peripheral role at the peace conference, being mainly concerned with developments in the Adriatic area where she had extensive territorial claims. These claims had received the support of the Allies in the Treaty of London, secretly concluded on 26 April 1915, which promised Italy not only the Brenner frontier (including a substantial German minority) but also Istria and the largest part of Dalmatia. Italian claims, however, were felt to have received insufficient recognition at the peace conference, and the Italian representatives withdrew altogether in April 1919 over the refusal of the other powers to accede to their demands for Fiume, a partly Italian city which had not specifically been promised to Italy under the Treaty of London, and to which the newly established Yugoslav state also laid claim. Italy duly signed the peace treaty, but with a rather bad grace, and in September 1919 the Italian government connived in the seizure of Fiume by the nationalist poet Gabriele d'Annunzio and a group of followers. A formal treaty with Yugoslavia was eventually concluded in November 1920 under which Fiume was declared a free city and its Istrian hinterland was partitioned between the two powers. Italian territorial ambitions nonetheless remained unsatisfied, and throughout the inter-war period Italy was generally a 'revisionist' power, determined to alter the terms of the Versailles settlement to her own advantage. The Italian elections of 1919, the first to be held on the basis of proportional representation, failed to produce a decisive result, and Italian affairs were presided over until 1922 by a series of unstable coalitions headed by a succession of Catholic or socialist prime ministers.[40]

Further away, Japan was also a revisionist power, and a power little committed (for obvious reasons) to the economic reconstruction of Europe. Japanese delegates took little part in the discussion of European matters at the peace conference, showing most interest in questions which directly affected Japanese interests such as racial equality and the disposition of the Shantung peninsula. The Japanese in the end were awarded not only the former German territory in the peninsula but also a mandate over the formerly German islands in the northern Pacific, and they took advantage of the collapse of the Russian empire to intervene in eastern Siberia, ostensibly to block the spread of Bolshevism. Japanese troops remained in the area until the autumn of 1922. Japan's expanding naval power appeared also to threaten American interests in the Pacific until a four-power pact, embracing both countries as well as France and Great Britain, was concluded at the Washington Conference in late 1921 and early 1922. Japanese pressure for the insertion of a clause on racial equality into the Covenant of the League of Nations – which would have had implications for the question of immigration into the United States and the British Dominions – was however resisted.[41] Of the other

Allies, Belgium (and the Netherlands, a neutral during the war) had a more obvious interest in European reconstruction, but both countries had only a limited influence in international affairs. The Belgian government was headed in the early 1920s by George Theunis, a member of the Catholic party and a banker by profession, and the Dutch government by C. J. Ruys de Beerenbrouck, also a Catholic.[42]

Among the defeated powers, the condition of Germany gave the Allies particular cause for concern. The Kaiser had abdicated, a Social Democratic government headed by Friedrich Ebert had come to power in Berlin, and a new and democratic constitution had been adopted at Weimar. The new regime nonetheless looked an insecure and vulnerable one. The German armies had been withdrawn in good order from France and Belgium, promoting the view that they had been 'stabbed in the back' by unreliable and cowardly politicians. The Versailles treaty was held to represent a departure from the terms that President Wilson had originally extended, and its imposition in virtually unrevised form was seen as a *diktat*. The clauses relating to war guilt and to the trial of war criminals were particularly resented. At the general elections which took place in June 1920 the popular response became evident: the parties committed to Weimar lost heavily, and a weak and shifting coalition of parties was left with the manifestly disproportionate task of supervising the implementation of an unpopular and unrealistic peace settlement.[43] During the later stages of the war and the early post-war period, indeed, it seemed at times as if no stable government of any kind was likely to emerge, as established authority, in Germany and elsewhere in central and eastern Europe, was threatened by the forces of the left. During the last months of the war there had been mutinies in the German fleet at Kiel; there was a left-wing rising in Berlin in the winter of 1918–19; and as shortages of food and civil disorder persisted, the Allies became increasingly concerned by the possibility that Germany might fall victim to the same contagion that had affected Soviet Russia. As Lloyd George pointed out in his 'Fontainebleau memorandum' of March 1919, the 'whole of Europe' was filled with the 'spirit of revolution', and there was the 'gravest danger' that Germany in particular might 'throw in her lot with Bolshevism and place her resources, her brains, her vast organising power at the disposal of the revolutionary fanatics' in Moscow, whose dream it was 'to conquer the world for Bolshevism by force of arms'.[44] As the premier's favourite military strategist and head of the

Imperial General Staff, Sir Henry Wilson, put it in his diary on 10 November 1918, 'Our real danger now is not the Boche but Bolshevism.'[45]

The Russian situation, Lloyd George pointed out in his memorandum, was one that the Allies would have to deal with as soon as possible. A settlement in the West and a settlement in the East, indeed, appeared to be closely interconnected. Russia had been a vital element in the European balance of power since at least the eighteenth century. More particularly, Soviet diplomacy and the operations of the Red Army bore closely upon the stability of the Versailles settlement in eastern Europe, above all upon the stability and independence of Poland. Outside Europe, Soviet policy had serious implications for the continued existence of western colonial possessions and of the British eastern empire in particular. In western countries themselves the labour and working-class movement had acquired an increasingly radical tinge since the October revolution of 1917, and soon afterwards a network of communist parties began to come into existence under the general auspices of the Communist International, established in March 1919 with its headquarters in Moscow. Fully communist regimes, indeed, came into existence in Hungary in 1919 and for shorter periods elsewhere. Apart from this again, Russia was a central element in the European economy. Before the revolution Russia had supplied much of Europe's grain and other foodstuffs; the absence of these after the war had led to shortages and high prices. Russia had also traditionally provided an important market for European manufactured produce and equipment, a market whose absence after the war was contributing to a mounting total of excess industrial capacity and unemployment. The repayment of Russian debts was also a matter of direct concern to many Allies. Russia, in other words, remained an essential element in the European political and economic equation; the central task of the Genoa Conference, and of the conference diplomacy that preceded it, was to find a means by which the new Soviet administration could resume that place in a manner which would be acceptable to all the parties concerned.

The assumption of power by the Bolshevik party in October 1917 had not, to begin with, aroused much interest or anxiety in Allied capitals. The 'Maximalists', as they tended to be known at this time, were seen as simply the latest in a sequence of aspirants to power in a country in which effective central government had already broken down and which was in any case making a negligible contribution to the Allied war effort. *The Times* on 23 November 1917 called the Bolsheviks a 'band of anarchists and fanatics' who had 'seized power for the moment, owing to the paralysis of the national life'; the *Daily Telegraph* declared on 5 January 1918 that 'no sane man would give them as much as a month to live'. Similar advice was received from foreign ministry officials and from diplomatic representatives in the field.[46] The Bolsheviks, however, survived; and they began to press, as they had promised, for a negotiated settlement of the war, ideally with Allied agreement but if necessary without it. The Decree on Peace, adopted on 8 November 1917, called for the 'immediate opening of negotiations for a just and democratic peace' and proposed an immediate armistice of three months. The appeal was directed to all belligerent governments and peoples, but more particularly – an innovation in diplomatic practice not welcomed by the governments concerned – to the 'class-conscious workers' of Britain, France and Germany, so as to bring about not only an end to the war but also the 'liberation of the toilers and exploited masses from all kinds of slavery and exploitation'.[47] The Decree was followed by further appeals to the Allied governments to join in the peace negotiations, which went without direct response.[48] Negotiations between the Bolsheviks and the Germans duly began on 3 December 1917; on 15 December an armistice was signed, and on 22 December formal peace negotiations were initiated. The Allies, in the event, did not join in (they could hardly have approved any agreement which was likely to allow German troops to be transferred to the western front), and after an extended period of negotiations the Germans were able virtually to dictate the one-sided Treaty of Brest-Litovsk, which was signed on 3 March 1918. The new Soviet regime lost about one-third of its population and its Ukrainian, Finnish, Baltic and Polish territories; it did, however, at least remain in being.[49]

The conclusion of a Russo-German peace led to some concern in Allied capitals that the Germans might be able to gain access to the substantial supplies of military equipment as well as food and raw materials that still remained within the country. It was to guard against the possibility of this occurring, at least in the first instance, that detachments of British troops were sent to occupy Murmansk in March 1918. In April 1918 a force of British and Japanese troops occupied Vladivostok, again at least ostensibly to protect military supplies and their own nationals in the area. The Allied action was tacitly accepted by the Soviet authorities at the time, as it appeared to offer some protection against the possibility of a further German advance upon Petrograd and Moscow. Some contacts, particularly those between Trotsky and emissaries of the British and American governments respectively, appeared to hold out the prospect that Russia might even resume the struggle against Germany provided adequate Allied military assistance was forthcoming. These overtures were not on the whole taken seriously in western capitals, however, in part at least because the Allies were more preoccupied with the vigorous German offensive that took place in the late spring and early summer of 1918. The Brest-Litovsk treaty was not acknowledged, the Soviet government remained unrecognised, and further troops were sent, in August 1918 and later, to occupy Archangel, Siberia, parts of Central Asia and the Caucasus. By the time the war ended the Allies had in effect acquired a substantial occupation army whose original anti-German rationale had now disappeared.[50]

The Allies, in the end, failed to discover an alternative rationale which was both convincing to their domestic publics and acceptable to all the parties concerned. The Japanese in Siberia pursued more or less openly annexationist objectives, while the Americans, at the other extreme, bound by the sixth of the fourteen points (which had specified the evacuation of all Russian territory) and by Wilson's fastidious conscience, sent only a small contingent which was to be used exclusively for the protection of supplies and of the Czech Legion, a substantial force of prisoners of war who were attempting to leave Russia through Vladivostok in order to fight for the Allies in France. The British and French governments were somewhat closer in their objectives, and indeed concluded an agreement in December 1917, subsequently extended, which defined their respective spheres of operation. Neither, however, was in a position to provide the enormous numbers of men that would have been necessary to instal an anti-Bolshevik government in power, the financial implications of attempting to do so were unacceptable, and the continued occupation of a foreign country for what appeared to be no valid reason was increasingly unpopular both with their respective populations and with the troops themselves. Despite intermittent pressure from ministers such as Winston Churchill for a more 'forward' policy, Allied commitments were first contained and then gradually liquidated. The last British troops left Murmansk in October 1919, French troops were evacuated in March 1920, and the last American

troops left Siberia in April 1920. The anti-Bolshevik forces they had
supported had in the meantime failed to dislodge the Soviet government, despite major offensives by Kolchak and Denikin in 1919 and
then by Baron Wrangel in the latter part of 1920, and with the latter's
defeat in November 1920 organised domestic opposition to Soviet
rule had come to an end.

The end of military hostilities between the Allies and the Soviet
government, and the failure of all domestic attempts to overthrow it,
left the way open for the resumption of some sort of relations between
the two sides. In January 1920 the Allied Supreme Council, meeting
in Paris, decided to end their blockade of Soviet Russia, and later in
the year negotiations began between British and Soviet representatives (the French declined to take part) towards the conclusion of a
trade agreement.[51] The negotiations were suspended during the
summer of 1920, when a Soviet advance into Poland, following a
Polish attack, appeared once again to threaten the stability of central
Europe and of the whole Versailles settlement. On 16 August 1920,
however, the Soviet forces were defeated within sight of Warsaw, and
two months later an armistice brought hostilities between the two
countries to an end. The British–Soviet negotiations resumed in
November, and on 16 March 1921 – not without misgivings on the
part of some members of the British Cabinet – the Anglo-Russian
Trade Agreement was signed. Its formal terms were unspectacular –
they mainly concerned the renewal of communications and the
removal of obstacles to trade – but its significance was in fact far
greater: it represented the first resumption of relations *de facto* if not *de
jure* between Soviet Russia and a major capitalist power. The agreement was itself to be followed by a more general treaty by which it
was intended to establish full *de jure* diplomatic relations and to
resolve all claims still outstanding between the two parties.[52]

The Soviet government had established diplomatic relations of
some kind with several other western states by this time. On 2
February 1920 a Soviet–Estonian treaty had been concluded, followed by treaties with Lithuania on 12 July 1920, with Latvia on 11
August 1920, and with Finland on 14 October 1920.[53] Treaties with
Persia and Afghanistan were concluded in February 1921, and a
treaty with Turkey was signed in Moscow on the same day that the
Anglo-Russian Trade Agreement was being signed in London.[54] A
formal treaty with Poland, the Treaty of Riga, was signed two days
later, on 18 March 1921; and treaties with Norway and Austria

followed later the same year.[55] Of rather more significance, a provisional agreement was concluded between the Soviet government and Germany on 6 May 1921. The agreement provided for the exchange of diplomatic missions, the granting of consular privileges, the return of the nationals of one country from the territory of the other, the renewal of postal and telegraphic communications and the facilitation of trade.[56] The resumption of diplomatic relations with Italy was complicated by the Italians' initial refusal to accept the Soviet government as the only legitimate representative of the territory over which they claimed to rule, but on 26 December 1921 a provisional agreement, modelled very closely on the Anglo-Russian trade agreement, was signed in Rome. The agreement, like the British one, sought to stimulate the revival of trade between the two countries and signified the *de facto* recognition of the Soviet government by its Italian counterpart.[57]

The resumption of diplomatic relations with the other Allied powers proceeded rather less smoothly. The United States, for instance, had been the most reluctant of the interventionist powers and had fewer differences with the Soviet government in terms of territory or debts than the other western powers. There appears to have been some recognition of this on the part of the Soviet authorities (American influence in the Far East was also seen as a useful counterweight to that of the Japanese), and it was American emissaries, Raymond Robins and William Bullitt, who had the closest contacts with the Soviet leadership in the spring of 1918 and 1919 respectively.[58] With the ratification of the Brest-Litovsk treaty, however, American government policy became more hostile towards the new regime in Moscow; American forces joined the Allied intervention, and scare stories about Bolshevik atrocities and communist agitation began to receive more coverage in the American press. President Wilson went so far as to describe the Soviet government, in the autumn of 1919, as the 'negation of everything that is American'.[59] In June 1919 the office of the newly appointed Soviet representative in New York, Ludwig Martens, was raided in search of subversive materials, and in December 1920 the agent himself was deported.[60] Secretary of State Bainbridge Colby formulated the considered position of his government on 10 August 1920 in reply to a query from the Italian ambassador. The United States government, Colby began, had 'profound sympathy' for the Russian people, and wished to render assistance to them in every way possible. The

Bolshevik administration, however, had come to power by 'force and cunning', and it maintained itself by the 'savage oppression' of all opposition. It had moreover repudiated its international obligations, and was wholeheartedly pledged to world revolution. 'We cannot', Colby concluded, 'recognize, hold official relations with, or give friendly recognition to the agents of a government which is determined and bound to conspire against our institutions.'[61] Succeeding American administrations, up to 1933, took the same view.

Relations between the French and Soviet governments in the early 1920s were scarcely more cordial.[62] France had been perhaps the most persistent of the interventionist powers, and had the most substantial differences with the Soviet authorities in terms of repudiated debts. The French, indeed, with the other Allies, had gone so far as to extend recognition to the Kolchak and Denikin administrations in 1919, and had been the only power to recognise Baron Wrangel's forces in southern Russia in August 1920. The French government, like its Allied counterparts, had eventually to recognise the failure of these movements, and it was a party to the Allied decision of January 1920 to bring the blockade to an end and subsequently to enter into negotiations with representatives of the Soviet government. The French, however, refused to take part in these negotiations, explaining (as Aristide Briand, who became prime minister as well as minister of foreign affairs in January 1921, put it to the French Chamber) that there could be no resumption of diplomatic relations with Russia until that country had a government which genuinely represented the Russian people, and which accepted the obligations of its predecessors.[63] There were several overtures from Moscow with a view to the establishment of more friendly relations, such as a message from Chicherin which was published in *L'Humanité* on 15 August 1921 urging France to follow the example of Britain and resume trading relations, and an official declaration from Krasin to the same effect.[64] French policy (which was closely associated with that of Belgium, another major creditor of Russia) nonetheless remained unyielding up to the beginning of 1922, and indeed beyond.

A number of issues, accordingly, lay between the new Soviet administration and its western counterparts at the beginning of the 1920s. Several of them originated from the war in which all had recently been engaged, and had also to be resolved between the Allies and the defeated central powers. The question of prisoners of war was an obvious example. Agreements to return all prisoners of war, together with all foreign nationals who wished to return to their own country, were generally incorporated into the provisional and trading agreements that were concluded between the Soviet government and its British, German, Italian and other counterparts in 1920 and 1921, and the matter was covered by more specific agreements as well, particularly with France and the United States.[65] The implementation of these agreements, however, took some time, and a series of contested individual cases arose which complicated relations among the governments concerned for several years.[66] The arbitration of territorial issues still in dispute also gave rise to difficulties, whether the Soviet government was a party to the negotiations or – as in the case of the Aland islands and the Straits – was (in its view improperly) excluded from them;[67] and even when territorial issues had been resolved there were frontier incidents to contend with, particularly along the Soviet–Finnish and Soviet–Polish borders. A further series of issues related to the resumption of diplomatic and commercial relations: procedures had to be agreed for matters such as the immunity of diplomatic and commercial staff, diplomatic communications and the provision of suitable premises, as well as for the resumption of postal and telegraphic communications, of shipping operations and so forth.[68]

Many of these matters, as we have noted, had also to be resolved among the other powers, and between the Allies and the defeated central powers in particular. Relations with Soviet Russia, however, were more complicated for at least two reasons, each of which related to the distinctive nature of the regime as the world's first established socialist state. The first of these was propaganda. From the outset, as we have seen, Soviet communications with the outside world were addressed as much to their populations as to their governments. Often, indeed, they were addressed to their populations as against their governments, seeking to achieve socialist as well as Soviet state objectives by encouraging the overthrow of western governments by their class-conscious proletariats.[69] The Soviet authorities had a variety of means at their disposal to bring about this desired outcome. To some extent they could rely upon their proclamations and upon appeals to the working class in the West, such as Lenin's letters to British and American workers respectively.[70] To some extent also they could attempt to subsidise the class struggle directly, as in the case of the assistance given to the British *Daily Herald* in the summer of 1920.[71] Appeals to the western working class, however, were often poorly judged and sometimes counter-productive, and the subsidies, sent abroad in the form of jewels contained in chocolates or in other guises, were often misappropriated, intercepted or too insubstantial to make a major contribution to the movement for which they were intended. A much more promising tactic, or so at least it must have appeared in the early 1920s, was to make use of the developing network of communist or workers' parties, many of which had substantial influence within their respective trade union movements, and which were organised internationally by the Communist International with its headquarters in Moscow. It was to the existence and propaganda activities of the Comintern (as it was known) that western governments took the most serious exception in their dealings with Moscow in the early 1920s.

The Communist International was not, in fact, a Soviet state organisation, and throughout its existence the Soviet government consistently maintained that it could assume no direct responsibility for its activities. As Maxim Litvinov, at this time a deputy commissar for foreign affairs, put it in a note addressed to the British government on 27 September 1921, the reason the Third or Communist International had chosen to base its executive committee in Russia was that Russia was the 'only country providing complete freedom for the spreading of communist ideas and personal freedom to communists'. The fact that several members of the Soviet government were on its executive committee, he went on, gave no more grounds for identifying the Communist International with the Soviet government than the location of the Second (Social Democratic) International in Brussels, and the presence on its executive committee of present or former British and Belgian ministers, gave for identifying that International with the British and Belgian governments.[72] Western diplomats, not surprisingly, found these arguments unconvincing, and in their dealings with the Soviet authorities they generally sought to ensure that all propaganda directed against them, whether it was organised by the Soviet government or simply emanated from the territory over which they ruled, was brought to an abrupt end. The Anglo-Russian trade agreement, for instance, bound both parties to refrain from hostile action or undertakings against the other party, whether within their own borders or beyond them. The Soviet–German agreement of May 1921 similarly bound the representatives of both parties to refrain from any agitation or propaganda against the government or political institutions of the other party; and the

Soviet–Italian agreement of December 1921 made analogous provisions.[73]

The matter, however, could not be quite so simply resolved. There was, in fact, a deep ambivalence at the leading levels of the Bolshevik party about the respective roles of revolutionary propaganda and of orthodox diplomatic relations. Although they had been disappointed by the collapse of the revolutionary regimes in Hungary and elsewhere and by the political stabilisation in Europe generally, the Soviet leaders remained committed to the view that the capitalist and socialist worlds could not indefinitely coexist, and that in the struggle between them socialism (led by Soviet Russia) would be triumphant. Whenever events abroad appeared to provide a warrant for it, as in Germany in the spring of 1921 and again briefly in 1923, the optimistic and more revolutionary tendency tended to gain ground. As an institution, the Communist International had also more political weight throughout the 1920s than the People's Commissariat for Foreign Affairs, which was headed by Chicherin. Grigorii Zinoviev, the chairman of the Comintern's executive, was a long-standing Bolshevik with a particularly close association with Lenin, and was a candidate member of the Politburo from 1919 and a full member from 1921 onwards. Chicherin, by contrast, was of noble origin and had worked for some time in the Tsarist foreign ministry; he had been first of all a Tolstoyan socialist and then a Menshevik before associating himself (on his return to Russia in January 1918) with the Bolsheviks. An outstanding linguist, cultivated (the author of a book on Mozart[74] and himself an excellent pianist), skilful and dedicated to his work, he was nonetheless not a member of the Bolshevik Central Committee in the early 1920s, much less a member of the Politburo, and was more of an executant than a maker of the foreign policy for which he was responsible.[75] The tensions between the two men and the institutions they represented, and more generally between a policy of revolutionary propaganda and one of normalisation of diplomatic relations with the outside world, were a major complicating factor in Soviet–Western relations in the early 1920s, and indeed beyond.

Apart from propaganda, the other major point at issue between the Soviet government and its western counterparts in the early 1920s was the question of nationalised property and debts. A series of decrees in the early months of Soviet rule had taken land, banks, oil and other sectors of the economy into state ownership.[76] Much more serious, from the Allied point of view, was a decree of the All-Russian Central Executive Committee (effectively the Soviet parliament) of 3 February 1918 which liquidated all state loans that had been contracted by the Imperial and Provisional governments with effect from December 1917. All previous state guarantees to enterprises and institutions were similarly annulled; and foreign loans, in particular, were annulled 'unconditionally and without any exceptions'.[77] The diplomatic representatives of the Allied and neutral powers, in a note to the Soviet foreign ministry of 15 February 1918, insisted that all decrees providing for the repudiation of loans and the confiscation of the property of foreign nations would be regarded as non-existing, and reserved the right of their governments, whenever they thought it appropriate, to demand restitution and compensation for any damage or losses that might have been suffered by foreign states in general or by their citizens in particular.[78] No agreement covering these issues had been made by the early 1920s, however, and the trading and other agreements into which the Soviet and western governments had entered generally reserved the matter for further discussion and for a separate and more specific agreement.

Not all the Allied nations were affected equally, and the proportions of nationalised property and of debts, and of public and private debts in particular, varied considerably from one country to another. France was in general the western nation which had lost most heavily. Estimates presented to the French government in 1920 suggested that a sum of more than 18 billion francs was involved, the larger part of which (over 11 billion francs) represented Russian government stock, railways bonds and so forth; the remainder (about 7 billion francs) represented the property or other interests in Russia of French nationals. Over 1.6 million individual claims had already been lodged in the latter connection.[79] A later estimate was prepared by Joseph Noulens, the president of the General Commission for the Protection of French Interests in Russia and a former French ambassador to the Tsar. According to Noulens's figures, the Russian debt to France amounted to not less than 25 billion francs, of which 4 billion represented state debts, 11 billion represented private debts guaranteed by the state, and over 10 billion represented the investments of French nationals in Russia.[80] French investments in Russia in 1902 were estimated at nearly 7 billion francs, by far the largest in any single foreign country at that time, and about 23.6 per cent of total French foreign investment at the same date.[81] The French stake in the pre-war Russian economy was also the largest of that of any of the powers, according to subsequent Soviet calculations; some 32.6 per cent of all share capital in foreign hands was French, followed by Great Britain with 22.6 per cent, Germany with 19.7 per cent, Belgium with 14.3 per cent and the USA with 5.2 per cent.[82]

British losses were also substantial. According to Hilton Young, Financial Secretary to the Treasury, in a speech to the House of Commons on 28 February 1922, Russian indebtedness to the United Kingdom up to 31 March 1921 amounted to £561.4 million, excluding interest payments since 31 December 1918, which had not been added to the capital sum. Russian debts to British private investors in the form of guaranteed bonds were not known, but a sum of about £180 million was suggested in this connection in early 1922.[83] British debts, however substantial, were nonetheless clearly less than those of France. According to an estimate prepared for the French foreign ministry in February 1922, France held some 43 per cent of all Russian foreign debts, followed by Great Britain with 33 per cent, Belgium and Germany with 6 per cent each, and the USA with 3.4 per cent. In some ways more important, however, was the structure of these various debts, and in particular the differences between Britain and France in this connection. According to the same French calculations, nearly three-quarters (73.9 per cent) of British debt represented government debt; in the French case, however, only 22 per cent fell into the same category, and much more was owed to private individuals.[84] Altogether there were about 1.2 million holders of Russian bonds in France, and they possessed, as a French treasury minister reminded the Genoa Conference, 'great political and electioneering influence'. British private claimants, in contrast, numbered no more than 38,000, and Italian private claimants a mere 400.[85]

The negotiation of a settlement to the Russian debt question in the early 1920s, already difficult, was greatly complicated by these various circumstances. The British government, holding the great majority of the Russian debt owed to that country, could itself determine the larger part of any general settlement so far as Britain was concerned; the French government, however, exercised much less control over the rather larger sum that was owed to that country, and was much more subject to pressure on the part of private citizens, in whose personal fortunes the Russian debt question generally occupied a much larger place. In Belgium, private Russian debts also

greatly exceeded intergovernmental debt, and Belgian policy was
generally in close accord with that of France; in Italy, however,
Russian debts were generally modest, and Italian policy, like that of
the British government, was generally more concerned to revive
trade and reduce unemployment than to insist upon the recognition
of obligations which were unlikely to be discharged for many years to
come.[86] The question of Russian and international debt in the early
1920s was accordingly not simply a matter that divided the Soviet
government from its major capitalist counterparts; the varied interests of the western countries themselves made it a challenge to
statesmanship of the highest order to devise a settlement that would
appeal to all the parties whose support would be essential for its
success.[87]

2

Approaching the Russian problem

The more remote origins of the Genoa Conference, it has been suggested, lie in the increasing realisation that urgent steps had to be taken to reconstitute the post-war European economy, combined with an increasing awareness that some form of relations would have to be established with the new Soviet government in Moscow. The Soviet government, it had become clear, was likely to survive for at least the foreseeable future, and no realistic alternative appeared to remain but to attempt to establish a political and economic relationship between the new regime and the rest of Europe, a task as great as any that European statesmen had experienced since the end of the French revolutionary wars. The more immediate origins of the conference lie in a number of further circumstances. It had become clear, first of all, that the two problems, that of European reconstruction and that of the establishment of some sort of relations with the Soviet government, were closely interconnected; and secondly, it had become apparent that the position of the Soviet government, although difficult, was not such as to allow the western powers to dictate their own terms to it. Thirdly, and perhaps most important, the Soviet government's own actions, as well as the declarations of its representatives in their dealings with foreign powers, suggested that the new regime might for its own part be interested in establishing a closer relationship with its western neighbours, in order, above all, to revive its own economy, and that it might not be inflexible in regard to the issues that the western powers regarded as most important in this connection, such as propaganda and debts. By the end of 1921 these various circumstances had led to their logical outcome, a proposal for an international conference to which the Soviet and German governments would both be invited and in which a new

European political and economic order, it was hoped, would be negotiated.

It appeared to begin with as if no such negotiations might be necessary. The introduction of the New Economic Policy in March 1921, in particular, with its denationalistion of small-scale industry and retail trade, seemed to suggest that the Soviet government's adoption of what were generally regarded as unworkable economic principles might prove no more than a temporary aberration. Lloyd George was particularly impressed by a speech of Lenin's of 17 October 1921 in which the Soviet leader was reported to have said that the Bolsheviks had 'suffered a heavy defeat on the economic front' and to have conceded that the New Economic Policy involved a 'transition to the re-establishment of capitalism to a certain extent'. Lenin, the premier told the House of Commons, 'admits they have been wrong, he admits they have been beaten'. The speech as a whole had been a 'very remarkable condemnation and exposure of the doctrines of Karl Marx by ... its greatest living exponent, the only man who has ever tried honestly to put these doctrines into operation'.[1] Reports from diplomatic representatives in the Soviet capital, and in the press, generally conveyed the same impression. The communist experiment in Russia was 'at an end', declared *The Times* on 2 December 1921; it was 'only a matter of hitting on a suitable formula for reintroducing capitalism', the paper reported on 19 November. Across the Channel, an article in *Le Matin* on 'Lenin, the apprentice bourgeois' put much the same view. In America, the normally cautious Walter Duranty reported the end of communism in a series of articles in the *New York Times*.[2] In many quarters in the West, recalled Lyubov' Krasin, the wife of the Soviet foreign trade commissar and diplomatic representative, in France, Britain and Germany, it was believed that Lenin was persuaded of the failure of Bolshevism and that it would 'not be long before foreign capital would reassume, under modified conditions, its former prominent place in Russia'.[3]

Weak as the Soviet government might be, however, the experience of the late summer and early autumn of 1921 showed that it was still too soon to expect it to capitulate entirely. In particular, the Soviet leaders showed no inclination to modify their position during the famine which overwhelmed the Volga area in the latter part of 1921. The Soviet government did, indeed, make an appeal to the governments of all countries on 2 August 1921, calling upon them urgently for assistance, and Lenin made a parallel appeal to the international proletariat on the same date.[4] The relief organisations already in the field, the Soviet note pointed out, were insufficiently informed of the real state of affairs in Russia, as were the press and governments in western countries. In ten *gubernii* and several *uezdy* a severe and continuous drought had ensured that the harvest would not exceed 10–15 per cent of its usual level, and in some cases it had been totally destroyed. About 18 million people lived in the regions concerned, and substantial supplies would be needed to feed them and their cattle, and to provide for future harvests. Only a small proportion of these needs could be met from other domestic sources, and a very serious disaster accordingly threatened the whole area. The Soviet government, the note went on, was making every effort to provide assistance, as were all Russian citizens, whatever their political views or social origin. A number of Soviet delegations had already travelled or would be travelling abroad to negotiate with relief organisations in various countries; western governments were urged to place no obstacle in the way of the work of these organisations, or of private individuals who wished to render assistance. The Soviet government for its own part would welcome assistance from whatever quarter and would make every attempt to facilitate it.[5]

The matter was followed up in more detail at a series of meetings between British and Soviet trade representatives at 10 Downing Street and later in the Board of Trade. At the first meeting, on 5 August 1921, called at the request of Jan Berzin, the deputy Soviet trade representative, he and his colleague N. K. Klishko met Lloyd George, the premier's adviser on Russian affairs E. J. Wise, and his personal secretary Sir Edward Grigg. Berzin raised the question of assistance; the British representatives, for their part, raised the issues of propaganda and of the outstanding debts, and asked if they would be acknowledged.[6] In a memorandum to the prime minister of the same date Wise had suggested that the Russian famine might best be countered by the provision of goods on commercial credit terms, which in turn might be made conditional upon a greater degree of recognition by the Soviet government of its public and private debts.[7] The Cabinet also urged against the allocation of government funds, but raised no objection to the provision of facilities in return for payment, to the raising of a voluntary fund, or to allowing Romania to provide wheat to Russia in return for the discharge of her debts, providing that the administration of any relief should be in British hands.[8] At a further meeting, on 6 August 1921 in the Board of Trade, with Sir Philip Lloyd-Greame, Director of the Overseas Trade Department, also in attendance, the Soviet representatives gave a detailed exposition of the situation in the famine areas, and of their needs and proposed purchases; Lloyd George, in reply, again raised the question of the recognition of the Russian debts, and also raised the question of collateral for any loans, whether in the form of gold, timber or whatever. The security presently being offered in return for assistance, he remarked at the conclusion of the meeting, did not seem likely to be sufficient to convince the advisory committee that supervised the operation of the relevant export credit arrangements.[9]

The matter was discussed further at a meeting of the Allied Supreme Council which took place in Paris two days later, and which was principally devoted to the question of Upper Silesia. The Russian question came up for discussion at the session on 10 August 1921. Briand, the French premier, began by arguing that it would be 'abominable' to treat the Russian question from any other than a humanitarian point of view, or for the powers to assume no responsibility for the great misfortune that had befallen that country. He thought it best to associate Allied efforts with those being made by the Red Cross and other relief organisations in their own countries. Lloyd George, for the British government, agreed with Briand that private efforts would not be enough; 'It would require the miracle of the loaves and fishes over again.' The consequences of the disaster, moreover, such as typhus, cholera and plague, had direct implications for the European nations themselves. All the Allied governments disliked working with the Bolsheviks; on the other hand they were the only effective authority of any kind in Russia. Lloyd George proposed the establishment of an international committee to deal with the matter; the Russian people, he thought, would not be ungrateful for its formation, and it was moreover the 'best way of saving Russia from something almost as bad as the plague – the Bolshevist system'. It was eventually agreed to establish a 'Commission for the study of the possibilities of affording urgent relief to the starving population of Russia'; three days later it was agreed that each power should appoint three representatives to the commission, and that it should meet as soon as possible in Paris and determine the best mode of cooperation with philanthropic and other bodies.[10]

The Commission duly met in Paris on 3 September 1921,[11] and the following day its chairman, Joseph Noulens, addressed a note to the Soviet government announcing its existence and seeking permission for a 'committee of experts' to visit the affected areas. The committee, Noulens explained, would consist of about thirty experts from the five Allied powers represented on the International Commission, and would attempt to determine the food, medical, transport and other needs of the famine area.[12] The Commission's request was considered by a meeting of the Russian Communist Party's Politburo on 6 August, and a reply was agreed on the basis of a draft by Lenin. Lenin drew particular attention to Noulens's openly counter-revolutionary role in the past, and to what he considered to be the impudent and insulting nature of his request.[13] The Soviet reply, issued the following day, began by casting doubt upon the wish of such a delegation to render genuine assistance to the famine-stricken population, and noted the anti-Soviet credentials of Noulens in particular. The Commission, moreover, was proposing a lengthy and detailed investigation of internal conditions in Russia in place of the assistance to the starving population that was urgently needed. Neither the American Relief Administration nor the relief organisation headed by Fridtjof Nansen under the auspices of the League of Nations had felt it necessary to make such preliminary inquiries (agreements with both organisations had been concluded on 20 and 27 August respectively),[14] and in any case there was little point in examining the opportunities for the sowing of new crops, as the season had almost ended. Any practical offer of assistance to the famine-stricken population would be welcomed; but the Noulens proposals, the note concluded, were an 'unheard-of mockery of millions of dying and starving people'.[15]

The International Commission, undaunted, held a meeting in Paris on 15 and 16 September 1921 to consider further moves. It was decided that no useful purpose would be served by entering into further correspondence with the Soviet government, but it was agreed that the Commission should nonetheless continue its work and that it should meet in Brussels on 6 October, with representatives of the border states in attendance, to determine what action should be taken in regard to the provision of relief and of credits.[16] The Brussels meeting, which took place between 6 and 8 October 1921, was attended by representatives of twenty-one nations, including German and American representatives in an observing capacity. After discussion of the rival merits of the American Relief Admin-

istration and Nansen agreements, the Commission approved a series
of resolutions and established a secretariat in Paris to coordinate its
future activity. The resolution on credits which was adopted again
insisted that the provision of credits to assist the export of supplies to
Russia would be feasible only if the Soviet government recognised its
debts and provided adequate security for future obligations (the
Commission disclaimed any motive, political or otherwise, in imposing such a condition).[17] The Soviet government, however, proved no
more receptive to these new proposals, rejecting them in a note to
Allied governments of 28 October 1921,[18] and the International
Commission played no further part in international famine matters.
Western governments, in the end, generally made bilateral arrangements of their own, often through the agency of the Red Cross; on 2
November 1921, for instance, it was announced that the British
government was providing £250,000 worth of medical stores,
clothing and tinned food to the British Red Cross for distribution in
Russia, and on 3 November it was announced that the French
government was allocating 6 million francs to the French Red Cross
for similar purposes.[19]

The Soviet note of 28 October 1921 did nonetheless appear to
represent a modification and the previous Soviet position in at least
one significant respect: the all-important question of the acknowledgement of debts. The Soviet position had in fact begun to move
rather earlier in the year, according to the records of a secret
discussion between a member of Lloyd George's staff and Klishko of
the Russian trading delegation on 9 September 1921. At the meeting,
which took place at 10 Downing Street, Klishko read out a secret and
personal message to Lloyd George signed by Krasin and counter-
signed by Chicherin. The Soviet government, according to this *note
verbale*, would be willing to recognise Russian external state debts,
other than war debts, provided that it was accorded full *de jure*
recognition, that it received a guarantee of non-interference in its
internal affairs, and that all support was withdrawn from counter-
revolutionary movements. A guarantee would also be needed that
Russian counterclaims for damages suffered directly or indirectly as a
result of foreign intervention during the Russian civil war would be
recognised. The precise terms for the conversion of debts, the dates at
which the payment of interest would begin and the method of
payment would be determined after having taken into account the
measures that would have to be taken for the economic restoration of

the country, which was itself to be assisted by the immediate granting of long-term trading and financial credits. Detailed arrangements on all these matters should be made by an international conference which would meet at a later date. Klishko sought Lloyd George's opinion on this far-reaching proposal, and expressed his willingness to travel to Scotland (where the premier was holidaying) to discuss it with him further.[20]

This secret communication (to which no reply is extant) in fact coincided fairly closely with the substance of Chicherin's note of 28 October 1921 to the Allied governments. The recognition of Tsarist debts, the note began, on which the Brussels conference had insisted, was also, under certain circumstances, the wish of the Soviet government itself. The Soviet government had from the beginning declared its willingness to cooperate in economic matters with other states, and to provide an adequate return for foreign capitalists who might wish to develop Russia's natural resources and to re-establish its economic administration. There could in fact be no genuine peace without Russia and her 130 million population, the note went on, and no relations could be established between Russia and the outside world without the agreement of the Soviet government. The Soviet government had already re-established private trade and private ownership of smaller enterprises, and had introduced concessions and leasehold arrangements for larger ones. Legal and other guarantees had also been introduced in order to provide security and an adequate rate of profit for foreign capitalist interests. No people, the note declared, could be required to pay for the chains they had had to bear for centuries. In the interests of a complete agreement with the other powers, however, and in order to satisfy the legitimate needs of the numerous private holders of Russian bonds, particularly in France, the Soviet government declared its willingness to make a series of 'major and significant' concessions in regard to Tsarist debts. The Soviet government, the note continued, would be prepared to recognise all state loans contracted by the Tsarist government before 1914, provided it was granted conditions sufficiently advantageous to make their repayment a real possibility. It would similarly have to be formally recognised, a general peace treaty with the western powers would have to be concluded, and the inviolability of Soviet frontiers would have to be guaranteed. An international conference, the note concluded, should be called for this purpose in the near future; its task would be to arbitrate the claims of each side against the other and to establish a firm and definitive peace between them.[21]

The British response to this communication was a measured but not entirely hostile one. The Soviet government, L. S. O'Malley, Senior Clerk in the Foreign Office, pointed out, had gone halfway to satisfying one of the resolutions of the Brussels conference in expressing its readiness to honour pre-war Tsarist debts. The note had said nothing, however, about the Russian war debt to the United Kingdom of some £600 million, nor about the claims of private citizens in respect of their property in Russia which had been seized or destroyed (about £200 million in total value), nor about other categories of claims such as railway or municipal loans. The aim of the note, O'Malley thought, was to shift the discussion to the question of recognition; the British reply should however be 'as little contentious as possible', and should not discourage the Soviet government from making further concessions. J. D. Gregory of the Northern Department added that a swift response would prevent the issue being 'diverted from the famine towards the dangerous question of recognition'.[22] The British reply of 1 November 1921 accordingly welcomed the general tone of the Soviet note but drew attention to some of the obscurities it contained, such as the questions of post–1914 Tsarist debts, municipal and railway loans, and the claims of those owners of private property in Russia which had been nationalised or destroyed. The note invited the Soviet government to make its attitude explicit in regard to these and all other such classes of claims.[23]

The Soviet note of 28 October 1921 was received with rather less enthusiasm in Paris. Indeed it was received with 'calm scepticism', according to a press report, because it covered only the pre-war and not the vast wartime debts, and was in any case excessively vague about the means of their repayment.[24] On 8 November 1921 the French government asked the British government for its views upon the matter. It referred to its previous communications to the British government on the subject of the Russian debts, and suggested that Chicherin's concessions showed the wisdom of France's firm stand upon the matter. The French government, the note made clear, continued to regard it as 'vain and dangerous' for the present to seek the resumption even of economic relations with the Soviet government. This, it thought, was also the attitude of the United States government, and had been shown to be correct by recent experiences, such as the failure of the negotiations between Leslie Urquhart, a British claimant, and the Soviet authorities. The restoration of economic relations with Russia, in the French view, depended upon the Soviet authorities abandoning the economic principles they had applied up to that time, which differed from those obtaining among all civilised nations. The recognition of debts in this connection was not a concession, but rather the recognition of a basic principle, and only means and guarantees of repayment could properly be discussed. The note drew attention to the omissions of Chicherin's communication, such as war and municipal debts and the claims of private citizens for damages or repossession, and also raised the question of propaganda. The only solution, the French note concluded, was for the Soviet government to recognise all its obligations without exception or qualification; only then could negotiations be considered. What, it asked, were the British government's views upon the matter?[25]

The British reply of 16 November 1921 avoided responding to all the issues that had been raised in the French note, commenting simply that the British government shared the French view that it was necessary for the Soviet government to recognise all its debts before normal economic relations with other countries could be resumed.[26] The French government, in reply, emphasised that all Russian, and not simply all Soviet, obligations must be accepted.[27] Meanwhile, however, British–Soviet discussions had advanced further. On 12 November 1921 Chicherin sent a telegram to Krasin for the British government welcoming the British reply of 1 November, agreeing that some aspects of the Soviet proposal needed further clarification, and suggesting that an international conference might be a more convenient means of reaching agreement upon such matters than the further exchange of diplomatic notes. Debts were seen, from the Soviet point of view, as only one aspect of the economic restoration of Russia and of the world generally. It was also necessary for both sides to manifest good will, which had not been evident in the exclusion of Russia from international gatherings where questions affecting her interests were being discussed and decisions binding upon her were being taken. No people, the note reiterated, could be expected to pay for the debts of a social order they had overthrown, but the Soviet government had always made it clear that it was at least prepared to pay its own debts in the most punctilious manner.[28] The recognition of pre-war debts, Klishko remarked to the Foreign

Office, was in fact a very important concession, opening the way to closer cooperation and to joint measures for economic recovery.[29]

The position was considered in more detail at a meeting between Krasin, Lloyd George and Sir Robert Horne, the Chancellor of the Exchequer, on 17 December 1921. Lloyd George began by suggesting that assistance to Russia could best be organised by a syndicate of British, French and German interests. Security for any loans might be provided through (for instance) the control of Russian railways by the interests concerned. Krasin reacted sceptically; full diplomatic recognition was a prior necessity, and Soviet public opinion had also to be considered when such far-reaching concessions were involved. Nor would private assistance be sufficient for the tasks involved without substantial state guarantees and direct participation.[30] On 24 December Krasin held two further meetings with E. F. Wise to consider a draft declaration covering the central issues involved: recognition, debts and assistance. The Soviet government, Wise suggested, should recognise all Tsarist and Provisional government debts, and agree to compensate private citizens and foreign governments for their losses. In return the western powers would agree to recognise any obligations they might have towards Soviet Russia, the amounts involved in both cases to be determined by an arbitral commission. Lloyd George had indicated that France might be prepared to recognise the Soviet government on such a basis, and that French representatives might be willing to take part in an international conference on the matter such as the Soviet government had been proposing.[31] Wise sent a draft proposal to Thomas Jones, Assistant Secretary of the Cabinet, along these lines on 29 December, adding that Krasin had in principle accepted it and had undertaken to recommend it to his government.[32] Lloyd George, Krasin reported to Moscow, was in fact resigned to the necessity of eventually recognising the Soviet government, but it would be much harder to persuade Briand to do likewise; the British had also no precise plans for the economic development of Russia, where their ideas had evidently been borrowed from the German industrialists who were taking an interest in such matters.[33]

Krasin's response to Wise suggested that the Soviet government might at least not prove entirely inflexible on some of the key questions that remained at issue. The Politburo, at its meeting on 13 September 1921, had in fact taken a decision that Russian debts to certain states might be recognised, with the exception of war debts, provided that Soviet counterclaims were allowed, that compensation was paid for damages arising from foreign intervention during the civil war, that loans were provided for economic reconstruction and that the Soviet government was fully recognised.[34] Chicherin, impressed by what he regarded as a worsening international situation for the Soviet government at this time, privately urged still further concessions upon the other Soviet leaders. Lenin and Trotsky, he suggested in a letter to Lenin of 15 October 1921, should leave the executive committee of the Comintern, and all the Tsarist debts should be recognised. He repeated his proposals in a further letter of 17 October.[35] Lenin, however, remained firmly opposed to all such suggestions, and at his initiative Chicherin prepared a new and more uncompromising draft of his proposals. This, with Lenin's amendments, was approved by the Politburo on 27 October and despatched abroad the following day under Chicherin's signature.[36] Krasin, in a letter to Chicherin of 2 November 1921, proposed that railway and municipal debts should also be acknowledged. Lenin, however, was once again opposed, arguing that there was 'no need to hurry' and that more attention should be given to the Soviet counterclaims.[37] Chicherin eventually suggested, on 4 November, that any discussion of private, railway and other debts should be deferred until an international conference could consider the matter; Trotsky disagreed, but Lenin this time sided with Chicherin, as did Stalin, and the Politburo took a decision accordingly on 8 November 1921.[38] Chicherin's reply to the British government of 12 November, which proposed that all remaining Soviet–Western differences be referred to an international conference, was in line with this decision.[39]

By this time a further element had entered into the equation, the proposal, already referred to in general terms by Lloyd George at his meeting with Krasin, that a western economic syndicate should be established for the economic development of Russia and perhaps of other countries in eastern and central Europe. The idea originated from several sources. In part, at least, it sprang from a suggestion originally made by Briand in a note to the British government of 25 November 1920 that an international organisation should be established which would take control of Russian assets so as to ensure the repayment of Russian debts, which the Soviet government (together with the other states which had come into existence on the territory of the former Russian empire) would be required unconditionally to recognise.[40] To perhaps a rather greater extent, as the former French president Raymond Poincaré explained in his regular article in the *Revue des Deux Mondes*, it sprang from the gradual renewal of economic links between Russia and Germany which had been encouraged by the trade agreement of May 1921. Russia, before the war, had been one of Germany's most important export markets, and Germany had in turn been by far Russia's most important trading partner in the outside world. With the conclusion of the trade agreement German–Russian economic relations began to resume their earlier intimacy, and the idea began to emerge of a more far-reaching arrangement including other western interests for the economic development of Russia on a much broader scale. Krasin, Poincaré believed, had been among the most active proponents of such an idea, and had held several discussions on the matter with leading German industrialists; American participation also seemed possible.[41]

The Germans, according to the British ambassador in Berlin, Lord d'Abernon, had in fact 'vast hopes' as to the benefits they could enjoy from an opportunity to develop the Russian market. The former foreign minister, Dr Simons, had remarked to d'Abernon that the 'best chance' for Germany appeared to lie in cooperating with Britain and America to regain her prosperity by developing Russia. German opinion generally held that economic recovery would come from this source more readily than from any other, but British political support was believed to be essential for the project to be successful.[42] Lloyd George, for his part, appears to have been convinced by the failure of the London reparations conference of May 1921 that there was no hope of moderating French policy and achieving an agreement unless the area of discussion was widened further. From this emerged the threefold formula of 'reparation, security and reconstruction'.[43] The premier was also concerned by the rapid rise in unemployment, noting in a speech at Inverness on 4 October 1921 that the country was facing not simply an ordinary trade depression but a collapse of credit, currencies and confidence throughout the world, the solution to which would require global and not simply domestic British measures.[44] The Chancellor of the Exchequer, Sir Robert Horne, took a similar view in a message he communicated to the *Amsterdam Telegraaf* of 10 November.[45] Hugo Stinnes, one of those most concerned in the proposals for the establishment of an international consortium in Germany, made a visit to London between 19 and 24 November 1921, and although he was unable officially to see Lloyd George he engaged in discussions with several people in the premier's confidence and with financial and industrial interests.[46] Walter Rathenau, the German minister for reconstruction and later foreign affairs, was also in London in November and December 1921; he met Lloyd George (who told him he had in fact met Stinnes) on 2 December 1921 and discussed the possible connection between Russia, reparations and western industry at some length.[47]

Most proposals for the establishment of a consortium assumed the participation of British, German and in a few cases American interests. French participation, however, was not normally envisaged, partly because of France's traditionally less intimate trading relations with Russia, and partly also because French public as well as official opinion remained sceptical of a proposal from which Germany appeared most immediately to benefit. There was also a relative lack of available capital and interested entrepreneurs. The French government, however, was kept fully informed of the progress of the discussions,[48] and on several occasions French ministers were invited to take a more active role. Rathenau, for instance, held up a vision of 'powerful syndicates directed by Frenchmen and Germans' operating in Russia in his discussions with French officials in September 1921.[49] The French ambassador in Tokyo reported a more elaborate scheme for the reconstruction of Siberia and Turkestan under American, Japanese and possibly French auspices. Projects of this kind were in fact doomed to failure, the financial service of the French foreign minister reported at the end of October 1921, and would lead to no concrete results.[50] The danger still remained, as Poincaré had put it in his article in the *Revue des Deux Mondes*, that other countries might lack the patience to allow Bolshevism to collapse of its own accord and that they might approach the Soviet government directly, seeking access to the largest market in the world. If they did so, Poincaré asked, could the French afford to be left alone, 'eternally lamenting at the roadside'? And could the French government afford to alienate its British counterpart at a time when it was seeking a bilateral alliance to take the place of the lapsed treaty of guarantee?[51]

A report in the *Manchester Guardian* early in December 1921 suggested that enthusiasm for the new scheme might be somewhat premature. Commenting upon an elaborate version of the consortium proposal which had been published in Paris by the *Journal des Débats*, apparently based upon Rathenau and Stinnes's discussions in London, the Russian trading delegation in Britain pronounced itself

'very sceptical' about the scheme. The idea of the economic exploitation of Russia by a western syndicate, it pointed out, was not new:
something of the kind had been in the minds of Kaiser Wilhelm II
and his advisers at the start of the war, and it had formed the basis of
the settlement they had imposed at Brest-Litovsk. Nor was there
necessarily anything new in the idea of a consortium: the western
powers, in fact, had constituted such a combination in their intervention in Russia after the revolution. The scheme, it pointed out, could
not be carried out without the support of the Soviet government and
people, who were not likely to wish to become an 'arena for economic
and political experiments' carried out by foreign powers, and it was
defective in technical and commercial terms also.[52] The proposal
nonetheless continued to gather weight in western capitals. On 8
December 1921 Lloyd George took the idea further in preliminary
discussions with Louis Loucheur, the French minister for the liber-
ated regions, and the basis of a Franco-British understanding on the
matter began to emerge more clearly. The prime minister urged, first
of all, that a combined effort be made to involve the United States in a
general settlement of war debts and indemnities. If this failed, as it
appeared likely to do, the prime minister believed an independent
initiative of the same character should be undertaken by Britain and
France; and though the moment might not yet be ripe, he thought a
consortium should also be established between Britain, France and
Germany for the economic reconstruction of Russia.[53] Rathenau,
with whom Loucheur had also discussed the proposal, had been
willing to allow Britain and France to take a 35 per cent share each in
the proposed consortium, leaving Germany with the remaining 30
per cent.[54]

The prime minister also sought the opinion of his Cabinet colleagues upon the matter. At a meeting on 16 December 1921, called to
consider British policy in advance of a conference with Briand which
was to take place the following week, it was reported that the United
States government had adopted a 'very hostile' attitude to the
possibility of discussing inter-Allied debts at any future meeting, and
it was agreed that no proposals of this nature should be presented to
the United States government for the time being. It also appeared
unlikely that the German government would be able to make the
reparations payments that were due in January and February 1922.
Both matters, it was thought, required the convening of an international conference at which appropriate measures could be con-

sidered. The Cabinet was reminded in this connection of the enormous importance to Great Britain of the economic restoration of eastern Europe and Russia. It was clear that this was a task which could most effectively be carried out by Germany; and it had been suggested that the Allies facilitate the task of Germany in this respect, provided that a substantial proportion of the income that resulted was devoted to the payment of reparations. Both Rathenau and Stinnes were reported to be strongly in favour of such a scheme. The consent and cooperation of the Soviet government would be necessary, and also some degree of foreign control of Russian railways and customs in order to guarantee the substantial sums involved. It was agreed that the prime minister should be empowered to discuss such a scheme further with the French ministers, provided that no commitment was made to the diplomatic recognition of the Soviet government without a further consideration of the matter.[55]

The decision, even in this qualified form, was not a unanimous one. Winston Churchill, in particular, objected to any steps of this kind being taken for the time being, and Edwin Montagu, Secretary of State for India, insisted that all Soviet anti-imperialist propaganda be ended before closer relations with the Soviet government were contemplated. Curzon, who had left before this point on the agenda had been reached, reserved his position on the question of recognition and argued for prior agreement with the French government before a decision on any of these matters was taken.[56] Curzon wrote to Churchill to inform him of his attitude, and Churchill, in reply, expressed his full agreement. When the right moment came, he explained to Curzon, he would be prepared to support a tripartite or (if the United States were involved) quadripartite plan for the economic reorganisation of Russia, including, if necessary, the diplomatic recognition of the Soviet government. He saw the 'gravest objections', however, to giving help and countenance to the 'tyrannic Government of these Jew Commissars', who were persecuting their bourgeoisie and carrying on a continuous war with their peasantry. Some improvement in the Russian internal situation, he thought, was imperative before external assistance to the Soviet government was seriously contemplated. From what he knew, the Soviet authorities were so desperate for foreign aid that they would be prepared to change their policies and broaden the basis of their government in order to secure it.[57] Curzon, in reply, agreed that the sole object of the Bolsheviks in seeking recognition was to strengthen their domestic position. Once they had done so, they would revert to type and the Allies would be confronted by the old absolutist and terrorist regime. Soviet propaganda, moreover, with Lenin's complicity, was continuing unabated. He hoped the Cabinet would be cautious before it gave the 'final leg up to Lenin, Trotsky & Co.'[58] It was a reminder that divisions within governments ran almost as deep as divisions between them.

The conference with Briand and Loucheur had been prompted by the situation in the Near East, where M. Franklin-Bouillon, a French representative, had recently entered into an agreement with the Turkish government which appeared to contravene a prior British–French understanding. The French, Curzon informed the Cabinet, had failed to consult Britain about the agreement, and there might be further secret provisions which would be to their disadvantage. The Cabinet agreed that French conduct had been 'most reprehensible'.[59] Relations improved somewhat thereafter – the French insisted that the agreement had been similar to ones previously proposed, and that the British ambassador had been kept fully informed – and it was agreed in early December that the matter should be resolved by negotiations between the British, French and Italian foreign ministers. Briand, under criticism at home for France's relative lack of success at the Washington naval conference, was keen to secure some tangible achievement in the foreign policy field by way of compensation. Agreeing to the meeting on 4 December 1921, he accordingly added that he would like to make use of the opportunity to have a 'more general discussion on the whole range of questions that interest France and Great Britain'.[60] In further correspondence with Lord Curzon the French ambassador made it clear that it was intended the discussions should touch on the proposed bilateral alliance, where France would not be satisfied with a simple guarantee against direct German aggression, and also on the consortium proposal, where French participation would help to allay the criticism that too much had been conceded at Washington.[61]

The meeting between Lloyd George and Briand began on 19 December 1921.[62] It was, the premiers agreed, to be concerned with all issues outstanding between the two powers. Lloyd George began by referring to his conversations with Loucheur, and emphasised the need to go beyond the immediate problem of reparations to deal with the economic situation of Europe more generally. The United States, he thought, would not be likely to take part in any plan they might devise, and any effective solution would therefore depend upon Franco-British cooperation. Briand, for his part, drew attention to the concern in French public and official circles about the possibility that Germany might default on her reparations payments. In contrast, it was believed that an agreement with Britain would 'put everything right'. Lloyd George pointed out that Germany would be able to pay only if German exports were increased, and that this in turn required the opening up of eastern and central Europe to German traders, an area with which they had historically strong connections. If half or two-thirds of the proceeds of such trade could be devoted to the payment of reparations, that problem would be very much alleviated; and France might also be enabled to raise a loan on an ordinary commercial basis for the reconstruction of her devastated provinces. A regular payment of perhaps £50 million per annum from Germany would provide sufficient security for a loan of perhaps £700 to £800 million. Briand agreed the plan was a good one in principle, but it would be necessary to wait a long time for any payment to ensue; there was no immediate prospect of extensive trade in Russia or central Europe, and the real problem, he thought, was that big businessmen in Germany were not helping the government to pay its debts. Lloyd George thought the Germans should be offered more inducements to fulfil their commitments; Briand replied that French opinion was more concerned by Germany's continual evasion of those commitments. It was agreed that a sub-committee should examine the matter further.[63]

The following day, 20 December 1921, discussion again centred on the reparations problem. After a series of further exchanges, Lloyd George announced to the French premier that he proposed to call a 'great economic conference' to which representatives of all European industrial countries would be invited, whose task would be to advise on arrangements for the rehabilitation of central and eastern Europe. As part of the scheme for the rehabilitation of Russia in particular, he suggested that Germany be granted facilities for the development of Russian industry and that 50 per cent of the profits that accrued from such activities be devoted to the payment of reparations. This would in turn offer good security for Germany to raise a loan. The British government, Lloyd George went on, was proposing a general settlement along these lines; he hoped the French government would be able to agree to cooperate, but if not it would have to pursue its own course. British public opinion would tolerate no further disturbance of the world situation; any undue pressure upon Germany in particular would simply drive that country into bankruptcy with 'incalculable' results throughout the world. The reconstruction of eastern Europe and Russia would be undertaken by a syndicate of French, British, German and possibly also Belgian and Italian interests, though these other countries would be unlikely to be able to make a significant contribution. The United States should also be invited to participate. The syndicate would need to exercise considerable control over railways and other services in the area concerned in order to guarantee its investment. The scheme as a whole, he thought, offered the only serious prospect of enabling Germany to meet her reparations payments. The British and French governments should agree first of all upon the basic principles, and then ask other countries to take part if they wished to do so. A group of experts should meanwhile be appointed to examine the proposal in more detail.[64]

A meeting between Horne, Loucheur and Sir Laming Worthington-Evans, Secretary of State for War, duly took place later the same day, and a more precise version of the consortium proposal began to emerge. It was agreed that the United States was unlikely to participate in any proposed arrangements, and that any action would have to be undertaken by private entrepreneurs, although governments could advise and assist. The establishment of a central syndicate was proposed, on which all European countries would be represented by industrialists of high standing. It should have an initial capital of £10 million, although if any extensive reconstruction work was to be undertaken a much larger sum would ultimately be needed. The central syndicate would also participate in separate but related ventures, for instance a special syndicate for Romania. It was agreed that the proposal meant 'sooner or later the recognition, *de jure* as well as *de facto*, of the Russian Soviet Government'. This appeared to be the only realistic approach; and that government was anyway, according to Rathenau, who attended the meeting, 'rapidly shedding most of its extreme communistic views'. Loucheur thought French public opinion might eventually be reconciled to such an arrangement provided it could be shown that this was the only, or at least the most promising, means of restoring France herself. Rathenau had doubted if any German profits could be allocated to the repayment of reparations, and had pointed out that the sums involved would, at least to begin with, be very small. He had, however, been told that some arrangement of this sort was psychologically necessary if French participation was to be envisaged. It was generally agreed that a scheme based upon the syndicate idea offered the best prospects for European reconstruction, provided it was possible to attract the right type of industrialist, and also that the necessary capital would be raised. Horne was less confident than Loucheur or Rathenau in this connection.[65]

At a further meeting on 21 December 1921, the two premiers agreed that the Supreme Council should meet at Cannes on 4 January 1922 to 'discuss the general economic situation in Europe'. Briand remarked that the proposal was not an easy one for his government to accept, and added that French public opinion would need some time to accustom itself to a new situation of this kind, even if some advantages were to be obtained as a result. He thought any recognition of the Soviet government, in particular, would be premature, and he urged that the scheme for the reconstruction of Europe if possible avoid all mention of Russia. Lloyd George, however, thought that influential elements in the Soviet leadership were ready for some recognition of their debts, and if this were so the French government would at least be able to secure a written guarantee for its bondholders. This did not mean that interest would immediately be payable – all the European countries, not only Russia, were in fact seeking to avoid interest payments on their foreign debts – but the bonds would undoubtedly increase in value and might have a significant value in a few years' time. Briand replied that it would help if the Soviet government gave some indication that it would behave in future as a government should behave. Lloyd George, however, pointed out that the old system of government had not been of a high moral order, and he thought it would in any case be unwise to wait until the Soviet government had collapsed. Its most serious opponent, Boris Savinkov, had told him he expected it to survive for up to three more years, and Europe could not go on starving until then. Savinkov, in fact, had urged the Allies to talk to Lenin and Trotsky, who were, he believed, now fighting the extremist wing of their own party, and would defy them if they thought they had the support of western Europe. The Bolsheviks could thus be split and turned into a 'respectable political party of somewhat advanced views'. Briand agreed that some form of relations was necessary and had indeed been involved in the arrangements for famine relief, but he continued to urge the need for caution.[66]

Horne reported later the same evening that the plan had been put
to Rathenau and that he had agreed upon a means by which the
German government could take part in the proposed syndicate.
About half of the German capital involved would be found by the
government and the remainder by commercial undertakings; all of
the dividends accruing to the German government would then be
allocated to the repayment of reparations. The details, it was agreed,
could be considered at Cannes; both the British and French governments undertook meanwhile to consult their own industrialists upon
the matter. Briand at this point announced his agreement with the
policy that Lloyd George had put forward, although he still wished
no mention to be made of Russia, if possible, for the time being. The
French bondholders 'would themselves become advocates of the
revolution', he thought, as soon as it was made clear that the Soviet
government would be repaying them.[67] There was some further
discussion of the proposed Anglo-French alliance, Lloyd George
again resisting French pressure for a comprehensive treaty instead of
a mere limited guarantee against a direct German attack on France's
eastern borders. It was agreed that the matter would be discussed
more fully at Cannes.[68] On 22 December 1921, at their final meeting,
the two premiers gave their attention to a British Treasury memorandum, entitled 'Proposals for re-establishing better economic conditions in Europe', which outlined the reasons for the proposed
consortium and suggested an organisational structure for it. An
amended version was approved and it was agreed that it should be
considered further by a meeting of experts in Paris on 30 and 31
December and then discussed at Cannes. Italian and Belgian
ministers were to be informed of the general nature of the proposals
by British and French ministers respectively. After some further
discussion of the reparations issue the meeting concluded.[69]

A meeting of British and French financial experts duly took place
in Paris on 30 and 31 December 1921, with Belgian, Italian and
Japanese delegates also in attendance. Discussion centred on a
French translation of the British Treasury memorandum that had
been approved by Lloyd George and Briand. The need to restore
nationalised property, not simply to compensate its former owners,
was actively pressed by the French representatives, and the document was revised to take account of both possibilities. There was also
a discussion of the currency in which the consortium should operate,
a difficult matter in view of exchange rate fluctuations. Loucheur, for

the French government, thought it might be better to set up a small
central syndicate with affiliated societies holding capital in their own
domestic currencies rather than to have a central body with a unitary
capital operating in all countries. It was agreed, however, that the
capital allocation of £10 million originally agreed in London should
be increased to £20 million, and a French proposal for the allocation
of the capital was approved (France, Britain, the USA and Germany
were to subscribe 20 per cent each, with Belgium and Italy each
contributing a further 5 per cent). It was also to be made clear that
half of the German income from the scheme was to be paid directly to
the reparations commission.[70] Later that day and the following day a
French proposal incorporating these revisions was considered further
together with Belgian, Italian and Japanese representatives. Differences still remained on points of substance, however, particularly on
the amount of capital and currencies in which it was to be denomi-
nated, and it was eventually agreed that the currency issue should be
put directly to ministers at Cannes, as it had political as well as
financial implications. The French version of the British Treasury
proposals, as amended, was thereupon approved.[71]

There were some grounds, then, for thinking that the Cannes
meeting might be able to reach a substantial measure of agreement
when it convened in early January 1922. Apart from the preliminary
agreements reached in London and Paris between the Allied powers,
an exploratory discussion on 27 December 1921 between Krasin and
two British business representatives, Lionel Hitchens and Allen
Smith of the engineering employers' federation, at the home of Sir
Edward Grigg, appeared to hold out some hope that the Soviet
government would cooperate in whatever decisions might be reached
at Cannes. The meeting, Grigg noted, had been a 'great success'.
Krasin had made clear that *de jure* recognition was essential so far as
the Soviet government was concerned, but had given 'quite satisfactory assurances' regarding the recognition of Allied debts and private
property in Russia. All had seen the formula that Wise had proposed
to Krasin the previous week, and Krasin had indicated that he
thought some such formula might be acceptable to his government.
The only points of difficulty were war debts – which Krasin thought
should form part of a more general European settlement – and the
private ownership of land, to which the Russian peasantry would be
implacably opposed. Both points, however, could be discussed
further. Russia, for her part, needed to secure the revival of transport

and food production, and credits were 'absolutely indispensable' for this. The railway system was part of the machinery of government and foreign management could not be accepted, but joint management might be a possibility. Further security could be offered provided that it was clear it would not be used as a means of organising covert attacks upon the Soviet government. French cooperation in such arrangements was highly desirable, particularly to reduce the danger of border skirmishes with Poland and Czechoslovakia. The most appropriate step forward, Krasin thought, might be for a small group of businessmen to visit Moscow and discuss these matters directly with the Soviet government.[72]

The response to the British–French discussion in Italy also appeared to be a favourable one. The provisional Italian–Soviet trade agreement had just been concluded, on 26 December 1921. On the same date the Italian ambassador in Paris received an invitation for his government to attend the Cannes conference, which was to examine the situation created by the notification by the German government that it would be unable to meet its reparations payments due on 15 January and 15 February 1922, and also to study a plan for the economic reconstruction of Europe.[73] The Italian ambassador in London had already been informed by Lloyd George that Italian participation in the proposed consortium was envisaged,[74] although at the Paris experts' meeting Loucheur had repeatedly hinted that Italian activities would be limited to Austria. The scheme that had been presented had been essentially a British, French and German one for the exploitation of Russian resources, the Italian ambassador in Paris reported to his government, and he had objected to this with, he believed, general approval.[75] The British ambassador in Rome, Sir Ronald Graham, called on the Italian prime minister, Ivanoe Bonomi, on 29 December 1921 before his departure for Cannes, and found that the premier was intending to offer his 'full and wholehearted support for the British point of view' at the Allied meeting. He understood and sympathised with French attitudes, but Italian interests in the matter were the same as those of Britain. He appeared also to be concerned that France and Britain might come to some private understanding without the participation of the Italian government, leaving it in an awkward and isolated position.[76] The Italian government had already outlined its position to the Chamber of Deputies, where it had declared in favour of the renewal of active economic relations with Russia, if possible by joint agreement with the other Allies, and had received firm parliamentary backir.g for its position.[77]

Elsewhere, however, the auguries were less auspicious. The Belgian ambassador in London, for instance, wrote to Curzon on 26 December 1921 to explain that his government could not associate itself with the proposals that were to be submitted to the Supreme Council in Cannes, as they appeared to affect the right of priority in regard to reparations that had been granted to Belgium by the Allies on 16 June 1919.[78] The British ambassador telegraphed from Brussels to inform Curzon that both the Belgian prime minister and minister of foreign affairs would be attending the Allied meeting, but that they would receive Cabinet support in defending the Belgian right of priority and also the backing of the Belgian public, which was greatly exercised about the matter. It was possible, indeed, that Belgian ministers might contact their French counterparts in order to present a united front at the Allied meeting.[79] The position of France, in fact, was a pivotal one. Briand's approval of the Anglo-French plan had been subject to many reservations, and the position of his government was in any case in some doubt, partly because of internal divisions and partly because of a scandal concerning the collapse of the Banque Industrielle de Chine, in which the head of the foreign ministry, Philippe Berthelot, had been obliged to resign.[80] Briand's position was not improved by news of the Allied meetings in London, and he had repeatedly to assure the Chamber of Deputies that no resolutions had been agreed in advance for the Cannes meeting, that France was not going to be asked (and would not in any case agree) to make sacrifices on the reparations issue, that none of the guarantees in the Versailles treaty would be surrendered, and that the treaty itself would not be modified unless and until a parliamentary vote decided accordingly.[81] These far-reaching concessions showed the strength of French parliamentary as well as public sentiment upon the matter, and showed how difficult it would be to agree upon and still more to implement a plan for the reconstruction of Europe (including Russia) of the kind that had been discussed between the two premiers.

3

From Cannes to Boulogne

The Cannes Conference began on 4 January 1922 with a series of bilateral meetings among the Allied premiers and their advisers. The first meeting, on 4 January, was between Lloyd George and Briand. Briand, who had left Paris the previous evening, was determined to secure a Franco–British alliance which would improve his domestic standing and indeed contribute to the long-term vision he was already entertaining of a European system of alliances, including Germany and Russia, to preserve a just and stable peace upon the continent. This vision found expression some years later in the Locarno Pact.[1] The public mood in Paris on his departure was reported to be one of 'uneasiness and depression'; there were doubts about the proposed treatment of Germany and Russia and about French security, and business opinion in particular was sceptical about the scheme for European reconstruction, which was seen as more of a palliative than a cure.[2] Britain, explained *Le Temps*, located as it was outside the European continent, saw European problems in a simplified form, rather as the distant spectator saw only mountain ranges while the local inhabitants sought with difficulty to make their way through the valleys and the summits. France, like Belgium and Italy, knew her continental neighbours better than Britain did, and knew better the conditions that must be satisfied if peace and prosperity were to be re-established. The basic requirement was that France and Britain should be prepared to resist German agression, whether in the framework of an alliance or otherwise.[3] Briand, on his departure, informed the foreign editor of the *Daily Mail* that he shared the same priorities; a Franco–British pact, he argued, would resolve the differences that stood between the two powers, and once it had been concluded, other alliances could be established on its basis.[4]

The two premiers addressed these issues directly in their meeting at the Villa Valletta, Cannes, on 4 January 1922. Lloyd George, in a preliminary statement, said he hoped for definite results from the Cannes conference. In the British government's view, the indispensable condition of such a success was a close understanding between their two countries. French opinion was naturally concerned about future security as against Germany; British opinion, on the other hand, was more concerned about trade and unemployment. The only solution appeared to be to deal with all these problems at the same time. The British government would be prepared to accept the agreement made in London regarding reparations, which had considerable advantages for France, and would also give France a guarantee against an unprovoked German attack. Both sides should also seek to avoid competition in regard to the construction of submarines. In return, the British government would expect its French counterpart to cooperate in the economic and financial reconstruction of Europe, or in other words to agree to the proposal to convene an international economic conference to be attended by all the countries of Europe including Russia.[5] Lloyd George discussed the same ideas with the Italian premier, Bonomi, who welcomed them.[6] Briand, at a further meeting on 5 January 1922, declared his entire agreement with the proposal to call a conference, but urged that precautions be taken in regard to Russia, particularly over propaganda and the security of the Baltic states.[7] In later meetings the two premiers devoted more attention to the proposed Anglo–French pact, Briand arguing for an agreement more extensive than the military guarantee that Lloyd George had proposed, and Lloyd George in turn resisting any undertaking that would make Britain responsible for the general peace of Europe. In the end no compromise proved possible between these two positions, and alternative proposals were put forward over which discussion continued intermittently throughout 1922 and into the following year.[8]

Formal proceedings opened on 6 January 1922 with American, Belgian and Japanese representatives in attendance as well as those of the British empire, France and Italy.[9] Lloyd George, who had been invited to open discussion on the 'methods by which the economic reconstruction of Europe could be carried out', began by remarking that he considered the conference perhaps the most important of those that had been held since the armistice. It would have to take decisions of a wider and more far-reaching character than any that the powers had previously adopted, in view of the grave condition of the world as a result of the devastation of the war which had just ended. He had no desire to seek to modify the undertakings into which Britain had entered as a result of the peace treaties. Reparations and other debts, however, would be impossible to recover unless there was a general improvement in the economic condition of Europe. Germany's ability to pay reparations, despite her considerable natural resources, was in the main a function of that country's foreign trade; and Germany's foreign trade, in turn, was suffering because her traditional trading partners to the east and to the south had collapsed, both industrially and commercially. The consequences of this were to be seen in countries that had no very direct trading links with the eastern and southern European countries themselves: in the unemployment, for instance, which was seriously affecting Britain and Belgium, as well as France and Italy. There were of course dangers involved in dealing directly with the Bolsheviks, as this strategy appeared to require. There were, however, much greater dangers in failing to attend to the work of reconstruction, which would encourage the growth of Bolshevism more effectively than any propaganda that the Soviet authorities themselves might undertake. It was, in any case, often necessary to do business with governments of whose domestic conduct one might not necessarily approve.

Towards these ends, Lloyd George concluded, he was proposing that a conference be summoned of 'all the Powers of Europe to consider the economic reconstruction of Europe, east and west'. If Russia attended, as the premier evidently intended, it must be made clear to that country's representatives that trading relations of the kind he envisaged could be established only if Russia recognised the 'honourable obligations which every civilised country imposes upon itself'. These were: that all the debts incurred by the present Soviet government or its predecessors should be paid; that all foreign nationals should be compensated for any loss or damage caused to them when their property was confiscated or withheld; that a legal system should be established which sanctioned or enforced trade and other contracts with impartiality; that all propaganda designed to subvert the institutions and social systems of other countries should cease; and that the Soviet government should join in an undertaking to refrain from attacks upon any of its neighbours, an undertaking which should also be binding upon the western powers themselves. If it were necessary in order to re-establish normal trading conditions, Lloyd George went on, the Soviet government should also be recognised, provided that it undertook to observe all these obligations. Lloyd George's proposals were welcomed by the Italian and the Belgian representatives and accepted by Briand, on behalf of France, with the proviso that the details should be examined more closely and at leisure. Briand added that the conditions outlined by Lloyd George for dealing with Russia in particular were generally satisfactory and likely to lead to a reconciliation with that country. On his suggestion the conference accepted Lloyd George's proposals in principle and remitted their more detailed consideration to a commission composed of the prime ministers and foreign secretaries of the government concerned.[10]

The commission began its work later the same day, 6 January 1922. A number of detailed amendments were made to the resolution submitted by Lloyd George to the earlier meeting, which was then adopted. The resolution, in its final form, announced that a 'financial and economic conference' would be held in Genoa in February or early March as an 'urgent and essential step towards the economic reconstruction of Central and Eastern Europe'. The resolution specifically included Russia and Germany, as well as Austria, Hungary and Bulgaria, among the powers that were to be invited, and it urged that the prime ministers of each nation should if possible attend so that action could be taken as swiftly as possible upon its recommendations. The conference, according to the resolution, would include among its objectives the removal of all obstacles in the way of trade, the provision of substantial credit for the weaker countries, and the cooperation of all nations in the restoration of normal prosperity. It was agreed that there were six fundamental conditions upon which alone this effort could be made with any hope of success. These, the 'Cannes conditions', were (i) that nations could claim no right to dictate to others the principles upon which they regulated their systems of ownership, internal economy and government, but (ii) that before foreign capital could be made available foreign investors must be assured that their property and rights would be respected and the fruits of their enterprise secured to them. This involved (iii) the recognition of all public debts and obligations, and the obligation to restore or compensate all foreign interests for any loss or damage they might have suffered when their property had been confiscated or withheld, together with the establishment of an impartial legal system; (iv) the provision of an adequate means of exchange; (v) an undertaking by all nations to refrain from propaganda subversive of order and the established political system in countries other than their own; and finally (vi) a similar undertaking by all countries to refrain from aggressive action against their neighbours.[11]

A further meeting was held on 10 January 1922 to consider the conference agenda and to settle the form in which the invitation to the Soviet government should be issued. M. Loucheur, the French representative, explained that his government took the view that the Soviet government must have explicitly accepted the six conditions before they were permitted to participate in the conference. It was not only Russian opinion which must be considered in such matters, he pointed out, but also French opinion. In the event the British draft letter of invitation was modified to refer to the importance attached by the Allied powers to the assurances and guarantees which it held to be essential if the task of European reconstruction was successfully to be accomplished, and after a number of less substantial amendments had been agreed the letter was thereupon adopted.[12] The Soviet government had in fact already accepted the invitation, in a telegram addressed by Chicherin to the Supreme Council on 8 January 1922. The Soviet government accepted the invitation 'with satisfaction', Chicherin announced; the Central Executive Committee would shortly meet in extraordinary session to proceed with the selection of the Russian delegation, and would confer upon it the broadest possible powers. If Lenin were unable to attend in person because of his numerous duties, particularly in relation to the famine, the composition of the delegation and its powers would be otherwise unaffected. 'Nothing that depends on Russia', Chicherin promised, 'will in any case impede the rapid progress of the conference.'[13] Wise simultaneously addressed a message to Krasin to inform him of the Supreme Council's decision and to ask him to make immediate enquiries in Moscow as to whether Lenin would be able to attend in person, on the understanding that Lloyd George and the other European premiers would also be present. Wise added that it was 'vitally important present opportunity of complete settlement on basis contemplated in discussions should be accepted'.[14] Krasin, in his reply, did not respond directly to all Wise's points; he did, however, express reservations about the choice of Genoa as a meeting-place, and suggested London instead. In a further message on 9 January he added that Lenin would be more likely to attend in person if the conference were held in London, as he would have to absent himself from Russia for a shorter time.[15]

These various matters were taken up by a full meeting of the Supreme Council on the evening of 10 January 1922. The meeting considered the draft letter of invitation to the Soviet government which the sub-committee had already approved, and again discussed whether the Soviet or any other governments should be allowed to attend the conference without having first accepted the Allies' six fundamental conditions. Briand pointed out that French public opinion would be strongly opposed to a meeting between French and Russian delegates unless the Soviet government had already accepted the Allies' conditions and acknowledged the debts they owed to French nationals. Lloyd George, however, argued that the acceptance by the Soviet government of the invitation to the conference meant that the conditions would ultimately be accepted, and he thought it would defeat the purpose of the conference if the Russian delegates were required to accept the conditions before they actually arrived. 'The object was to get the Russian delegates to come to Genoa, as this was the only chance of doing business', he pointed out; they should not unnecessarily be antagonised. It was finally agreed that the invitation to the Soviet government should emphasise the importance attached by the Allied powers to the assurances and guarantees that had been laid down, but that it should not necessarily insist that these conditions be accepted in advance of the conference itself. The meeting approved a list of the countries which were to be invited to the conference, and agreed that Bonomi, on behalf of the Italian government, should be empowered to proceed with the necessary arrangements. It was also agreed that an 'international corporation with affiliated national corporations' should be established, and an organising committee was set up to examine the project in more detail.[16]

A further meeting on 11 January 1922 approved an outline agenda for the conference. The first point of the agenda, reflecting French pressure, was to be an examination of the means by which the Allies' six fundamental conditions of 6 January were to be put into practice, thus precluding a discussion of their intrinsic merits. The conference was also to consider the establishment of European peace on a firm basis, the 'essential conditions for re-establishment of confidence without injury to existing treaties', and a number of more detailed financial, economic and transport questions.[17] Discussions were also

held with a delegation of German representatives, headed by the
minister of reconstruction, Walter Rathenau, on reparations
matters.[18] On 12 January, however, Lloyd George announced to the
conference that Briand, who had returned to Paris for a vote of
confidence in his government, had resigned and would accordingly
be unable to take any further part in their proceedings. In the
circumstances, Lloyd George continued, he and his colleagues were
of the opinion that it would be impossible to do any further business
at Cannes. The discussion of reparations had not been concluded and
would have to be deferred for further consideration; it had, however,
been definitely agreed that a conference would be convened, that
certain powers would be invited to attend it and what its agenda
would be. He felt certain that the new French government, whatever
its composition, would honour the undertakings of its predecessor in
this respect. Bonomi, for the Italian government, concurred in these
views, and proposed to issue invitations straight away. It was agreed
that the conference should open, subject to amendment, on 8 March
1922, and a small committee was set up to prepare a more detailed
agenda and draft resolutions for the conference to consider. With this
the proceedings terminated.[19]

Briand's position had in fact begun to deteriorate since the beginning of the conference, if not before. President Millerand, who
presided over the Council of Ministers in Briand's absence, wrote to
him on 7 January 1922 to express his 'regret' and 'anxiety' concerning the resolution the conference had adopted at its opening the
previous day. It appeared to be possible, Millerand pointed out, for
Lenin and Trotsky to attend the conference without having accepted
the six conditions beforehand; and so far as the pact of non-aggression
was concerned, the French government could not possibly renounce
whatever means were necessary to enforce the Versailles treaty. This,
Millerand thought, should be made more precise, and he also
thought the participation of the United States should be made an
essential condition for holding the conference.[20] Briand sought to
clarify the position somewhat in later correspondence – the Cannes
resolution, he wrote to Millerand on 8 January, would indeed have to
be accepted in advance by the participating powers[21] – but on 10
January Millerand wrote to him again to inform him of the views of
the French government upon the matter. The Council of Ministers,
Millerand explained, had decided that the Soviet government could
not be allowed to attend the proposed conference until it had

explicitly accepted the Cannes conditions, and demonstrated that it intended to observe them. The Council had also decided that France must expressly reserve her rights under the Versailles treaty to apply sanctions in the event of Germany defaulting on her payments, and that no moratorium on German reparations could be accepted.[22]

Briand, in his reply of 10 January 1922, insisted that recognition of the Soviet government would be subject to conditions and guarantees, that there was no question at this stage of abandoning the French right to impose sanctions, and that the decision to allow a moratorium on German reparations had been justified by recent developments. He had also secured an agreement with the British government by this date which he would be submitting to the president and Council of Ministers for their approval.[23] The Franco-British treaty, the text of which was handed to Briand by Lloyd George before the premier's departure for Paris on 12 January, provided for a ten-year British guarantee of military assistance to France in the event of a direct and unprovoked attack upon the latter by Germany.[24] Briand explained to *Le Temps* that his discussions with Lloyd George had been directed towards the revival, in the form of *accords mutuels*, of the pact of guarantee of 1919 which had not entered into force. It had been suggested that such a result could be obtained by France only at the price of concessions on (for instance) national defence or Allied rights in the Rhineland. In his discussions with Lloyd George, however, 'absolutely nothing' of this kind had been suggested, and the plenitude of French rights had 'not for a single minute' been at issue. Briand himself had hoped for a more far-reaching accord than the one eventually submitted, but British ministers had been unwilling to go beyond the limited terms of a military guarantee. He hoped the treaty would soon be ratified.[25] The terms of the proposed agreement were also considered in the British Cabinet on 10 January, where they met with 'general concurrence'. An Anglo-French alliance of a bilateral character would be open to 'serious objections', it was thought, as it would impose heavy military burdens on both sides. On the other hand Britain was under a moral obligation to defend France against an unprovoked attack by Germany, and the draft articles would leave the British government a free hand in relation to Germany – a former enemy, but a major trading partner and the 'key to the situation in Russia'. The terms of the treaty were 'generally approved' and a telegram was despatched to the prime minister in this sense.[26]

Millerand, however, had made it clear to Briand on 11 January 1922 that the Council of Ministers would not support the treaty in the form in which it had been drafted.[27] Pictures of a golf match on Sunday 8 January, a day on which no formal meetings had been scheduled, did not improve Briand's domestic standing. The game appears to have been suggested by the journalists attending the conference, and Briand apparently acquitted himself rather well for a beginner. A photograph of the occasion in the French press, however, showing Lloyd George instructing an apparently docile Briand how to play, aroused particular indignation.[28] The foreign affairs commission of the Senate and the finance commission of the Chamber of Deputies both adopted resolutions amounting in effect to votes of censure on the policy Briand had been pursuing, and only eighty-five deputies voted against a resolution on 11 January calling for an extraordinary sitting of the French parliament to 'consider the new situation created at Cannes'.[29] Briand duly returned and defended his policies on the Chamber on 12 January. There was, he insisted, a need to secure an international agreement to strengthen peace, the Versailles treaty would not be open to discussion, and the proposed conference would in any case be purely financial and economic in nature. A moratorium might also be granted for German reparations, although the French representatives had opposed any concessions of this sort (there were shouts of 'traitor' at this point).[30] Faced by a hostile Chamber and with a majority of his own government opposed to him, Briand resigned the same day without pressing the matter to a vote.[31] The following day President Millerand asked Raymond Poincaré, a former president and a Lorrainer who had been among the most vociferous of Briand's critics, to form a new administration. It duly took office on 15 January.[32] Lloyd George, sitting in the dining car on his way back from Cannes, asked a French colleague who was going to be the next French premier. Told it would be Poincaré, he reportedly grimaced.[33] It was already clear that the scheme for European reconstruction, successfully negotiated through Cannes, would require a good deal of further advocacy.

The extent to which the change of government in Paris would impede the holding of the conference became apparent on 14 January 1922, when Lloyd George and Poincaré held a meeting in the British embassy in Paris on the prime minister's return from Cannes. Poincaré told the prime minister that he had 'always been a firm believer in the Franco-British Entente'; in particular, he had always supported the idea of a written understanding between the two countries, and would like to continue the negotiations from the point at which Briand had left them. French public opinion, however, would not like the idea of a unilateral guarantee, and an agreement without a military or naval convention attached to it would be seen as having a rather limited value. The aims and policy of the French government would, he thought, be generally the same as before, though perhaps with different nuances, and he believed that relations with the British government in particular might actually be better. Regarding Genoa, Poincaré told the prime minister that he would of course honour the undertakings of his predecessor in this respect, but he was anxious about the preliminary acceptance by the Soviet government of the six conditions agreed upon at Cannes. Lloyd George pointed out that it had been decided that the acceptance of the Allied conditions should be preliminary to the recognition of the Soviet government, not to its participation in the conference, and it was in any case clear that conditions of this kind would have to be accepted if the economic restoration of Europe was to be accomplished. Poincaré, nonetheless, was concerned that the conditions might be amended if it became possible to discuss them, and he remained little mollified by Lloyd George's urgings that the two countries should 'march together'.[34] Public accounts of the meeting suggested that it had been of a 'very cordial nature' and that it had been a 'good augury for the future'; Lloyd George told the Cabinet, however, that the French attitude had been 'hostile', and it was agreed that no further steps should be taken in relation to the Anglo-French pact for the time being.[35]

Presenting a statement of the new government's foreign policy to the Chamber of Deputies on 19 January 1922, Poincaré began by assuring deputies that it was his main aim, in association with parliament, to ensure respect for the treaties which had established the conditions of peace. If Germany were to escape from her reparations obligations it would be the 'most scandalous of iniquities'. He too was keen for a restoration of the European economy, but the first steps must be taken in the two countries attacked by Germany, namely France and Belgium. Further controls on the German budget, currency and exports might be necessary in order to ensure that Germany discharged her obligations in this respect. Turning to the Genoa conference, Poincaré repeated his view that all the Cannes conditions must be accepted before the conference opened and not discussed directly or indirectly at the conference itself. Without

adequate guarantees from the Bolsheviks, he made clear, France
would be compelled to resume her liberty of action. He hoped also
that meetings such as that at Cannes, which inevitably took on a
public and rather oratorical form, would become much rarer in the
future, and he re-emphasised his determination to defend essential
French interests and above all to prevent any direct or indirect
discussion of Germany's reparations obligations at the conference, or
of the other terms of the peace settlement.[36] The policy of the new
government was approved by a massive 434 votes to 84 and met,
according to the British ambassador in Paris, with the 'almost
unanimous approval' of the French press.[37]

Reactions to the Cannes proposals elsewhere in Europe were less
unfavourable. The 'whole bulk of the Italian press' had expressed
satisfaction that Genoa had been chosen as the site of the conference,
the British ambassador, Sir Ronald Graham, reported from Rome.
The question of Italian sacrifices in relation to reparations had been
mentioned by some papers, and it was generally felt that Italy should
not forgo the small amount due to her in this respect. There was also
a 'certain fear that Germany may be let off too lightly'.[38] A further
telegram on 13 January 1922, however, reported that Italian public
opinion was 'definitely favourable to the principles indicated by Mr.
Lloyd George's proposals', and that they had been received with
'very great satisfaction by almost all of the principal newspapers'.
The Italian government had generally been urged to associate itself
with the British government, whose interests in the matter were
largely similar, while keeping a close watch on the details of any
formal arrangements.[39] From Belgium, Sir George Grahame
reported that the prime minister, M. Theunis, had commended the
conference to the Chamber of Representatives in the warmest terms,
noting that the present state of Russia had not only practically ended
all exports from that country to the rest of Europe but that it had also
had serious indirect effects. Neither Germany nor Austria could
export to Russia as a result, and their purchasing power in Belgium
had suffered a corresponding decrease. The weakness of any member
of the European system, Theunis believed, inevitably reacted upon
all its other members, and he described the success of the conference
as of 'really enormous importance for the whole world'.[40] German
press and official opinion was similarly favourable to the idea of the
proposed conference;[41] the French ambassador in Berlin, Charles
Laurent, wrote to Poincaré to point out in particular that it was

believed that reparations could not in practice be excluded from the conference agenda, linked as they necessarily were with the economic restoration of Russia and eastern Europe.[42]

French attitudes towards the conference were not improved by such reports, nor by reports from London that Wise, who had been in touch with Krasin and was believed to be under his influence, had persuaded the prime minister to share some of his illusions with regard to the likely economic opportunities to be obtained by opening up the Russian market.[43] He was 'not too hopeful of your coming to terms with Poincaré in his present mood', the British ambassador wrote to Curzon on 20 January 1922, although the French premier still attached importance to the conclusion of a Franco-British pact.[44] A week later, however, Hardinge reported to London that Poincaré was not necessarily resolved to block the conference altogether. According to the Belgian ambassador in Paris, a close friend of Poincaré's, the premier believed that the French people wanted an Anglo-French pact more than anything else, and that they would make any sacrifice to obtain it. He would accordingly be willing to go to Genoa, meet the Soviet representatives and discuss with them the establishment of a more general agreement. This, Hardinge noted, was a 'considerable advance'.[45] A note communicated by the French ambassador in London on 6 February, however, conveyed a rather different impression. It raised a series of questions with regard to the conference agenda, spoke of the need for the Allies to reach a clear understanding among themselves before they found themselves in the presence of the Soviet delegates, insisted once again upon the prior acceptance by all parties of the Cannes conditions and upon the inviolability of the peace treaties, and urged, in view of the amount of preliminary negotiation and discussion that would be necessary, that the conference be postponed for at least three months.[46] The message was reinforced by a memorandum to French representatives abroad of 9 February 1922, published in the French press the following day, which was similarly uncompromising in tone.[47]

The note was considered on 7 February 1922 by the British interdepartmental committee which was making preparations for the conference. The committee interpreted the note as 'designed to make difficulties and delays, without definitely excluding French participation at the conference', and suggested the terms of a reply.[48] The possibility of holding the conference without France was briefly considered in the Foreign Office, but finally rejected. It was agreed instead that the French should be invited to send a team of experts to discuss the agenda in detail with their British counterparts.[49] A conference of ministers considered the matter further on 10 February. Curzon, opening the discussion, reported that he had had a conversation with the French ambassador the previous day[50] in which he had pointed out that the French note was susceptible of two different interpretations. It might either be regarded as expressing legitimate doubts as to the meaning of the resolution adopted at Cannes on 6 January, or else it might be regarded as an attempt to prevent the conference taking place at all. The ambassador had unhesitatingly replied that the former interpretation was the correct one and that the French government had every intention that the conference should indeed take place; it was simply concerned to ensure that adequate preparations were made for it. Curzon, however, pointed out that a delay of three months would be seen as an adjournment *sine die*, and that the Italian government, which was responsible for convening the conference, had seen no necessity for an adjournment of this kind. If further delay occurred in the formation of a new Italian government some slight postponement might be necessary, but no more than this.[51] Ministers approved Curzon's proposal that French experts be invited to London to discuss the details of the conference with the British interdepartmental committee; it was also agreed that the Italian government, and perhaps also the Belgian and Japanese governments, should be invited to send their representatives to attend the meeting.[52]

The conference of ministers also agreed that the prime minister should see Krasin, who was shortly to depart for Moscow. The meeting took place later the same day, 10 February 1922. Krasin began by asking if a postponement of the conference was possible in view of the attitude of the French government. The Soviet government regarded the Cannes proposals as the basis of a possible agreement, but if its approval of the Cannes conditions was regarded as a condition of its attendance it would be placed in a 'very difficult position'. The Soviet view was that the conditions were excessively one-sided in character, and there were further more detailed objections. Lloyd George, however, insisted that the Cannes conditions must be accepted; they were, after all, 'only the conditions on which every civilised Government conducted its affairs', particularly so far as the recognition of debts was concerned. There was no expectation that all the Russian debts would be paid at once, any more than in the case of the inter-Allied debts. Unless the Soviet government accepted its debts, however, the prime minister feared the business community would not be brought to take a full part in any new arrangements that might be proposed. He thought the German government took the same view. The Soviet authorities, he urged, should declare their acceptance of the Cannes conditions in principle, while reserving the right to discuss their application in more detail. The Soviet government could for its part make claims against western countries on a basis of reciprocity. The prime minister hoped for an unqualified response; if the Soviet government declined to accept the conditions or hesitated, the conference would not take place. Curzon, who was present, added that the French government at all events would not attend. Krasin, in reply, continued to emphasise the one-sided nature of the Cannes conditions, and asked about the measures of economic assistance which might be proposed at Genoa. Lloyd George referred to the consortium proposal, and again urged the Soviet government to accept the Cannes conditions, at least in principle. Krasin took due note of this appeal, but pointed out that Soviet Russia had her own public opinion to consider as well, which might change but would do so 'very slowly'.[53]

Curzon, in his reply of 11 February 1922 to the French ambassador, took the firm but sympathetic line urged by his colleagues. He welcomed the proposal that the subjects proposed for discussion at Genoa be considered further, and suggested that French representatives with the necessary technical qualifications be sent to discuss the points in question with the British officials who had been examining the matter for some weeks. The Belgian, Italian and Japanese governments should also be invited to send their representatives to attend the meeting. In a personal communication to Lord Hardinge, enclosing the text of this communication, Curzon added that there was no reason for the preparatory work to take a long time, and that a postponement of three months, as had been proposed, was 'wholly unnecessary'.[54] Two days later the French ambassador called on Sir Eyre Crowe, Permanent Under-Secretary of State for Foreign Affairs, to give him a verbal reply from Poincaré for the foreign secretary. Poincaré, according to the ambassador, rejected the idea that he was putting obstacles in the way of the conference. Now that it had definitely been decided to convene it, the French government were simply concerned to ensure that it was a 'real success' and for this reason were anxious to make sure that it was well prepared in advance. An interdepartmental committee had been set up to study the conference programme and would be meeting on 15 February;[55] the inter-Allied meeting of experts, Poincaré thought, could take place immediately afterwards, and preferably in Paris. Poincaré particularly emphasised that such a meeting could not take place until the British government had responded to the issues raised in the French note of 6 February, and he urged that Czech, Yugoslav, Romanian and Polish representatives be invited to attend as well, as their interests were directly involved. This committee, the ambassador suggested, could prepare definite proposals for Genoa.[56]

Crowe pointed out that this procedure would lead to very serious delays, since it amounted to the holding of a preliminary conference in Paris before the Genoa conference itself could begin, and he took particular exception to the presence of the Little Entente states at their deliberations. He was also reluctant to agree to change the place of meeting from London to Paris.[57] Curzon, in a message to Saint-Aulaire of 14 February 1922, endorsed Crowe's refusal to change the place of meeting or to widen the scope of the discussion any further. The permanent representatives of the other states in London, he pointed out, could be asked to give the views of their governments if necessary. The Italian government had already nominated two representatives to take part in the talks, and Curzon hoped the French government could do likewise.[58] Poincaré, according to the French ambassador in an interview with Curzon on 16 February, was willing to accept that the meeting should take place in London, and it could begin when the French experts were ready to depart, probably in about ten days' time. He regarded the discussions as embracing technical questions only, however, and he continued to seek a formal reply to the French memorandum of 6 February, which had dealt with questions of political principle on which prior agreement was necessary. Curzon replied that he would be willing to send an official response if this was necessary, but on balance it seemed wisest to avoid discussion of the matters in question by means of formal diplomatic memoranda which were likely to be communicated to the press the next day. He suggested instead that the issues in question be discussed directly either with the ambassador himself or with any other representative that Poincaré might nominate. Afterwards, if necessary, a formal reply could be issued. He also thought it a 'great mistake' to include the eastern European states in their discussions.[59]

The French ambassador, in a further visit of 18 February to the

Foreign Office, continued to reiterate Poincaré's request for a detailed and formal reply to the French memorandum of 6 February. The absence of a reply of this kind, the French premier was reported to believe, created real and practical difficulties. A number of the points in the French memorandum raised political issues and were not suitable for discussion by experts; a clear statement of the British government's view on these points was necessary, in the absence of which the French government would be unable to attend the conference. Nor could the French experts be despatched to London as quickly as had been hoped.[60] A more precise reference to these issues of political principle arrived the following day in a communication from the French ambassador to Sir Eyre Crowe. Nine points in the earlier French memorandum were singled out for particular attention. It was to be stated at the outset of the conference that all the states represented, by virtue of their presence, were deemed to have accepted the Cannes conditions; Russia and the neutral countries were to be required to recognise the peace treaties, which were to remain inviolable at all stages of the conference's proceedings; and the role of the League of Nations was to be given more prominence in relation to the proposed agreement by all the states concerned to refrain from attacks upon their neighbours. In addition, the definition of non-intervention and the undertaking not to engage in political propaganda were to be examined more closely, and various matters concerned with debts, Russian claims and the establishment of European peace were to be considered further among the inviting powers before the conference began.[61] Curzon commented wearily: 'It is difficult to know how to deal with M. Poincaré.'[62]

On the afternoon of 20 February 1922 Curzon met Lloyd George to consider what action should be taken in response to this latest statement of the French position. They agreed that the best course of action would be a meeting between the prime minister and Poincaré himself. Lloyd George explained that he had proposed such a meeting to Poincaré through the Czech prime minister, Edward Beneš, whom he had seen on 17 February,[63] and Curzon added that he had suggested the same course of action in his meeting with Saint-Aulaire the previous day, although this had been before the letter of 19 February had been received.[64] The prime minister discussed his communication to Poincaré with Beneš later the same evening.[65] Curzon meanwhile wrote to Hardinge to ask him to see Poincaré and reiterate the foreign secretary's objections to an extended correspondence on the matters that the French premier had raised. He was to add, however, that the British government was perfectly prepared to discuss these matters, 'but in a preferable form'. Towards this end, the British government proposed that a confidential discussion be held with one or more French ministers, in Britain or in France as Poincaré preferred; this appeared to be the 'only possible way of terminating an impasse which is much to be deprecated and for which there is no real excuse'.[66] On 21 February Hardinge reported that he had just seen Poincaré, who had expressed his willingness to discuss the political issues connected with Genoa with any member of the British government,[67] and on the same day Curzon replied that the prime minister in person would be glad to come to France to discuss these issues with Poincaré the following Saturday, 25 February 1922, at either Calais or Boulogne.[68] The meeting duly took place in Boulogne on the day that had been arranged.

Poincaré opened the proceedings by assuring Lloyd George that France had no desire to prevent or delay the holding of the conference. French public opinion, however, was concerned about three points in particular. These were, first, that there should be no encroachment at Genoa upon the Covenant or the prerogatives of the League of Nations; secondly, that no clause of the peace treaties should be the subject of discussion; and thirdly, that the question of reparations should not be raised, because neutral countries would be present at the conference which had not been a party to the original settlement of those questions. If there was agreement on these points then the French government would be glad to cooperate with the British and other governments in making the necessary arrangements to hold the conference at the earliest possible opportunity. Lloyd George, in reply, regretted the deterioration in the relations between the two countries which had occurred over the previous months, and welcomed Poincaré's assurance that there was no desire to impede the holding of the conference. In Britain, however, a very different opinion prevailed, and as an industrial country with nearly 2 million people unemployed the matter was seen as an important one. Three by-elections in Britain that month, in each of which the government candidate had been defeated, had shown the strength of popular feeling on such matters. The general belief, regrettably, was that France had imperialistic and chauvinist tendencies, and was standing in the way of the peace of Europe. It would be a tragedy, the prime minister continued, if the British government were driven by these pressures to reach an accommodation with Russia, Germany and Italy while France was left to her own devices.

Poincaré, for his part, regretted these apparent misunderstandings, which, he thought, the French government had done nothing to create. France had no, and had never had any, desire other than to respect the Treaty of Versailles, which both countries had signed. He asked if the prime minister could express a view upon the three points he had raised at the outset, after which they might proceed rapidly to other matters. On the League of Nations, Lloyd George replied that he was, of course, in favour of using it as much as possible, but Germany was not a member, Russia was hostile to it, and if League machinery was employed he thought the United States government might use this as an excuse for not participating in the conference. On reparations, similarly, he agreed that the fundamental aspects of the question could not be discussed, but if the economic condition of Europe were to be considered at all it would be difficult to avoid any reference whatever to the matter. This was not enough for Poincaré, who told the prime minister that there had been absolute unanimity in the Chamber of Deputies that questions of reparations could not be raised. He thought that there was only one secure and effective method of doing this, namely, to make clear that the amount of reparations fixed by the reparations commission could not be touched upon at Genoa, and similarly that the conference could not encroach upon the powers of either the Allied governments or the reparations commission. He was broadly satisfied by the formula which Lloyd George proposed to this effect, which specified that the 'question of reparations must not be settled by the Genoa Conference, but through the machinery set up by the Treaty of Versailles'.

Poincaré then turned to the date on which the conference was to be convened. He explained that it had proved impossible in practice to make serious preparations for the conference until a few days previously, and that it would not be possible for the experts to begin their work in London before 6 March 1922. If the British government were willing to consider a postponement of no more than three weeks, the consequence would be that nothing would be properly prepared. He understood that several other governments took the same view. Would it not be better, he suggested, to arrange for the conference to meet at a later date, when the necessary preparatory work had been completed? Lloyd George, however, was unwilling to agree; the matter was seen by the British public as an urgent one, and the British government had almost completed its arrangements. He thought that France was hardly responding adequately to an ally's difficulties. 'Would the whole thing be frozen up until the French government were ready to thaw?' Poincaré pointed out that the questions involved were complicated ones which would not necessarily be resolved by conversations among the powers, but nonetheless he was prepared to do his best. 'If Mr. Lloyd George would agree to a date in April, he would do a service to the French government and to France, so that France would be in a better position to do him a service at Genoa.' Lloyd George replied that if some date between 28 March and Easter (16 April) would suit M. Poincaré, he would do his best to oblige him.

Poincaré secured agreement upon two further matters. In the first place, it was agreed that the machinery of the League of Nations should be used as much as possible, although Lloyd George asked that there be no 'rigid resolution' on this subject in view of the considerations he had mentioned, and that the conference should not become a permanent institution existing alongside the League of Nations and infringing its prerogatives. ('The reconstruction of Europe', as *Le Temps* had put it on 20 February, was 'not an enterprise which can be undertaken like a game of golf, from hole to hole.')[69] There was also agreement that existing treaties, particularly the peace treaties, should not be called in question. Poincaré urged further that the general question of disarmament should not be raised at Genoa; Lloyd George replied that he had no wish to raise such matters himself since the whole question was being considered by the League of Nations, and that the proposed non-aggression agreement would not in any case preclude the Allies exercising their rights under the peace treaties to apply sanctions against Germany. There was agreement on this point. The principal political questions having been clarified at the meeting, Poincaré went on, the experts could not be set to work as rapidly as possible on the more technical economic questions with which the conference was concerned. Both governments agreed to propose to the Italian government that the opening of the conference be postponed until 10 April 1922. The *entente* between France and Britain in all political questions that had been apparent at the meeting, the two leaders declared in a press communiqué with which the meeting concluded, could 'confidently be expected to produce the most fruitful results'.[70]

A preliminary meeting of the international consortium took place in London earlier the same week, attended by British, French, Italian, Belgian, Japanese, German and Danish representatives, together with an unofficial representative of the United States government. At the meeting, which lasted from 21 to 25 February 1922, the delegates pledged their best endeavours to bring about the establishment of national corporations in the various countries affiliated to the central corporation, which was itself to be established in London. A memorandum and articles of association for the British national corporation had been approved, and these were adopted as a model for the corporations to be established in other countries. The aggregate capital of the national corporations was to be £20 million, of which 25 per cent was to be called up immediately. Government guarantees would be required where necessary to enable this capital to be raised. The initial capital of the central international corporation would be £2 million, subscribed by the various national corporations. There would, it was agreed, be no dealings with any state which did not recognise basic principles of economics such as the obligation to restore all property that had been seized or nationalised, or (where this was impossible) to provide satisfactory compensation. A legal system which guaranteed commercial activities must also be established, and it must be shown in practice that such activities could indeed be engaged in without undue restriction. These principles clearly applied above all to operations in Soviet Russia.[71]

Sergent of the Banque de l'Union Parisienne, one of the French representatives at the meeting, reported to Paris that he had been able to secure some improvement in the original British proposals, which would have given the central corporation too much power. He had been supported in this by the Belgian and occasionally by the German representatives. The British representatives, however, had appeared rather vague about the objectives of the consortium, other than the economic reconstruction of eastern Europe and particularly Russia, and some British financiers with interests in that country were known to be hostile to the idea. The main proposals were that banks (with capital in sterling) would be set up in the Baltic states, and that the Russian railways would be re-established. The British, Italians and Germans would guarantee the capital subscribed, but it was not clear that the French government would do likewise, and if not the French public would be unlikely to contribute to the scheme. This matter had to be clarified by 11 March. The main danger,

Sergent pointed out, was that the consortium was essentially a plan for the economic exploitation of Russia, where it might lead to an upsurge of popular xenophobia; it might also prejudice French interests in that country, particularly since Poland would not be taking part in the scheme. Sergent, however, believed that France should nonetheless participate, in order (if nothing else) to defend the French interests concerned, and he expected the scheme to develop rapidly because of the British and German interest in it.[72] On the face of it, at least, the main elements of the Cannes programme had successfully been brought into being.

4

Diplomatic preliminaries

The Boulogne meeting removed perhaps the most substantial obstacle to the further progress of the conference proposal so far as inter-Allied relations were concerned. Lloyd George announced on his return that he and Poincaré had been in 'absolute agreement' and that no further meetings would be necessary before the conference itself began. 'Undoubtedly all difficulties have been swept away', *The Times* commented on 27 February 1922.[1] In Paris, *Le Temps* noted that the meeting had taken place in an atmosphere of the 'greatest cordiality and also a great spirit of conciliation'. Like its London counterpart, it thought the signature of an Anglo-French pact could not be long delayed, and it thought it 'certain' that both Lloyd George and Poincaré would attend the conference in person, at least for the first two or three weeks.[2] Lloyd George himself saw an official in the French embassy after the meeting, and declared himself 'extremely satisfied'; accord had been reached on all points, and the pact, although not discussed at Boulogne, was likely to be concluded in the near future.[3] Hardinge wrote to Curzon from Paris, however, having examined the protocol of the meeting, and remarked that there appeared to have been an 'atmosphere of bickering without very great results'. He noted, in particular, that Poincaré had avoided giving unequivocal commitments in respect of either his own attendance at the conference or the recognition of the Soviet government.[4] The Italian ambassador in Paris reported similarly that differences had remained on the recognition of the Soviet government, Lloyd George insisting upon Soviet acceptance of the Cannes conditions but Poincaré upon their implementation.[5] Lloyd George and Poincaré, it later emerged, had in fact lunched separately at Boulogne, and Lloyd George had been taken to the meeting in a 'dirty and badly battered car'.[6] For all their formal agreement, the two premiers had evidently failed to develop a personal relationship of any intimacy.

The most immediate problem, however, concerned the Italian government, which had been threatening to collapse since late January 1922 and which appeared unlikely to be able to fulfil its obligation to convene the conference on 8 March. Rumours that the conference would have to be postponed were current from the end of January onwards, and although they were officially denied the British ambassador in Rome was privately told that the government was experiencing great internal difficulties and that it was unlikely to survive very long after the Chamber reconvened.[7] Bonomi duly resigned on 2 February 1922, although the King refused to accept his resignation and the government remained in office until 19 February. Opinion in Paris was that a postponement of the conference was now inevitable, and although the rumours continued to be denied in Rome they began to be given credence by some sections of the Italian press.[8] On 22 February *The Times* quoted an 'official source' to the effect that the conference would be unable to meet on 8 March, and that it would take place rather later in the month; two days later foreign governments were officially informed that the persistent ministerial crisis in Italy would indeed make it impossible for the conference to be convened on the date originally agreed, and that a new date would be decided in agreement with the other Allied powers.[9] The French ambassador in Rome made a formal request for a three months' postponement on 20 February, quoting the support of the Swiss, Romanian and Yugoslav governments,[10] but on 26 February, following the Boulogne meeting, both the French and British governments agreed to urge the new Italian government to accept the date they had agreed upon, 10 April 1922.[11] This proposal was accepted in a letter of 9 March to foreign governments; although 10 April was rather soon, Carlo Schanzer, the new foreign minister, commented, and although the beginning of the conference would now fall in Holy Week, the Italian government through 'special deference towards Mr. Lloyd George' would accept the date proposed.[12] Luigi Facta, who headed the new administration, explained in a newspaper interview that he intended to fulfil all the obligations of his predecessor so far as the conference was concerned, and added that the problems to be discussed were 'of too great importance to be made the subject of disputes between political parties'.[13]

The Soviet government, in contrast to the French, was strongly opposed to any postponement of the conference. On 22 February 1922 the Russian trade delegation in Rome inquired from the Marchese della Torretta, foreign minister in Bonomi's government, when the conference was going to take place. The Soviet delegates were reported to be ready to leave and the delegation sought confirmation of the original opening date.[14] The following day della Torretta replied in the same terms as to the other governments invited to the conference, explaining that a short delay would be necessary and that a new date would be advised in due course.[15] Chicherin replied on 25 February expressing his 'astonishment' that the Soviet government should have been informed of a decision of this kind at such a late stage, and without a firm alternative date being given. Members of the Soviet delegation, he pointed out, had been obliged to relinquish important state responsibilities, and had in some cases been required to travel to Moscow from distant parts of Soviet Russia and its allied republics. The convocation of the conference, discussed and agreed upon by a number of powers, should not, he thought, depend upon personnel changes in any one of them. The conference, moreover, was intended to tackle business that Lloyd George himself had described as particularly urgent. For its part the Soviet government hoped that any further delay for 'accidental reasons' would be avoided, and 23 March was proposed as a new date on which the conference should open.[16] A further telegram of 15 March, addressed to the British, French and Italian governments, expressed concern that it appeared to be intended to present some of the powers invited with a series of decisions taken in advance by some of the other powers. This, instead of a free exchange of opinions, would represent a 'new form of boycott', and if such decisions were incompatible with the sovereign rights of the Soviet government and the Russian state the conference would assuredly fail. Chicherin concluded by expressing the hope that all the powers attending the conference would be enabled to take part freely in the discussion of all the subjects on its agenda.[17]

The participation of the Soviet government in the conference, albeit on terms it might not find satisfactory, was not at least in doubt. Rather more serious from the point of view of the conference's promoters was the decision of the United States government not to take part. The United States had been a participant in the Cannes discussions, and that country's great wealth and position as a major international creditor made its participation in the conference of particular importance. On 16 January 1922 della Torretta issued an invitation to the United States government in the same terms as those to other powers, and on 20 January Krasin visited the US consul-general in London to urge that the invitation be accepted.[18] Harding, however, remained uncommitted, and from Rome the US ambassador, Richard W. Child, drew attention to some additional considerations. The conference, he pointed out would be primarily political in character, and Chicherin's telegram to the Italian foreign minister of 25 February suggested that the Soviet government would be likely to adopt an abusive and uncooperative position in its deliberations.[19] Finally, on 8 March 1922, the US Secretary of State, Charles E. Hughes, wrote to the Italian ambassador in Washington to announce formally that the American government would not be able to accept the invitation to take part. The conference, Hughes explained, despite its designation, was evidently to be political rather than economic in character, and the American people were not inclined to become involved in European questions of this kind. The Soviet government, he thought, must itself be responsible for taking the essential steps which could alone restore that nation's future prosperity. He hoped nonetheless that the conference would be a successful one.[20] The US ambassador in Rome was instructed on 24 March that he should keep his government fully informed of the proceedings of the conference; he was not to participate formally, although he might proceed to Genoa if he thought this advisable.[21] Child did, in the end, go to Genoa for the duration of the conference, but his government, one of the most important if the conference's objectives were to be achieved, was officially unrepresented.[22]

The establishment of the international consortium, another essential element in the proposals for European reconstruction, also began to look increasingly doubtful. Soviet representatives had made it clear from the outset that they had serious reservations about the proposal for a single Anglo-Franco-German consortium, since it represented a political threat and was also clearly intended to exploit Russia on a quasi-colonial basis. Several consortia might be acceptable, each working in a different part of Russia on terms agreeable to the Soviet government, but not an 'international capitalist front for the exploitation of Russia', as Chicherin later described it.[23] The consortium clearly required the approval or at least the consent of the Soviet government if it was to come into being, and the hostile reception accorded to the idea in Moscow was already sufficient to raise doubts about its eventual establishment. German participation, moreover, began to look increasingly unlikely, at least in the form originally envisaged. The German government, as Chancellor Wirth told the Reichstag on 26 January 1922, was keen to assist the economic restoration of Russia, a task which could successfully be accomplished only with the support of the Soviet government. It had the 'gravest mistrust', however, 'for a policy which would consider Russia as a colony and treat her as such'.[24] Even more important, German business opinion was losing interest in Allied proposals and was becoming increasingly favourable to the idea of establishing bilateral links with the Russian market and perhaps even monopolies in certain areas. Rathenau continued to favour German participation in the consortium, as well as direct relations between the two countries, but he began to place increasing emphasis upon direct German relations with Russia, receiving support for his views from Stinnes and major industrial and political interests.[25] The Dutch had already decided not to participate,[26] the Belgians were doubtful about the state guarantee of investments that appeared to be necessary,[27] and the French found objections to the whole scheme under French law, were hostile to the extent of British control over the corporation that appeared to be involved, and in the end declined to provide the state guarantee which alone was likely to encourage French private investors to take part.[28]

Nor, indeed, had all the differences between the British and French governments been resolved by this point. The French government, for its part, continued to resist the overtures for more friendly relations extended by various representatives of the Soviet government, most notably by Karl Radek, who was based at this time in Berlin. Radek gave a lengthy interview to *Le Matin* on 9 February 1922 on which he urged the desirability, on the eve of the Genoa conference, of establishing direct relations between Paris and Moscow.[29] Radek also saw Marcel Cachin, the Communist deputy and editor of *L'Humanité*, while Cachin was travelling to Moscow to attend an executive committee meeting of the Communist International. It was reported, though strongly denied, that Cachin had seen Poincaré after his return from Moscow, and that he would be travelling back to Moscow with Poincaré's reply.[30] Rumours circulated that a formal agreement had been signed, and Radek even produced the purported text of a Franco-Russian treaty (its signatures turned out to be false).[31] The French foreign ministry, in an official statement, insisted that no negotiations of any kind had been entered into, and Poincaré himself poured scorn upon the 'veiled ladies' and others who were supposed to have acted as intermediaries.[32] French business opinion appears in fact to have had some interest in developing relations with the Russian market, and there was an obvious French interest in frustrating a Russo-German rapprochement, particularly one from which Germany was likely to benefit economically.[33] Soviet representatives, for their part, professed to favour France as a diplomatic partner rather than Britain (which wanted a weak and divided Russia) or Germany (which wanted a colonial relationship), and they had every reason to seek a relationship which would reduce Soviet diplomatic isolation as the conference approached and also increase their leverage upon potential partners elsewhere, such as Germany.[34] It appears even to have been discreetly suggested that France might support Russian claims to German reparations under article 116 of the Versailles treaty in return for Soviet recognition of French public and private debts.[35] In the end, however, the differences between the two sides proved too great to be overcome and the hesitant exchange of feelers came to nothing. A more serious French concern was the possibility, reported in diplomatic communications, that Germany might seek to raise the reparations issue and even French disarmament at the conference, and that Lloyd George might seek for his own domestic ends to make the conference no more than the beginning of a whole series of international meetings whose ultimate objective would be the renegotiation of the peace treaties.[36]

The French government, accordingly, continued to seek firm assurances from its British counterpart about the limitations upon the conference discussions that had already been agreed at Boulogne. On 15 March 1922 the French ambassador in London sent a note to the Foreign Office summarising the views of his government upon the treaties that the Soviet government had concluded, and also emphasising that the Genoa conference must not be allowed to concern itself with the peace treaties and related matters.[37] Saint-Aulaire followed this up with a visit to Lord Curzon's private residence on 18 March. Poincaré, he reported, was still somewhat uneasy as to the position that the German and Russian delegations would occupy at Genoa; the opening statement of the conference, he thought, should make it clear that all the states represented, by virtue of their presence, would be deemed to have accepted the Cannes conditions. Curzon replied that this had already been agreed upon by the Allies, but he was willing to reaffirm the point. Poincaré, the ambassador went on, also thought that the League of Nations should be invited to send delegates to attend the conference. Curzon replied that the League question would have to be 'very carefully handled'; he was against the League sending a delegation as such, but he thought they might be kept informed of developments and invited to send representatives whenever any matters came up which concerned the League directly. Saint-Aulaire was inclined to agree with these views, and thought Poincaré would do likewise; a further discussion also took place upon the proposed pact and Anglo-French relations in general.[38]

British technical arrangements for the conference were by this stage reasonably far advanced. The interdepartmental committee established shortly after the Cannes conference under the chairmanship of Sir Sydney Chapman of the Board of Trade had produced an interim report for the Cabinet on 8 February 1922. It suggested that the conference, after passing a resolution confirming the Cannes conditions of 6 January, should immediately appoint committees to deal with the proposed non-aggression pact, a proposed treaty with Russia, and the financial, economic and transport matters that would also be necessary for the economic reconstruction of Europe. The proposals that were formulated by these committees, it was suggested, should then be remitted to the full conference for their approval and be embodied in international conventions.[39] A second and more elaborate report followed on 20 February, containing further proposals for economic, financial and other matters and also a preliminary draft of the proposed Russian treaty. This made it clear that far-reaching concessions would be required on the part of the Soviet government. It would, for instance, be required to accept liability for all the public debts of its predecessors, and for the debts of municipalities and public utilities. A fixed sum would be payable in respect of Soviet liabilities towards the British and French governments, after which no further claims could be raised by either side. The Soviet government would also have to accept liability in respect of losses incurred by private citizens, which wherever possible were to be met by the restitution of the same or equivalent property. Further provisions bound all the parties concerned to refrain from 'propaganda subversive of the order and established political system

in one another's territories', and covered matters such as church
buildings, consular conventions and the administration of justice.[40]

Chapman took these proposals to Paris on 7 March and discussed
them further with Jacques Seydoux of the commercial relations
department of the French foreign ministry, with M. Avenol, a financial expert, and also with Francesco Giannini, a trade counsellor at
the Italian embassy in London who had been nominated to take part
in the discussions. The French representatives expressed themselves
in general agreement with the British proposals, both in relation to
the reconstruction of Europe in general and to Russia more particularly. There were some reservations, however, Chapman later
reported, about the role of the international consortium and about the
role that the League of Nations was intended to play in their arrangements. More generally the French appeared to Chapman to have
made little real progress with their preparations for the conference;
they might, Chapman thought, for this reason be more willing to
follow the general outlines of the British proposals.[41] Seydoux for his
part noted that Chapman had undertaken to think over the French
objections on such matters as war debts and counterclaims and to
modify his proposals to accommodate them. Seydoux also informed
the Belgian authorities of the substance of the Franco-British discussions, and their delegates to the experts' meeting later met the
corresponding French officials in Paris, at which a common approach
to the British proposals was agreed.[42] Poincaré, in his instructions to
the French delegates, insisted that the experts' discussions must be
'exclusively technical' in character, and that all political issues must
be excluded. The French delegates, he made clear, could not commit
the French government to whatever the meeting might decide; their
decisions could be only *ad referendum* and final approval would have to
be reserved for the government in Paris.[43]

The British proposals, as amended, duly formed the basis of the
work of the inter-Allied experts' meeting, which took place in London
at the Board of Trade between 20 and 28 March 1922. Belgian and
Japanese representatives were present as well as experts nominated
by the British, French and Italian governments. According to
Chapman in a report circulated on 26 March, a 'friendly and
accommodating spirit' had been shown throughout and rapid progress had been made. The *de jure* recognition of the Soviet government had not been considered, as this was a political rather than an
economic question. Nonetheless it was clear that there were differ-

ences on this point, the French, largely supported by the Belgians, taking the view that there should be no formal agreement with Russia until the Soviet government had given some effect to the undertakings on past debts and future security for investment which would have to form part of any such agreement.[44] The French, in particular, refused to discuss a draft treaty with Russia put forward by the British and also by the Italian representatives; the most that Poincaré could do, Seydoux told Sir Edward Grigg, was to undertake to recognise the Soviet government 'after a probationary period provided all guarantees were faithfully carried out'.[45] Two other French delegates told Sir Maurice Hankey, the Cabinet Secretary, that it would in fact be impossible for France to recognise the Soviet government, whatever the outcome of the conference, because of domestic public opinion.[46] The French, supported by the Belgians, also took the view that the proposed debt commission would have to be given the power to administer resources in the countries for which it was responsible.[47] The document that ensued, while not necessarily binding upon any of the governments concerned, nonetheless became known as the 'experts' report' and became, in effect, the agreed position of the inviting powers in the early stages of the conference proceedings.[48]

The report dealt first with the reconstruction of Russia. The economic restoration of that country, it was suggested, was largely dependent upon the support of foreign enterprise and capital, which would in turn require a considerable change in the conditions affecting Russian trade and industry. Measures would be necessary to ensure the liberty of action of employers and employees and to protect their industrial operations and capital. Foreign employers would also need guarantees in respect of their movable and immovable property and their right to import whatever they required and to dispose of the production of the enterprises as they wished. The report went on to consider the guarantees that would have to be provided to give effect to these principles. So far as the liquidation of past obligations was concerned, the Soviet government would have to accept the financial obligations of its predecessors towards foreign governments and their nationals, as well as the financial engagements entered into by municipal bodies and public utilities. It would also have to accept liability for all losses that had been incurred by the citizens of other countries due to the actions or negligence of the Soviet government or of its predecessors, or of any provincial or local body or of its agents. The liabilities thus incurred

and the method of repayment would be determined by a Russian
debt commission and by mixed arbitral commissions, a scheme for
the establishment of which was appended to the report. Intergovernmental debts, liabilities and obligations of every kind would be
discharged by the payment of a fixed sum on a basis to be
determined.

Turning to the future, the Soviet government was to be required to
establish an impartial system of justice, with judicial authority
independent of the execution and judges who must be independent
and irremovable, applying a law which must be known, equal as
between persons and without retrospective effect. Foreigners, in
particular, must be guaranteed against arbitrary arrest and domi-
ciliary visits, and they must have free access to the courts and the
right to be represented by a counsel of their own choosing. Their
conditions of residence and commercial activity in Russia would have
to be satisfactory; they would need to be able to move freely across
borders in accordance with normal international practice, they must
be exempt from compulsory service and forced loans, they would
have to be able to communicate freely by post, telegraph and wireless, and neither they nor their employees could be subject to any form
of discrimination on account of their nationality. Foreign firms or
individuals could be subject to rates of taxation no higher than those
of corresponding Russian firms or individuals, and they must have
the same rights of travel and transportation on roads, railways and
waterways. Foreign undertakings, moreover, were to be worked
under 'conditions of freedom', including the right to hire or dismiss
workers subject only to the laws on hygiene and the regulations
governing employment that applied in other countries. The report
concluded with a series of less controversial proposals intended to
provide for the economic restoration of the remainder of the continent, covering financial, transport and other matters.[49]

Commenting on the report on 29 March 1922, Commander Maxse
of the Northern Department of the Foreign Office pointed out that
although a satisfactory measure of agreement had been reached on
technical questions, there had nonetheless been a marked divergence
of opinion on political issues. It was quite clear, for instance, that the
French government had no intention of recognising the Soviet
government, at least for the time being, although the Cannes resolutions had explicitly contemplated such recognition. The Soviet
government for its part appeared to attach great importance to the

question of recognition, and if it was excluded from the scope of the conference it was more than doubtful if representatives would attend. Nor had the question of the prior acceptance of the Allies' funda-mental conditions by the conference participants been resolved. It appeared that the French government might be unwilling to discuss any matter with the Soviet delegates until they had explicitly accepted the Cannes conditions, in which case either the French or the Russian delegations would be compelled to withdraw from the conference. The French experts had also objected to the notion of reciprocity of obligations between the Soviet government and the other powers, and no mention at all had been made of the Red Army, although this was clearly a subject that would have to be considered at the conference.[50] The experts' report, at least in Maxse's view, represented an Allied agreement of a very limited and provisional character.

Perhaps even more serious than these differences among the experts were the emerging disagreements within the British govern-ment itself. To the coalition, already beset by serious problems over Ireland, India, Egypt and public spending, it was an additional and potentially serious source of strain. The most vocal and determined critic of the government's Russian policy, as he had been during the years of intervention, was Winston Churchill, at this time Secretary of State for the Colonies. The whole concept of Genoa, he wrote to his wife on 7 February 1922, was deeply distasteful to him. 'It is not a national British but only a purely personal Lloyd George affair', he added.[51] Churchill was particularly incensed by a Special Branch report of 17 March, which appeared to show that the Russian trade delegation in Britain was subsidising the Labour Research Depart-ment, the Communist party and other bodies. Should there not, he wrote to Austen Chamberlain, be a meeting of ministers to discuss the matter?[52] Writing to Lloyd George on 18 March, he pointed out that Genoa would not be popular with the Conservative party generally, but he thought it would not break up the government unless the issue of the juridical recognition of the Soviet government was raised.[53] This was, of course, at least implicitly the prime minister's position, and it exposed the difficulties in which the government had now been placed.

Chamberlain, who at this time was Conservative party leader in the House of Commons, wrote to Lloyd George on 21 March to underline the problem. Churchill, he wrote, had said that he could not remain a member of the government if *de jure* recognition were granted to the Soviet government. The position of the remaining Conservative members of the government would obviously be impossible if Churchill resigned because he was 'more Tory than the Tory Ministers'. Chamberlain urged the prime minister to have a quiet personal talk with him before the next Cabinet meeting took place. More generally, he thought the whole matter would repay further consideration. There would certainly be serious misgivings within the Conservative party, for instance, if Britain were to confer recognition on the Soviet government but neither the American nor the French government did likewise. Britain, moreover, should be 'entitled to expect from Russia something more than paper recognition of the ordinary obligations of a civilised State before we grant recognition. Our experience in regard to the assurances given at the time of the trade agreement do not encourage us to place much faith in her word.'[54]

The prime minister was not disposed to compromise. If Churchill, obsessed by the defeat inflicted upon his military projects by the Red Army, was determined to resign rather than assent to any recognition, however complete the surrender of the communists and whatever the rest of Europe might decide, the Cabinet would have to choose between Churchill and himself, he replied to Chamberlain. If, as it appeared, the Communist party was gaining the upper hand in Moscow, then there could be no question of recognition. But if 'on the other hand the party that is prepared to surrender its Bolshevism and to make terms with the Western Capitalists has captured the Soviet authority, then it would be folly not to help Russia to return to the community of civilised nations'. It was in any case an essential part of the Genoa programme that there should be a European pact of peace which would involve an undertaking by Russia not to attack her neighbours and by Poland and Romania not to attack Russia. 'I cannot see how that is possible without recognising Russia', the prime minister told Chamberlain.[55] To go to Genoa under conditions that would satisfy Churchill, he wrote to Sir Robert Horne, would be 'futile and humiliating in the extreme'. He could not go to Genoa under these conditions, which meant that he would have to resign if it were proposed to insist upon them. They could not put the Cannes conditions to the Russian delegates, and then if they accepted still refuse recognition. They had been put forward at Cannes as conditions upon which recognition could be granted. 'We must act straightforwardly even with Revolutionaries', Lloyd George insisted.[56]

On 23 March 1922 Chamberlain replied that he had looked again at the Cannes conditions and accepted that they went further than he had originally supposed. He begged the prime minister, however, to 'take trouble with Winston, for we cannot afford to impale ourselves on either of the horns of the dilemma which you put to me'. Nor, as Churchill might well claim, had there as yet been a formal Cabinet discussion and decision on the issue of recognition.[57] Horne wrote to the prime minister the same day to point out the ambiguities involved in the recognition question. If, for instance, Churchill were appeased, he believed there would probably be no objections on the matter from the Unionists other than the Diehards, provided at least that the Soviet government had publicly and solemnly accepted the Cannes conditions. If, at the other extreme, Churchill said he would refuse to recognise the Soviet government, or at least not for a long period of years, he would be unlikely to receive more than minority support. If, however, he took the line that the Soviet government must formally accept the Cannes conditions and should then be required to carry them out for a period of time before formal recognition was considered, Horne thought he would probably obtain the support of a majority of Unionists. This, Horne believed, was probably the position that the French, the Belgians, Beneš and the Little Entente would also adopt, and there was a danger that the British government would be almost entirely isolated if they went further than this. The Lord Chancellor, Lord Birkenhead, also took the view that immediate *de jure* recognition in return for no more than paper promises would be difficult to accept. If both Churchill and Birkenhead were to resign on this issue, Horne added, the coalition would certainly collapse.[58]

Chamberlain, writing to Curzon (who had been absent at a conference on the Near East) on 24 March 1922, explained that the government was in a 'very difficult situation' over the whole matter, as Churchill was refusing to consider recognition while Lloyd George was inclined to resign if recognition was excluded in all circumstances. The basis of a compromise, he thought, might be found by insisting, first of all, on firm adherence to the Cannes conditions as the necessary preliminary to recognition and, secondly, by imposing a probationary period during which the Soviet government would be required to show that it not simply verbally accepted the Cannes conditions but that it was also prepared to implement them. This, Chamberlain believed, would be a sound policy, although it might not please the extremists on either side, and the prime minister might well refuse to accept the idea of a probationary period.[59] Horne, writing to Lloyd George the same day, added that the whole issue in fact appeared to be of no particular concern to anyone but Churchill. If the prime minister took the view that the Soviet government must be given immediate *de jure* recognition if it formally accepted the Cannes conditions, Horne made clear that he would himself feel bound to take the prime minister's side, since this seemed a legitimate interpretation of the Cannes conditions which they had both negotiated. On the other hand, this was not the view taken by other Allied countries which were bound by the same agreement, and if their view was the same as that of the majority of the Cabinet he thought it was doubtful if the matter should be pressed to a rupture. It was a great disappointment to him, Horne added, that there should be 'all this bother over a plan which at the moment doesn't really excite anybody but Winston. George Younger [chairman of the Conservative party organisation] says that on a vote of confidence *sans phrase* you would have the whole Unionist party in the House behind you with the exception of the Die-Hards and many of them would also vote for you.'[60]

Finally, on Saturday 25 March, Lloyd George received a further communication from Chamberlain, informing him that Chamberlain had made every effort to persuade Churchill to make no public statement in the meantime which would prejudice the Cabinet's subsequent deliberations, and reviewing the general merits of the issue. The prime minister's general policy of appeasement, Chamberlain thought, was 'clearly right', and he did not think that any of his colleagues would disagree with it. Some might be more, and some less, optimistic as to the outcome of the conference, but they would all agree in wishing the prime minister every success in bringing matters to a satisfactory conclusion. The only real difficulty was the conditions under which recognition was to be accorded to the Soviet government. Chamberlain himself was opposed to isolated action by the British government in this regard, but he agreed at the same time that Poincaré and his representatives could not be given a right of veto over whatever the British government might propose. Chamberlain thought that there was no serious difference of opinion with regard to the terms of the Cannes resolutions. The difficulty arose when the guarantee of the acceptance of those conditions by the Soviet government was considered. Since the Soviet government had not, he thought, honoured the undertakings that they had made at the time of the conclusion of the trade agreement in 1921, something more substantial than paper assurances would be needed. Anxious as he was to remove difficulties, he could not affront the opinion of practically the whole of his party over a matter of this kind; nor did he think that the Cabinet had implicitly or explicitly given its assent to *de jure* recognition on the basis that was being proposed. His own view was that the Cannes conditions did not in fact necessarily imply that recognition would be given if they were accepted by the Soviet government; they seemed rather to suggest that recognition would be considered in such circumstances, but not otherwise.[61]

The issue was confronted directly at a conference of ministers the following Monday, 27 March 1922. Lloyd George, opening the discussion, began by referring to the evidence which had just been circulated by the president of the Board of Trade that the country was likely to experience a period of bad trade for at least the next two years.[62] This was in large part the result of the failure to revive European trade, which was in turn due to the fact that this task had so far been attempted only by experts rather than by ministers with the necessary political authority. The prime minister thought it was 'now essential that the political representatives of Governments should meet and endeavour to arrange something to re-establish the trade of Europe'. Owing to the attitude of the French government the question of reparations could not be discussed at such a gathering. There remained, however, the important questions of the exchanges, transport and the reconstruction of Europe, more particularly of Austria and Russia. The most difficult of these questions was Russia. He then read out the resolution on this subject which had been agreed at Cannes, and which had been implicitly accepted by the German and Russian governments when they had accepted the invitation to come to Genoa. This, admittedly, was not sufficient; it would be necessary to have a clear and definite acceptance of these principles as well, and perhaps also a probationary period to make sure that the acceptance was not purely formal. If the Soviet government was not prepared to accept the Cannes conditions the question of recognition could not even be considered. If, however, it was prepared to accept the conditions, the question would arise as to whether the British delegation should be precluded from recognising it under any circumstances. His own view was that the Cannes resolution gave the Allies the power to consider the question of recognition in such circumstances, and the right to take their decision 'according to the view they formed from the conduct of the Russian delegates as to whether they had practically abandoned Communistic principles in dealing with foreign Powers, or not'.

There were two parties in Russia, the prime minister went on, one entirely communist, the other prepared to abandon communism in dealing with foreign countries. He did not know which of these parties was in the ascendancy at this time. If, however, it were the latter, he thought it would be a mistake to send them away with a refusal to do business. It would, in fact, be useless to go to Genoa with instructions that under no circumstances could recognition be granted, and he could not undertake to go there on that basis after having agreed to the Cannes resolutions which defined the terms on which the Allies might agree to do so. Assuming that the Soviet delegates accepted the conditions, and assuming that the Allies were convinced by their demeanour and declarations that they genuinely intended to accept them, the question would then arise as to whether recognition should be immediate, or for a probationary period. He understood that there was a strong feeling in the Cabinet and in the House of Commons against recognition. He respected this view and wished to go forward together with his colleagues on the issue. It was clear, however, that it would be impossible to trade in Russia unless the traders concerned had some status in the courts in that country, and vice versa. It was even more important, indeed absolutely essential to trade, that there should be peace in Europe, and he hoped that a pact would be signed at the conference which would help to achieve this. If an agreement of this kind were concluded, he went on, Russian and Allied subjects and diplomatic representatives would have an appropriate status in the courts in each other's countries. Full diplomatic recognition, however, would be withheld until the pact had been substantially implemented by the governments concerned, and until the Allies had been satisfied of the *bona fides* of the Soviet government in particular.

Churchill, commenting on these views, pointed out that the Cabinet had not been consulted about the Cannes resolutions, and that the question of the diplomatic recognition of the Soviet government had been specifically reserved for subsequent discussion. Now, it appeared, the British delegation at Genoa was to be given complete discretion in this matter, and the Cabinet would be bound in advance without having been able to form its own view as to whether the Soviet representatives were likely to carry out their side of the bargain. According to his own sources of information, Krasin had in fact already informed the Soviet government that the recognition of the Cannes resolutions, at least in the form in which they had been published, could not possibly be contemplated. This had also been made clear by *Pravda*, which was the official journal of the Russian Communist party, and in a speech by Lenin to the Congress of Metal Workers on 6 March 1922 in which Lenin was reported to have stated, among other things, that any attempt to force conditions upon Russia as if she were a conquered nation was an 'absurdity' to which it was not worth replying.[63] The British government, he thought, was moving from point to point without ever obtaining a definite answer from the Soviet authorities on these matters. He also felt that Parliament should be consulted, not just about the possibility of recognition, but also about the granting of credits to the Soviet government.

Austen Chamberlain intervened at this point to make clear that there was in fact no question of giving complete discretion to the British delegates at Genoa. On the contrary, their discretion was limited and qualified. The prime minister had said that he would not discuss or consider the recognition of the Soviet government unless it accepted the substance of the Cannes conditions. In addition there would be no question of full diplomatic recognition in the first instance, but merely such limited recognition as was required to make business possible. Churchill accepted this, saying that he had simply wished to present the argument that 'giving full sovereign recognition was to take sides against Russia as a whole in favour of a band of dastardly criminals', and that there should be no recognition by Britain alone under any circumstances. The prime minister pointed out that in any event it was not proposed to grant full diplomatic recognition to the Soviet government; they would wait until that government had proved its *bona fides* before considering any measure of this kind. It was agreed that the Lord Privy Seal, the Lord Chancellor, the Secretary of State for Foreign Affairs, Sir Eyre Crowe of the Foreign Office and the prime minister himself should meet before the following day's Cabinet to draft a formula defining the limited degree of recognition that was contemplated.[64]

The meeting took place at 11 a.m. on the morning of 28 March 1922. The prime minister, opening the discussion, said he thought that all powers were in favour of recognition of the Soviet government, provided that some probationary period was involved. He himself thought that, if there was a decision to recognise, there should be merely a chargé d'affaires in London and in Moscow for the time being; full diplomatic recognition would come later and would depend upon the extent to which the Soviet government had carried out the terms of the agreement. It would first of all be necessary to decide whether it would be possible to do any kind of business with the Soviet representatives at Genoa. He hoped, however, that the British delegates would be given the freedom to act along the lines he had indicated. Austen Chamberlain, amplifying this proposal, said that there would be three stages in such a process; first of all, the Cannes resolutions would have to be accepted by the Soviet representatives; then, if they were accepted, the Allied representatives would have to judge from the demeanour and general attitude of the Soviet delegates if they were acting *bona fide*. Thirdly and finally, if they came to the conclusion that the Soviet representatives were indeed acting *bona fide*, they would go so far as to agree to representation at the level of chargés d'affaires.

Curzon expressed some misgivings about these proposed arrangements, and indicated that he personally was not in favour of any degree of formal recognition at this stage. His principal concern, however, was that the British government should not act alone in the matter. The prime minister agreed, although it might not be advisable to make this known publicly, as the French might take unfair advantage of it. Curzon added that at his meeting in Paris to discuss the Near East Poincaré had told him that he would not be coming to Genoa himself at the outset but would be sending some other minister. His reasons for not doing so had been 'somewhat lame'. As soon as he had satisfied the French chauvinists by not attending at the outset, however, Curzon thought he might be willing to put in an appearance. Both Poincaré and Schanzer, who had also been present at their discussions, had taken the view that the conference might last for some time, perhaps from two to six months. Curzon pointed out that even a qualified recognition such as the prime minister proposed would amount to *de jure* recognition. Lord Birkenhead agreed that technically this was correct, but pointed out that in international law *de jure* recognition was normally spoken of as full admission to the comity of nations. A country which in former circumstances had had an ambassador but was now to be represented only at the level of chargé d'affaires could hardly be said to have been accorded this status. Curzon suggested that the main difference in practice would be that the representative thus accredited would have access to the Foreign Office, but would not be received individually by the King. Lloyd George at this point read an extract from a letter which had been communicated to him by the Home Secretary, indicating that Lenin appeared to be abandoning his communistic principles. If this were the case, by recognising him the government would be supporting those in Russia who were in favour of moderation. He did not contemplate what he called 'ceremonial recognition' at this stage. The conditions which were being asked of Russia, he thought, were necessary but somewhat humiliating, and it might be necessary to give the representatives some idea of the extent of the recognition they might receive before progress could be made. He might have to return to explain the situation to Parliament from time to time during the course of the conference, but he hoped that the hands of the delegation would not be unreasonably tied in advance.[65]

A full meeting of the Cabinet followed immediately at 12 noon. The Cabinet first of all approved the resolution concerning the Genoa conference which it was proposed to submit to the House of Commons the following Monday, 3 April, and then passed on to the question of the instructions which were to be given to the British delegates who were attending the conference. The prime minister began by pointing to the disturbed state of politics in eastern Europe and elsewhere, which made it difficult to re-establish normal trading relations. The first business of the Genoa conference, he thought, should be to conclude a pact among all the nations of Europe against aggression. Russia, for instance, must undertake not to attack Romania, Latvia, Lithuania, Poland and Finland, and vice versa. Until some such conditions of peace was established, he pointed out, there would not be an effective revival of trade. The president of the Board of Trade, after consultation with leading businessmen, had prepared a report which had indicated that industrial and commercial prospects would be extremely unfavourable for at least the next two years. Very little reduction in the level of unemployment was to be expected either, for reasons that were at least in part connected with the international situation. So far as Russia was concerned, the prime minister went on, efforts had been made to restore trading relations with that country, but they had not been entirely successful. This was in part because the Soviet government had not carried out the provisions of the trading agreement of 1921 as strictly as the government had a right to expect, but also because Russia was still outside the comity of nations, failing which the full restoration of trade would be difficult. The government's first objective, he thought, should be to establish peace, and secondly to establish complete commercial relations with Russia.

This raised the question of the extent to which those objects involved the recognition of Russia. The prime minister himself did not believe it would be possible to get trade going unless there was some degree of recognition. Access to courts of law, in particular, was essential to the carrying on of trade. Therefore some measure of recognition was absolutely essential. This raised three questions: Should recognition be complete? If it was complete, should a time element be introduced? And thirdly, to what extent should Britain be prepared to act alone? He thought it was generally agreed that Britain should not act entirely alone. On the other hand, if it were decided that Russia should not be recognised until all the powers had agreed to do so, this would give countries which, such as France, had least need of Russian trade, a veto over any possible agreement. No self-respecting delegation could go to Genoa on such a basis. So far as the probationary period was concerned, it appeared, from a recent interview with Mr Vanderlip, an American with extensive interests in Russia who had just returned from a visit to that country, that Lenin had been personally largely responsible for the promulgation of the recent economic laws, which amounted to an abandonment of communism.[66] 'If the Russian Delegation came to Genoa having practically surrendered their Communistic principles and willing to enter into negotiation with capitalistic communities', the prime minister went on, 'we ought to give all necessary support to the anti-Communistic elements in Russia, and declare that if Communistic principles are abandoned we are ready to assist in the economic development of Russia.' They would not however be accorded full diplomatic recognition until the powers had been able to satisfy themselves that a genuine attempt had been made to carry out the terms of such an agreement. He thought the French and also Beneš would agree to cooperate upon this basis.

Curzon was disposed to attach the greatest importance to the desirability of acting in association with the other European powers on this question. Only in the later stages of the conference, he thought, would the delegates be in a position to decide upon the issue of recognition, and the Russian delegates would by then have made it clear whether their assurances would justify the confidence of the other powers. It would be ridiculous for the British government to stand out either for or against recognition at this stage if the other European powers were agreed upon a different course of action. He himself attached more importance to acting with Europe than to any other point. Churchill had even greater misgivings. He was reluctant, in the first place, to give the British delegation final authority in this important matter without requiring them to refer back to the Cabinet for further instructions. The trade agreement had been concluded on the understanding that if its terms were violated it could be revoked. The Soviet government had in fact repeatedly violated the terms of agreement, and yet it was now proposed to make still further con-cessions to that government. He thought it was right to meet the Russian delegates at Genoa. He was doubtful, however, if much trade would result in the two or three years thereafter, and there was also evidence to suggest that the Soviet delegation would simply use the opportunity the conference provided in order to improve their pres-tige at home. The delegates would go back having signed papers they did not mean to honour, and would be enabled to 'rivet their shackles even more closely on the ignorant peasants'. He was 'bitterly sorry that at a time of strong Conservative majorities in a country deeply devoted to the monarchy it was proposed to accord this supreme favour and patronage to the Bolsheviks'. If there were going to be a substantial revival of trade it would be different, but on that score he was doubtful.

Austen Chamberlain pointed out that a number of ministers would be at Genoa while others might be dispersed for the Easter vacation, and that it would therefore be desirable to give the British delegates a certain limited discretion within which they could make their own decisions. The prime minister added that the decisions of the Genoa conference, whatever they were, would in any case come before the House of Commons for its approval. The Cabinet accordingly agreed that the British delegates should be given authority to conduct negotiations at Genoa, subject to the limitations in respect of the Soviet government that had been suggested by the Lord Privy Seal. The British delegation was not to act in isolation or without a general consensus among the states represented at the conference; and there could be no advance in British diplomatic relations with Russia unless the government of that country fully accepted the substance of the Cannes conditions. If those conditions were accepted and the British delegates were convinced that the acceptance was in good faith, the British government would be prepared to receive a Soviet chargé d'affaires in London and to send a British chargé d'affaires to Moscow for a probationary period to facilitate the execution of the agreement. The British government would not, however, grant full and ceremonial diplomatic representation to the Soviet government until experience had shown that the agreement had been loyally observed by that government. The results of the conference would also be subject to the approval of Parliament.[67]

A conference of ministers the following Sunday, 2 April 1922, approved the main lines of the speech that the prime minister proposed to give to the House of Commons the next day in explanation of the government's policy towards the conference.[68] Addressing the chamber on 3 April, Lloyd George moved that the House approve the resolutions passed by the Supreme Council at Cannes as the basis of the Genoa conference, and that it support the government in endeavouring to give effect to them. The prime minister, opening the debate, announced that the vote would be regarded as one of confidence in the government as a whole. The conference, he informed Members, had been called to consider the problem of the reconstruction of the European economy, which had been devastated by war and its consequences. Trade had collapsed; currencies had become worthless as mediums of exchange; and vast areas of the continent, vital for the supply of raw materials and food, had been destroyed commercially. International tensions were also high, and the military burdens that these tensions produced had led to further economic difficulties. The purpose of the Genoa conference was to restore order in place of this disorder, and to recover prosperity out of this desolation.

The two questions of the peace treaties and of reparations, the prime minister continued, were very properly outside the agreed scope of the conference, which was concerned rather with the establishment of peace, confidence and credit, with currency exchanges and transport, and with the machinery of international trade. Conferences had been held on these subjects since the war, but to very little effect, since those represented had been technical experts rather than politicians who could commit their governments to the resolutions that were adopted. The restoration of Europe, the prime minister emphasised, was of vital importance to Britain in particular, because upon it depended the revival of British exports and the alleviation of unemployment. Nor could trade with other parts of the world offer a satisfactory substitute, because the ability of these countries to buy British exports was also dependent upon the income that they were able to generate from their trade with Europe.

The prime minister then turned to the question of Russia. It was, he admitted, a matter on which the doctrines and behaviour of the Bolsheviks made it difficult for a balanced judgement to be formed. He commended the example of William Pitt in this connection, in particular Pitt's willingness to seek peace with the French revolutionaries despite his repugnance towards the doctrines with which they were associated. The establishment of a genuine peace with Russia, the prime minister believed, would discourage military preparations, real or alleged, in that country; it would assist Germany to repay her reparations to the Allies; and it would enable Russia to resume the supply of foodstuffs and raw materials which were urgently needed by the rest of Europe. Russia, however, would have to recognise all the 'conditions imposed and accepted by civilised communities as the test of fitness for entering into the comity of nations'. The Soviet government, for instance, would have to accept the obligations of its predecessors, though their immediate repayment would not be demanded. Where the property of British nationals had been confiscated it would have to be returned, if it was physically possible to do so, or else an appropriate sum of compensation would have to be paid. An impartial system of courts would have to be established, and attacks on other countries would have to cease.

Would Russia be prepared to accept these fairly far-reaching conditions? The prime minister thought so. There were indications in that country, he believed, of a 'complete change of attitude'. The famine had helped to bring about this change, as it had shown the weaknesses of the Soviet government's administrative arrangements and also the extent to which the country depended upon its neighbours. The decrees that had been introduced in Russia over the previous few months, in fact, now recognised private property and the need for impartial judicial procedures. Lloyd George called the attention of the House in particular to a 'very remarkable speech' by Lenin on 1 November 1921 in which the Soviet government's new policies had been propounded. The speech, in the prime minister's view, had been an 'admission of the complete failure of the Communist system ... a very remarkable condemnation and exposure of the doctrines of Karl Marx by its greatest – not merely its greatest living exponent, but its greatest exponent, the only man who has ever tried honestly to put these doctrines into operation'.[69] If this represented the real attitude of the Soviet government – respect for private property, respect for the rights of individuals, fair play to those who made investments in that country, acknowledgement of honourable debts – then there was, the prime minister thought, a 'real basis upon which we can treat'.

The prime minister turned next to the question of the degree of recognition of the Soviet government that would be involved. The House of Commons, he promised, would have to approve any advance in this or any other direction that was agreed upon at the conference. If the circumstances were appropriate, however, it was proposed that a limited degree of recognition should be extended to the Soviet government. This would be sufficient to permit access by nationals of the other European countries to Russian courts, and vice versa, and agents would also be appointed in the usual way for the protection of traders and other interests. Before exchanging ambassadors and establishing full diplomatic relations, however, a reasonable time would have to elapse in which the Soviet government would have to give proof of its *bona fides*. It was, the prime minister suggested, a moderate, even over-cautious policy that the government was proposing. It was doing its best to work in partnership with France, and to make due allowance for the reasonable prejudices that might be felt towards a country, Russia, which had 'outraged every sentiment that is dear to the vast majority of the people of this country'. The British people, he believed, demanded the measures that the government proposed to undertake; Europe needed them; and the world was crying out for them. A number of Members felt that the government's proposals went either too far or not far enough, but in the event the policy was approved by 372 votes to 94, a very substantial majority in favour of the government.[70] For the time being, at least, the prime minister had won the day.

5

Soviet Russia and Genoa

The decision to invite the Soviet government to Genoa, essentially a personal one by Lloyd George, rested upon the assumption that the Soviet government would be willing not simply to attend but also to make substantial concessions in return for western economic assistance. The adoption of the New Economic Policy in March 1921, as we have seen, had led substantial sections of western public and governmental opinion to conclude that the Bolsheviks' early revolutionary enthusiasm was subsiding and that a more moderate and acceptable form of politics would gradually emerge in its place.[1] The attempt to establish an economic system on a basis completely different from any that had previously existed was widely believed to be more than a temporary aberration from economic laws which were implacable in their operation and as applicable to Soviet Russia as anywhere else. The example of the French revolution also suggested, at least to Lloyd George, that revolutions were periodic but essentially transient convulsions in the course of history; once the peasantry had secured the land, as in France, they would support the new government which guaranteed their possession, stability would return and normal relations with the outside world would gradually be restored.[2] In any case, it was believed, the Bolsheviks, in the difficult economic situation in which they found themselves, had no alternative but to turn to the West for assistance, in the absence of which the economy would collapse and with it their own regime. The task of western statesmanship, or so at least it appeared to Lloyd George and those who shared his views, was to accelerate this natural development so that the economic unity of Europe could be restored as soon as possible for the benefit of all its members, and so that a stable peace could be established in place of

97

the protracted disputes that had followed the conclusion of the Versailles treaty.[3]

The early months of 1922 provided a good deal of evidence to suggest that these were by no means unrealistic assumptions. Reports reaching western governments, at least, suggested that the evolution of public policy in Russia that had begun with the introduction of NEP was continuing further and indeed acquiring a momentum of its own. They also suggested that the Soviet government was attaching a good deal of importance to the invitation it had received to attend an international conference at Genoa together with the other powers. H. M. Grove, the British consul-general in Moscow, for instance, wrote to Curzon on 20 January 1922 informing him that since the invitation to the Soviet government had been received 'practically every column of the local press' had contained some reference to the subject, and it had been the 'principal topic of conversation on all sides'. The resignation of Briand had been seen, not as a warning that the conference might not now take place, but rather as an indication that the British government intended to insist upon the full *de jure* recognition of its Soviet counterpart. Internally, Grove noted, there were new signs of confidence and stability; the powers of the Cheka were being reduced, a new criminal code was being prepared, and new civil and commercial legislation was also under consideration. Profiteers such as the apocryphal Limon Milliardovich were also making their appearance.[4] 'Russians who formerly held large commercial interests', he added on 21 February, 'think that a turning-point has at last been reached'.[5] Grove warned that there were indications in the Soviet press that their delegation at Genoa might raise issues such as self-determination for the British colonies and for Alsace–Lorraine, and there had been assertions that the West needed Russia more than Russia needed the West.[6] Reports emanating from the Commissariat of Foreign Affairs, however, suggested that the Soviet authorities were 'most anxious to come to terms at Genoa' and that they were likely to accept 'almost any conditions which may be put forward by Great Britain, not excluding the abolition of the monopoly of foreign trade and the return of private property to British claimants'.[7]

Lloyd George drew upon these and similar reports when he met the Czech prime minister, Beneš, on 20 February 1922. Without European assistance, Lloyd George believed, Russia would collapse, and with it the Bolshevik regime. For this reason he thought the

Soviet government would accept any terms the Allies might demand. 'If Lenin came back from Genoa with nothing in his hands', as the prime minister put it, 'he would be overthrown.'[8] Lloyd George referred in support of these views to a report he had received from the British official agent in Moscow, R. M. Hodgson, who was at that time in London on a short visit. The Soviet government, Hodgson had written, was most anxious to obtain official *de jure* recognition from the western powers, believing that this was essential for the country's development, and would probably be prepared to abandon important elements of what still remained of the communist programme in order to obtain it.[9] Lloyd George appears to have been particularly impressed by an interview with Simon Eisenstein, the manager of the Marconi company in Russia since 1916, who visited London at the end of February 1922 and was interviewed on a 'strictly confidential' basis by British intelligence. Eisenstein, who at the request of Lenin had just erected a wireless station in the Kremlin, reported that Lenin himself had been largely responsible for the adoption of the new economic legislation, which effectively represented the abandonment of the main principles of communism (Lloyd George marked this passage in the margin and drew upon it in his speeches).[10] Lenin's own prestige and influence were so great, Eisenstein believed, that for the time being opposition both from the trade unions and from the extreme left wing of the Communist party had been defeated. The true nature of the change of policy had not yet been understood by the Soviet working class; when this occurred, the regime would be in 'acute danger'. Eisenstein thought the Soviet delegates at Genoa would begin with an ultra-communist programme, but that they would then accede one by one to the Allies' demands; they realised their danger, but believed that if they could persuade the working people their defeat had been an honourable and temporary one they might nonetheless be able to retain power.[11]

Further evidence of the changes that were taking place in Russia arrived in the form of a memorandum on legal reforms which was communicated to western governments on 1 April 1922. So far as personal rights were concerned, the memorandum began, the Soviet government had ended the prohibition upon employees of state institutions leaving their work, and had also ended periodic labour mobilisations. The rights of local administrative bodies to settle and resettle private citizens had been curtailed, thus strengthening the inviolability of the home, and the privacy of postal and telegraphic

communications had been legally recognised. Of particular importance, the memorandum suggested, was the decree adopted at the
Ninth All-Russian Congress of Soviets reorganising the Cheka and
limiting its powers of arrest and detention. A new criminal code,
submitted for approval to the Council of People's Commissars, had
established the principle of equality before the law for both Soviet
and foreign citizens, and the basis of a new court system had been
drawn up by the Commissariat of Justice. So far as the economy was
concerned, the memorandum went on, the government was limiting
its responsibility to major state enterprises, and transferring the
remainder to commercially operated trusts or to private entrepreneurs. The property of foreign concessionaires would be guaranteed for as long as their agreements were valid, and their property
would be exempt from any kind of nationalisation or confiscation.
Provision had also been made for private trade, for mixed companies
and for an independent bar. The perfection of the legal system, the
memorandum concluded, was the constant object of the Soviet
government, but already a legal order had been established to which
foreigners, as well as Russians, could safely entrust their property
and other rights.[12] Hodgson, writing from Moscow, pointed out that
arbitrary evictions and arrests continued to take place, whatever the
law might provide;[13] legal changes of this nature, however, were
among the conditions on which the Allies had insisted most strenuou-
sly, and for these governments at least they clearly represented a step
in the right direction.

Summing up the evidence that had so far been received in early
April 1922, Commander Maxse of the Northern Department of the
Foreign Office noted that there had originally been a great deal of
excitement about the conference, but that there had subsequently
been some disillusionment. The Soviet government, he thought,
would probably attend, but it might be pushed by its extremists into
making a gesture of defiance towards the western capitalist powers
and might after all refuse to come. Assuming it did attend, he thought
the issue of pre-war national debts would present no particular
difficulties. War debts, however, might raise some complicated issues
of principle. There would probably be no difficulty in securing the
recognition of private claims, but it was more than probable that the
burden of repayment would then be thrown back upon the Allies in
the form of counterclaims. The Soviet delegates, moreover, would be
unlikely to agree to anything unless they received credits for

economic reconstruction.[14] A telegram from Grove in mid-March suggested that 'extremists' were 'gaining the upper hand' in the Soviet government; the repeated postponement of the conference and the elaborate conditions that were being required for all participants had enabled more left-wing elements to increase their influence, and it was possible that the policy of economic cooperation with the western countries might be replaced by what Grove described as 'more aggressive tactics'.[15] The latest information received from the British minister in Riga at the end of March, however, was the Bolsheviks would ask for many things, but that they were 'ready in their hearts to make practically any concession provided that they get *de jure* recognition, large credits and, most important of all, retain their power'.[16]

The French government, lacking a diplomatic representative in the Soviet capital, was less fully informed than its British counterpart about the nature of the changes that were taking place in Russia. Reports from newspaper correspondents, however, suggested (as did other sources) that the situation was rapidly changing and in a manner congenial to French interests. The Soviet government, *Le Matin* reported, was becoming more and more convinced that communist ideas were leading to economic ruin. Having destroyed the economic foundations of the country, it was now having to relearn the basic truths it had earlier disregarded. The Bolsheviks, 'feeling their end near', were now offering 'appetising concessions' to foreign interests, Germans, Americans and Japanese among them; the country as a whole was likely to become a 'vast colony, where there will be enough work for all the nations of the globe'.[17] The French chargé d'affaires in Tallinn, offering his general impressions on the eve of the conference, thought it was 'beyond doubt' that Genoa was the 'last hope of the Bolsheviks'. In order to obtain enough to remain in power they would probably be modest in their demands and would be content with the recognition of their government and the guarantee of their frontiers for a period of time; they would also be likely to seek an international loan, which would assure the food supply and thus the support of the Red Army and the Cheka.[18] A report from the French ambassador in London, based on Foreign Office information, suggested that communism as a term would be retained only as the 'etiquette of a political party'; the clear direction of policy was towards the relaxation of state control and the expansion of private enterprise, and the communism of the early post-revolutionary years was now 'definitely dead'.[19]

According to a French intelligence report based on Soviet sources, there were in fact two main tendencies in the Soviet government and in the Central Executive Committee with regard to the conference. There was a radical or extreme tendency, headed by Litvinov, which insisted that the Soviet government, in order to retain its prestige among the world proletariat, must demand immediate recognition, a revision of the Versailles treaty, and compensation for the civil war and foreign intervention, and there was also a more moderate tendency, headed by Lenin, which believed that in view of the delay in the world revolution and the failure of the proletariat to come to the aid of Soviet Russia all aggressive policies must be abandoned. The general policy favoured by the latter (apparently dominant) faction was to open negotiations on general disarmament, to negotiate an international loan for economic reconstruction, and to attempt to secure the *de jure* recognition of the Soviet government, a guarantee of the integrity of Soviet frontiers, a readjustment of the Bessarabian frontier in favour of Russia and the revision of the treaty of Versailles.[20] The French agent at Riga reported on 1 April that according to the latest information, based on conversations with Chicherin, the Russians would be aiming above all at full *de jure* recognition at Genoa; they would be prepared to make concessions for this, such as permitting the establishment of joint Russian and foreign-owned companies and foreign leases of Russian forests, mines and less important railway lines, but no overall financial control of Russia by foreign interests would be tolerated, nor could there be any division of Russia into zones of influence.[21] A further report received as the conference opened suggested that the Soviet government was in fact in such desperate straits that Chicherin had been telegraphed to make whatever concessions were necessary in order to secure western economic and financial assistance.[22]

If these reports had anything in common, it was perhaps a tendency to exaggerate the internal divisions, lack of preparedness and willingness to make concessions of the Bolshevik administration. As early as December 1921, before the Cannes conference had taken place, Krasin had in fact written to Lenin to warn him of the need to make urgent preparations for the international conference that appeared to be in prospect, determining the limits of any possible concessions and inviting the leading members of the Supreme

Council of the National Economy (VSNKh) to undertake the necessary work. The forthcoming conference, he added, would be the most difficult the Bolsheviks had ever encountered, not excluding Brest-Litovsk.[23] Their opponents, he warned in a further letter, had very precise data at their disposal on the question of debts, and it would be necessary for the Soviet diplomats at any conference to have full and detailed evidence of the losses suffered during the civil war and intervention if they were to negotiate successfully on this matter.[24] The Communist party Politburo accordingly decided on 5 January 1922, before an invitation had been received or the Cannes proceedings had even opened, to establish a commission under the auspices of the Commissariat of Foreign Affairs to undertake the necessary preparatory work for the conference and for negotiations with the western powers. Chicherin was named as chairman of the commission; its other members were Litvinov, G. Ya. Sokol'nikov, A. A. Ioffe, A. M. Lezhava and N. N. Krestinsky. Later G. M. Krzhizhanovsky, E. A. Preobrazhensky, S. S. Pilyavsky (a staff member of the commissariat) and Krasin were added.[25] A parallel investigation into the losses suffered during the civil war and intervention period was entrusted to N. N. Lyubimov, a Moscow University professor.[26] The NKID commission was required to present the draft speeches of the conference delegates to the Central Committee by 15 February, and a detailed statement of the Soviet counterclaims was to be made by the same date. The commission met regularly, about twice a week, from 7 January onwards; altogether it held twenty-two meetings, each of which could last five or six hours, and leading state officials, experts and others were invited to take part in its deliberations.[27]

The work of leading members of the foreign commissariat was almost entirely devoted to Genoa from about the same date. The prospect of Genoa kept every junior member of the commissariat 'wide awake', recalled a former Soviet diploment; the people's commissar himself was 'driven mad by an endless stream of tiresome requests'.[28] Arthur Ransome, visiting the commissariat in March as a journalist from the *Manchester Guardian*, found that Chicherin had been forced to take extreme measures: a large printed notice on his door read 'It is forbidden to everybody, whosoever he may be, to speak with the People's Commissar on the subject of GENOA'. Ransome found that it was in practice impossible to get away from the subject of the conference. In the commissariat itself a whole series of rooms was filled with people exclusively preparing briefs for the

Soviet delegation. Ransome found Ioffe in a room near Chicherin's
behind a 'mountain of purple typescript on thin, flimsy paper, such a
mountain as a hardened publisher's reader could hardly get through
in a month'. A secretary beside him was similarly burdened, and on a
side table were 'Himalayan ranges' of the same kind. He had no
difficulty in understanding when Ioffe mildly remarked that a short
postponement might perhaps help the Soviet government to prepare
its case better. Ransome, who also met Litvinov, found that Soviet
officials believed the conference might meet for six months, or even
semi-permanently; although unwilling to make any sort of capitulation, they believed they were bringing enough goodwill and readiness to make concessions to give them a genuine belief that if there
was good will on the other side it should be possible to come to a
useful agreement.[29]

Soviet preparations for the conference took place in considerable
secrecy; Chicherin refused to discuss with visiting journalists the
policy the Soviet government would adopt,[30] and Lenin issued
instructions that no details were to be sent abroad, even in code,
about their plans.[31] Lenin also urged that there should be 'not a
word' about the Soviet counterclaims.[32] A version of the Soviet
programme for Genoa did however reach western governments at the
beginning of March 1922, which suggested that preparations had
been concentrated upon (i) the liquidation of old accounts (debts
and liabilities) and (ii) the re-establishment of Russia as an essential
part of the world economy (the financing of transport, state and
private industry, taxation, the re-establishment of agriculture and
famine relief).[33] The work of the NKID commission seems to have
exposed some differences: Krasin, for instance, in a set of theses
presented in the latter part of February, argued against surrendering
the monopoly of foreign trade but in favour of satisfying the claims of
the former owners of nationalised enterprises (he was nonetheless
allocated the task of exploring relations with foreign governments in
more detail),[34] and reports of a meeting of the commission which
came into the possession of the Foreign Office suggested that 'long
and heated debates' had taken place about the extent to which
concessions could be made to western interests.[35] A considerable
amount of preparatory work also took place in Gosplan and the other
economic commissariats,[36] and a plan for agitational work – repudiating the false assertions about Soviet Russia in the foreign press,
developing the notion of Soviet Russia as a partner in a general peace

treaty and so forth – was prepared under the auspices of the party Central Committee.[37]

The detailed preparation of the Soviet position at Genoa took place under the close supervision of the party leadership and of Lenin personally. Although Lenin spent much of the winter of 1921–2 outside Moscow at his retreat in Gorki, Chicherin later recalled, he took a 'close and keen interest in all questions concerned with the Genoa conference' and sent out a stream of memoranda which defined the Soviet position at the conference.[38] The first decision of major consequence was to accept the invitation to the conference, which was officially communicated by the Italian prime minister, Bonomi, on 13 January 1922. On 19 January Chicherin duly replied with a formal acceptance.[39] The Politburo approved the text of Chicherin's reply on 17 January, and also agreed upon the composition of the Soviet delegation that would attend the conference.[40] The delegation's membership was formally approved at a meeting of the Central Executive Committee on 27 January and communicated to the Italian government a few days later.[41] The delegation was to be headed by Lenin, but Chicherin, as vice-chairman, was to enjoy the same powers if Lenin was unable to attend. The other principal delegates were Krasin, Litvinov, Ioffe, the Ukrainian prime minister Christian Rakovsky, the Soviet trade representative in Italy Vatslav Vorovsky, and the general secretary of the Soviet trade union organisation Yan Rudzutak. These delegates, the Politburo decided, were to constitute the 'bureau' of the delegation; it was also decided that Soviet Russia and its associated republics should send a single delegation to the conference, and a formal protocol to this effect was signed by Ukrainian, Azerbaidzhani, Armenian and other representatives in Moscow on 22 February 1922.[42]

Lenin devoted particular attention to the precise terms in which the Soviet delegation had been invited to Genoa. On 26 January 1922 he telephoned Chicherin to ask for a copy of Bonomi's letter of invitation in the language in which it had been received. He also asked if it had not been the case that at least one of the Entente papers had published the text of the Cannes resolutions (which had been attached to Bonomi's letter) in the same form in which they had appeared in the Soviet press, which had made specific reference to the right of nations to choose their own 'system of property'.[43] Chicherin replied later the same day, sending Lenin a copy of the *Petit Parisien* of 8 January in which the full text of the resolutions had been printed. Bonomi had indeed omitted the term 'system of property' from the text of the resolution he had submitted.[44] The full text of the first point of the Cannes resolution, as adopted on 6 January and published in the *Petit Parisien* and other papers on 8 January, ran as follows: 'Nations cannot claim the right to dictate to each other the principles according to which they propose to organise, domestically, their system of property, economy and government. Each country has the right to choose for itself the system it prefers in this respect.' The text communicated by Bonomi to the Soviet government on 13 January, however, had reserved for nations the right to choose their own 'internal economic life and mode of government', but had said nothing about their system of property.[45] The omission was a particularly significant one in the Soviet case; it was, however, apparently an innocent mistake, as the text of the Cannes resolutions which was communicated to the other powers together with their invitations was couched in identical terms.[46] Lenin, nonetheless, rightly identified the issue as a crucial one, permitting, at least in principle, a non-capitalist form of economic organisation, and in his instructions to the Soviet delegates he urged them to quote this article of the Cannes resolutions 'particularly often'.[47]

Chicherin, who had already pressed for a compromise on the matter of foreign debts and whose uncertain health was suffering under the strain of preparations for the conference, was among those in the Soviet leadership who were willing to make the most far-reaching concessions to western pressure at this time. On 16 January 1922 Lenin wrote to the other members of the Politburo to ask if Chicherin should not be given immediate sick leave for a month or more in view of his evident ill health. In the event, because of the serious lack of qualified staff and Chicherin's own resistance to the idea, he was allowed to remain uninterruptedly at his post until the conference had ended.[48] On 20 and 22 January, however, Chicherin wrote to Lenin to urge that changes be made in the Soviet constitution to satisfy foreign (in this case American) opinion, such as permitting the representation of 'parasitic elements' in the soviets. This suggestion, Lenin wrote to the other members of the Politburo on 24 January, showed that Chicherin was seriously ill, and they would be fools if they did not send him immediately to a sanatorium. Any concessions of this kind, Lenin pointed out, would prejudice the Soviet position at the conference; more generally it suggested the need for preliminary but still precise guidelines to be drawn up as soon as possible for all members of the delegation.[49] Chicherin's letter, Lenin wrote to the foreign minister on 7 February, and still more a letter from Krasin, showed signs of panic. There was nothing more dangerous than this. A breakdown of the conference was, from the Soviet point of view, of no great importance; if it failed, there would certainly be another and a better one. They were not afraid of isolation or a blockade, or of ultimatums; they wanted an agreement with the West, but only if the conditions were known in advance and if all Soviet counterclaims were taken into account.[50]

General guidelines for the Soviet delegation began to emerge in the early part of February 1922. Lenin's first directives for the delegation were in fact drafted on 22 January 1922;[51] a more elaborate set of proposals was circulated to the Politburo on 1 February. All the delegates, Lenin began, should be required to prepare themselves for the whole range of political and financial questions that might arise at the conference; in addition, each member of the delegation should make a detailed study of one particular diplomatic and one particular financial topic. Chicherin and Litvinov should be asked to make the necessary arrangements, and also to supply the necessary literature. An additional group of financial experts should be asked to assist in the preparation of this aspect of the conference agenda in view of its complexity. All members of the delegation, Lenin went on, should have an excellent knowledge of Keynes's *Economic Consequences of the Peace* and of similar bourgeois-pacifist writings, and should quote them in support of their proposals rather than simply putting forward the communist viewpoint.[52] A further, more detailed set of proposals followed on 6 February. The Soviet programme as a whole, Lenin suggested, should be 'bourgeois-pacifist' in character, and should indicate a series of measures which would at least alleviate the world's economic difficulties if not resolve them entirely (this would require a break with the capitalist system as such). The main points in the Soviet programme, he thought, should be the cancellation of all debts, the application of an 'Irish' solution to all colonial and dependent countries, a radical review of the Versailles treaty, loans for those countries most in need of them, the establishment of a single gold unit of currency, measures to reduce inflation and to make better use of energy resources, and connected with all this, the reform of international transport. These directives were approved by the Politburo on 8 February.[53]

A further and, it appears, final set of directives for the Soviet delegation was circulated by Lenin on 24 February 1922. These conferred all the powers of the chairman of the delegation upon Chicherin, the deputy chairman, implicitly indicating that Lenin himself would not be attending. In the absence or ill health of the foreign minister, Litvinov, Krasin and Radek, or Litvinov, Ioffe and Vorovsky, were to exercise the chairman's powers collectively. The delegation, Lenin went on, should seek to avoid endorsing the Cannes conditions; but if it proved impossible to do so, it should propose a slogan suggested by Krasin: 'All countries recognise their state debts and bind themselves to make good the damages and losses caused by the actions of their governments.' If this in turn was not allowed, the conference should be allowed to collapse, the Soviet delegation nonetheless announcing for its part that it would be ready to recognise private debts but that it regarded these and all other obligations as covered by the Russian counterclaims. The maximum concession that could be offered to western interests was that previous owners could be allowed priority in the allocation of concessions. The full Soviet programme, Lenin suggested, should be indicated, at least in outline, at the first available opportunity; in general terms it should consist of an attempt, without concealing their communist views, to strengthen pacifist elements within the bourgeois states and to break up the united capitalist front. The detailed elaboration of such a pacifist programme should be left to the delegation itself. A detailed plan for the economic development of Russia and the European economy, based upon proposals prepared by Gosplan, should also be put forward. So far as loans were concerned, guarantees could be offered in the form of forests in the northern areas and so forth, but no infringement of the rights of the Soviet state could be considered and no treaties could be concluded without Central Committee approval. The draft resolution was approved by the Politburo, with minor amendments, on 28 February.[54]

Chicherin expressed no enthusiasm for the idea that he and the other delegates should be responsible for putting forward a pacifist rather than a socialist programme. All his life, he wrote to Lenin, he had criticised petty-bourgeois illusions, and now in his advanced years the Politburo had instructed him to prepare a programme of such a character. He had in fact no idea how to draw up such a programme, or of the sources on which he might rely. Could Lenin make some more detailed suggestions in this regard?[55] Lenin agreed that they had both struggled against pacifism as such, but it could be used in this case to weaken the bourgeoisie, not to strengthen them.[56] Chicherin eventually composed a 'broad pacifist programme' and sent it to Lenin for approval on 10 March 1922. Workers' organisations and colonial peoples, the foreign minister began by suggesting, should be invited to take part in future international conferences of this kind. The principle of non-intervention in the internal affairs of other states should be recognised, a world congress for economic development should be held, there should be a general reduction of armaments, and submarine, aerial, chemical and various other forms of warfare should be banned. Lenin expressed his full agreement with these proposals on 14 March, suggesting in addition the cancellation of all war debts and the revision of Versailles and the other post-war treaties.[57] Lenin made some further amendments in a pacifist sense to Chicherin's draft speech for the opening of the conference.[58] In the end, as Lenin explained to the Eleventh Party Congress at the end of the month, the party leadership had taken steps to select a delegation of the best Soviet diplomats to go to Genoa, and had given them a set of fairly detailed directives. How successful they would be in realising these objectives would depend, at least in part, upon the skill with which the Soviet delegates conducted themselves at the conference; but whatever its outcome, the development of economic relations between Soviet Russia and the outside world would undoubtedly continue, as the interests of the capitalist states themselves demanded it.[59]

Not only were Soviet preparations for the conference more thorough and detailed than most western government had realised, they also reflected a public opinion which the Soviet leaders could not lightly have disregarded even if they had wished to do so, and which was particularly concerned lest the achievements of the revolution be sacrificed for minor gains and the country itself be allowed to fall under the control of foreign powers. The decision to summon the conference itself had been widely welcomed in the Soviet press. It was 'undoubtedly the first major moral victory of Soviet Russia on a world scale', Yu. Steklov wrote in an editorial in *Izvestiya* on 11 January. Although there would undoubtedly be difficulties ahead, by their decision the Allies had recognised the stability of the Soviet government, forsworn at least open intervention into its domestic affairs, and accepted the economic necessity of an accommodation with Moscow. The conference would not succeed, however, if the

Allies made demands upon Russia which they had been unable to impose by military means, and there could be no 'one-sided capitulation'.[60] Radek, writing in *Pravda* on 10 January, described the invitation to the Soviet government as a 'major turning-point in the international situation'. The Allies, he believed, had now decided that the Soviet system was the only possible form of government in Russia, and that its cooperation was necessary for the restoration of the world economy.[61] But only 'absolute necessity', *Trud* pointed out, had compelled the international bourgeoisie to take this step and, as *Pravda* pointed out on 12 January, there was a continued need for vigilance to defend the country against any attacks upon its independence and material assets.[62] The plans to establish an international consortium aroused particular anxiety. Among the powers invited to take part, noted Steklov, was Japan, a country which was still effectively waging war on Soviet Russia in the Far East. Other writers noted that parallels had been drawn between Russia and China in this connection; but Russia was more powerful than China, and 'methods, applicable to China, will not do for Russia'.[63]

Concerns of this kind were also reflected in the discussions which were taking place at the same time in party and government circles. There had already been considerable controversy about the changes of policy involved in the transition to the New Economic Policy. The French minister in Warsaw reported a particularly vigorous attack upon official policy in this connection by the left-wing metalworker T. V. Sapronov at the Ninth Congress of Soviets in Moscow in December 1921, which had been reported in the emigre newspaper *Za Svobodu*. Sapronov, according to this report, had accused the party and state leadership of abandoning communism at the behest of bankers in Berlin, London and elsewhere. They had, he noted, been told that changes were necessary or else that there would be a catastrophe. He, Sapronov, could not imagine a revolution made to re-establish the stock exchange, the banks, or private exporting and importing concerns. The workers and peasants had revolted to abolish all that, not to restore it. Did things seem different at the elevated level of the Council of People's Commissars, he wondered? At all events the Russian people would refuse to be used as a simple labour force. They had long suffered in the hope that peace, equality and prosperity would be secured; now they were being forced to suffer for the 'needs of the state' as interpreted by bourgeois bankers. Their patience was at an end, and calls of 'For whom are we working?' were more and more to be heard in Moscow factories. The government appeared to be intending to denationalise foreign-owned property and return it to its former owners, to establish special labour legislation for these factories, and to offer attractive 'concessions' to foreign interests. If the factories were returned to their former owners, Sapronov asked, what guarantees would there be for the workers, whose experience was written on their skin? Concessions already granted to Swedish interests in the Archangel area had led to forced labour and armed surveillance. Evidently, he concluded, not only were the national riches and labour of the people to be sold to foreign interests, but an armed force would also have to be provided to repress the protestations of the exploited.[64]

Sapronov's views were perhaps extreme but they were by no means isolated. At the session of the Central Executive Committee at which the Soviet delegation for Genoa had been named, for instance, several delegates expressed rather similar concerns. Sharov, a deputy from the Petrograd area, urged against excessive concessions being made to western interests at the conference, and in general against concessions being made other than on a reciprocal basis. 'No concessions, because four years have cost us dear', he urged, expressing what he represented as the views of the Petrograd working class upon the matter. Another speaker, who had just returned from the countryside, testified to the enormous interest in the conference at the local level, but added that there was some concern lest its decisions result in further burdens for the already hard-pressed peasantry. The Soviet delegates, he urged, should declare that the Russian workers and peasants would recognise no debts.[65] Other views were even more uncompromising. Ioffe, for instance, one of the conference delegates, suggested that the conference be used as a forum for political propaganda and that little importance be attached to the economic issues – debts and nationalised property – with which it would have to deal.[66] A discussion club under the auspices of the Moscow party committee provided an opportunity for many similar views to be put forward. Several speakers at the club condemned the 'renting out of Soviet power' that appeared to be envisaged, asserting that the conference delegates had been given a plan for the leasing out to foreign interests of three-quarters of the railway network and of the entire electrical industry.[67] There were particular objections to a speech by Lenin at a congress of metalworkers on 6 March in which he had suggested that the Soviet delegation should go to Genoa 'as merchants'; more than twenty members of the Workers' Opposition who were present at the congress were reported to have directly charged him with the abandonment of communist principles.[68]

These views found further expression at the Eleventh Congress of the RCP, which met from 27 March to 2 April 1922, on the very eve of the conference. V. A. Antonov-Ovseenko, one of the main leaders of the armed insurrection in 1917, took issue with Lenin's assertion that economic necessity would force the bourgeois states to establish trade relations with Soviet Russia either at the conference or later. Lenin, Antonov-Ovseenko suggested, had 'illusions' about the possibility of a 'peaceful union' with the West in the near future, and he suggested that more emphasis be placed upon the development of the country's own resources.[69] Alexander Shlyapnikov, one of the Genoa delegates, took a similar line, arguing against the sending abroad of orders for railway carriages and the closing of factories when the same goods could be made more cheaply in Russia.[70] David Ryazanov, the Marxist theoretician, took issue with Lenin's suggestion that the Soviet delegation should go to Genoa 'as merchants', proposing instead that they should go both as communists and as merchants and that they should develop a broad agitational campaign addressed to the European and also the Russian working class. There had been too much emphasis upon foreign political games, he thought, instead of following the basic principle of a proletarian foreign policy and campaigning to develop the class consciousness of the proletariat.[71] Sokol'nikov, the Commissar of Finances, also took a hostile view of Lenin's proposals, arguing both at the congress and at the party conference which had preceded it that the development of closer economic relations with the western world should take place only on the assumption of a forthcoming proletarian revolution in Europe, which would prevent them becoming the captives of foreign capital. A revolution of this sort seemed likely, in view of the instability of western capitalism; if capitalism recovered its stability, however, Sokol'nikov believed that in one way or another it would overcome all Soviet resistance.[72]

Party and state leaders who were more regularly in contact with western representatives, among them members of the foreign affairs and foreign trade commissariats, on the whole took a rather different and more moderate view. They tended, in general, to take a more pessimistic view of Russia's ability to develop industrially on the basis of her own resources, and they were rather more willing to make

concessions to outside interests in order to engage their support for
the task of Russian economic reconstruction. Chicherin, as we have
noted, had already proposed a number of concessions to western
interests which Lenin and the other party leaders had rejected.[73]
Further evidence of his views was provided in a set of 'Supplementary
considerations on the tactics of the Russian delegation at Genoa'
which he issued, apparently for the benefit of the preparatory commission established under the auspices of the Foreign Affairs Commissariat, on 25 February 1922. The main thrust of Chicherin's
paper was to argue against using Genoa as an opportunity for
revolutionary propaganda, but rather to exploit the opportunities it
provided for initiatives of a pacifist or economic character. From the
documentation provided by the economic commissariats, Chicherin
wrote, he had been convinced that for the time being the restoration
of Russian transport, agriculture and most branches of industry
would be impossible without foreign capital. The Soviet diplomatic
representatives at Genoa, he believed, should orient themselves
accordingly.[74] Litvinov and Krasin took a similar position, arguing
that the Soviet delegates should refrain from communist propaganda, and taking a pessimistic view of the possibility of economic
development in the absence of foreign aid. Krasin, in particular,
appears to have been prepared to undertake a 'realistic' foreign
policy, recognising war debts and even the claims of private
property-owners in order to secure an agreement with the West.[75]
Lenin, in resisting these and similar proposals, was evidently reflecting not simply the views of more radical members of the party and
state leadership; more important, perhaps, he was reflecting the
views of the Soviet population at large, by whom any concessions of
this kind would ultimately have to be repaid.

Something of the strength of popular feeling on these matters may
be inferred from the fact that even domestic anti-communist and
Russian emigre opinion was generally hostile to the Allied proposals
for Russian economic reconstruction, believing that they went much
too far and that they would prejudice the prosperity and even
independence of their native land. The Committee of the Constituent
Assembly, for instance, according to a report received by the French
government, accepted that the Bolsheviks were, at least for the time
being, in power. The country was also experiencing an economic
crisis. In these circumstances the Committee was firmly of the belief
that there must be immediate foreign aid and the restoration of

economic relations with Russia, even if the Soviet government was strengthened as a result. It was easy, the Committee declared, to preach isolation; those who had remained in Russia knew that this was a 'mad and impracticable' position. All sections of opinion, from Socialist Revolutionaries on hunger strike to the more fortunate, condemned the effective continuation of the blockade from which the country was dying, and also the attempts that had been made to precipitate local revolts in the absence of an alternative government capable of establishing itself and maintaining order.[76] Mensheviks in Russia took a similar view, arguing in an appeal of 18 February 1922 in support of the Soviet government's own position: recognition and credits. They later called for the immediate and unconditional recognition of the Soviet government itself.[77] Some 'almost Marxist' circles of the Russian intelligentsia, remarked *Pravda*, were coming increasingly to the view that the Soviet government was effectively a 'government of national salvation' of the French revolutionary type; the working class, the paper added, would indeed save Russia just as the revolutionary bourgeoisie had saved France in the 1790s.[78] The Soviet government, in the view of all these groupings, had to be supported if the national interests of Russia itself were to be defended.

The views of 'Russia No. 2', as Lenin described it,[79] or in other words of the Russian emigre community beyond Soviet borders, were rather more varied. This was hardly surprising, given the wide diversity of anti-Bolshevik opinion and the dispersion of the emigres across a wide range of countries, particularly in central and eastern Europe. The largest emigre communities were in Poland (about 400,000) and in Germany (about 300,000), but there were substantial emigre communities in France (80,000), Turkey (65,000) and Yugoslavia (50,000) as well.[80] At least three distinct currents of opinion, however, emerged relatively clearly. The first of these, the most hostile towards the Soviet government, inclined towards the view that the Soviet system was bound ultimately to collapse and that any development of economic relations with the Soviet government, such as appeared likely to occur at Genoa, would simply help it to survive and thus artificially prolong the suffering of the Russian people. Bolshevism 'organically cannot survive', as the Paris emigre daily *Obshchee Delo* put it in an editorial on 15 December 1921. If there was an agreement with the West the Soviet government would be strengthened, even if it presided over a country which had become bourgeois. The proposals for a conference, the paper thought, showed that the West was insufficiently informed about the real situation in Russia.[81] The Bolshevik regime would collapse in the 'near future', the paper added on 11 January 1922; the invitation to the Soviet government to attend the Genoa conference was therefore a 'huge, historic mistake', as the French government at least appeared to have realised.[82] Views of the same character were contained in a memorandum addressed to western governments by Prince A. Kartachov, president of the Russian National Committee, on 18 February 1922. Russia, the Committee argued, was absolutely essential to the restoration of Europe, but the means chosen to secure such cooperation were 'absolutely inadmissible'. No agreement was possible with the Bolsheviks, who were themselves responsible for their country's ruin, and foreign aid was their last chance of avoiding their inevitable downfall.[83] Similar views were pressed upon the Allied governments by the Russian Financial, Industrial and Commercial Association, by the Russian Parliamentary Committee in Paris, by the Supreme Russian Monarchical Council and by other interested parties and associations.[84]

A rather different line was taken by the representatives of Russian liberal and Cadet opinion, who tended generally to take a sharply hostile attitude towards the Soviet government but who also objected to the Allies' proposals for Russian economic reconstruction, most of which appeared to be in contradiction to the country's best interests and even its survival as an independent nation. The Berlin daily *Golos Rodiny*, for instance, edited by the former Cadet minister and historian P. N. Milyukov, argued that a general economic recovery of Russia under the Bolsheviks was impossible, but that the economic domination of Russia by foreign interests was no more acceptable. The paper therefore favoured some sort of conference at which a reasonable *modus vivendi* between West and East could be established. There had been a 'decisive transformation' in Russian emigre opinion, the paper argued on 1 January 1922. Few saw any prospect of the restoration of the old regime; some were now very pessimistic, while others were more inclined to seek some kind of understanding with the Soviet government.[85] The Paris paper *Poslednye Novosti*, which took a similar position, argued against the recognition of the Soviet government, but also against 'economic intervention' which would turn Russia into a backward agricultural colony exploited by the Allies.[86] The proposals for economic reconstruction that had been agreed at Cannes, the Paris section of the Cadet party declared in a memorandum addressed to the Allies on 16 January, would achieve 'not the economic restoration of the country, but its exploitation with an extreme rapacity'. The party was opposed to the Soviet regime, but also to the use of Russia for vast international enterprises contrary to the interests of the Russian people. The plans elaborated at Cannes, it believed, would 'destroy the Russian state and reduce its people to economic and political slavery'. The Soviet government would have to be supported by the Allies, militarily if necessary, if these purposes were to be realised, and the Russian people would end up being persecuted by international capitalism as well as by communism.[87]

A third view went even further and argued that the Soviet government had in fact become the most effective defence of the Russian people against the domination of foreign capital, and that it was the duty of all patriotic Russians to support that government in its contest with the Allied powers at Genoa and elsewhere. These views were promoted with particular force by the Paris weekly journal *Smena Vekh* (which took its name from the celebrated emigre volume published in Prague in 1921) and by the Berlin daily paper *Nakanune*, which succeeded it. In an editorial of 7 January 1922, for instance, the editor of *Smena Vekh*, the lawyer and former Cadet minister Yu. V. Klyuchnikov, argued that the Bolsheviks were defending 'inviolable rights and interests' which concerned 'not parties, but the very existence of Russia'. On this there could be no division between Russia and the Bolsheviks; the division was rather between Russia and the creditors. A further editorial of 21 January declared that the Cannes proposals represented an attempt to reduce Russia 'to her knees', and called for all Russian patriots to resist them.[88] As *Nakanune* put it in its first issue on 26 March 1922, everything would be done at Genoa to force 'poor, hungry and ruined Russia to pay foreign governments for the war they had all lost and for their general inability to correct their past mistakes'. The paper called for all those who still loved Russia to end their defeatism and support those who were carrying forward the cause of Russia and establishing the firm foundations of the new state within the family of nations.[89] The paper had a Moscow office and frequently published Soviet authors; it was widely rumoured to be in receipt of a Soviet government subsidy, but opponents of the Soviet government were in turn accused by other journals of fearing the loss of their diplomatic status and privileges if the Soviet government was recognised.[90] Klyuchnikov was in fact invited to join the Soviet delegation at Genoa on Lenin's advice, and the following year he returned to Russia and resumed his academic career.[91]

The forthcoming conference received a great deal of attention in the Soviet press more generally, and popular interest in the whole subject appears to have been considerable. After the formal proceedings had started *Izvestiya* received a letter from a group of peasants in the Gomel' *uezd*, enclosing money and asking 'Please, please send us the newspaper more quickly and regularly, as we very much want to know everything, exactly about Genoa.'[92] A stream of letters reached Chicherin personally from all parts of Soviet Russia; a village in the Odessa *guberniya* was even renamed in his honour.[93] Children began to play games in which each would play a particular power at the conference; the only difficulty was that none of them would agree to take the part of France.[94] A 'nervous state' was reported to prevail as the conference approached, with rapid shifts taking place from pessimism to exaggerated optimism. Party spokesmen were reported to be addressing at least fifty or sixty meetings a day in Moscow alone to keep the population fully informed of developments.[95] The official versifier Dem'yan Bedny devoted a whole cycle of poems in *Pravda* to developments at the conference, from 'Cannes Elegy' on 14 January 1922 to 'The Results of Genoa' on 18 May.[96] Mayakovsky composed a poem entitled 'My Speech at the Genoa Conference' and published it in *Izvestiya* on 12 April as the conference opened.[97] The cartoonist and poster artist Viktor Deni contributed a series of sketches to *Pravda* of the main *dramatis personae* of the conference, most notably Lloyd George, who was depicted, after Pushkin's *Evgeny Onegin*, as a 'Genoa Tat'yana'.[98] Popular opinion of a different kind was apparent in the report that an effigy of Barthou had been burned on the Field of Mars in Petrograd to express popular indignation towards the policy he was believed to be promoting.[99]

There was particular concern about the possibility that Lenin himself might attend the conference. At the Central Executive Committee meeting of 27 January 1922 at which the choice of delegation was approved several speakers voiced their concern for Lenin's safety in such circumstances. How could the bourgeoisie, who had fought Soviet Russia for three years, be expected to guarantee his safety, one delegate wondered? The conference, another delegate urged, should be moved to Moscow, where alone adequate guarantees of personal

safety could be given. Chicherin, in his reply to the debate, promised
that these 'voices from the factory' would be given 'primary importance' when the decision came ultimately to be taken.[100] The tram-
workers in Sokolniki part, at the Marx factory and at a spring factory
in Moscow, among others, were reported to have passed resolutions
urging Lenin not to attend; in fact 'hundreds' of such petitions were
reported to be arriving daily at party headquarters.[101] The dangers of
an attack upon Lenin were by no means imaginary. An attack by
Russian monarchists in Berlin at the end of March had led to the
death of the Cadet Konstantin Nabokov (brother of the writer) and
the wounding of five others.[102] Genoa itself had been the scene of
violent struggles between left and right; early in March, for instance,
there had been a clash between fascists and communists, followed by
an attack upon the offices of the socialist paper *Il Lavoro*, a series of
bombings and shootings, and a general strike. It was, the French
ambassador in Rome remarked, a strange location for a conference.[103] Anti-Soviet groups in the West had in fact threatened serious
disorders if the Soviet delegation appeared at the conference; in a
Paris emigre paper on 29 January, for instance, V. Burtsev, a Savinkov associate, warned that there would be an 'explosion of legitimate
anger' if even one Bolshevik delegate attended.[104] Savinkov duly
made his way to Genoa while the conference was in progress under a
false name and with a forged passport; he and his associates were
found to have a plan of the hotel in which the Soviet delegates were
staying, and fifteen arrests were made.[105] Krasin had already
warned, in a telegram of 7 January 1922, that in view of the activities
of Savinkovites, Wrangelites and fascists in Italy it would be 'imper-
missible' for either Lenin or Trotsky to travel there.[106] In the light of
these circumstances it was not perhaps surprising that an
announcement was made on 25 March that Lenin, because of his
'excessive burden on state duties and insufficiently good health',
would be unable to head the delegation as had originally been
intended.[107]

It was to some extent to reassure their own population, as well as to
impress foreign powers, that the members of the Genoa delegation
emerged from their self-imposed silence towards the end of March
1922 and gave a series of interviews to the local press. Krasin, who
was interviewed in *Pravda* on 10 March, welcomed the idea of the
conference but warned that Russia could not accept a 'regime of
capitulation'. The Soviet government, he added, was firmer than any

other government in western Europe, and it would wait patiently for the outcome of the conference, whatever it was. The western states were in fact more interested in developing relations with Soviet Russia than vice versa.[108] Rudzutak, speaking to *Izvestiya* on 28 March, argued that the European powers were attempting to conduct a new war, not by military but by economic means, and that they were hoping to restore the old order in Russia. The Soviet delegates, he promised, would defend this 'front' just as energetically as they had defended its military equivalent during the civil war.[109] Krasin, in a further interview on 9 April, warned that if the capitalist countries treated Russia as a defeated nation, restricting her sovereign rights and seeking economic domination, the conference would make no progress. The Soviet delegation, he warned, would rather leave the conference than sign any agreement of this kind.[110] Chicherin himself gave an interview to both *Pravda* and *Izvestiya* on 26 March. The Soviet delegation, he promised, was prepared to sustain a 'vigorous struggle with the leading bourgeois governments'. The details of Soviet preparations for the conference had been kept secret, like those of the other powers, and they would be revealed only at the conference itself. The delegation, however, would fight to the last to defend the inviolability of the Soviet order, the sovereign rights of the Russian state and the economic foundations of the Soviet system. Subject to these reservations, agreements with foreign capitalist interests might be possible or even advantageous, for instance for the restoration of the transport system or for the development of the country's natural resources. There must also be full diplomatic recognition of the Soviet government, for practical business and not purely ceremonial purposes.[111] Speaking to *Izvestiya* a few days later, Chicherin added that the delegation was ready for negotiations but would 'not allow their country to be turned into a colony or a dependent state'.[112]

The delegation duly left Moscow on 28 March 1922, in circumstances of great secrecy because of fears of attack, and escorted by three aircraft.[113] Arriving first at Riga, the delegation took part in a two-day conference with representatives of the Estonian, Latvian and Polish governments, at the end of which (on 30 March) a final protocol was signed. According to the protocol, the governments concerned, desirous of securing the restoration of economic life in eastern Europe, the development of trade between their countries and the strengthening of peace, agreed that these aims would best be served by coordinating their actions at the Genoa conference. The treaties that existed between the other three states and Soviet Russia were reaffirmed, and the Estonian, Latvian and Polish representatives added that in their view the economic restoration of eastern Europe would be facilitated by the diplomatic recognition of the Soviet government. A series of more particular measures designed to improve trade and reduce the level of border hostilities among the countries concerned was also agreed, and the protocol concluded with a joint declaration in favour of the limitation of armaments more generally.[114] The Soviet delegation, according to the Estonian foreign minister, Anton Piip, had been 'nervous and depressed', partly because of fears for their own safety and partly because of the desperate economic situation in Russia.[115] The agreement, nonetheless, represented an appreciable strengthening of the Soviet position on the very eve of the conference. A further and more substantial contribution was made by the negotiations into which the delegation entered while passing through Berlin, which, although inconclusive, were to be resumed in Genoa.[116]

The *Daily Herald*'s special correspondent Frederick Kuh, who boarded the Soviet delegation's train as it left Bavaria on its way to Italy, found the delegates in a mood of 'resolute determination, tempered by patience'. Chicherin, who was reading Keynes's *Economic Consequences of the Peace* and his recently published *A Revision of the Treaty*, told Kuh that the Soviet government's basic conditions for any agreement at Genoa were that Russian sovereignty must be respected, that the economic system must remain under the control of the Soviet government and that the social achievements of the revolution must not be prejudiced. The Soviet government's strength, Chicherin believed, had generally been underestimated abroad; NEP had in fact largely satisfied the peasants, and Lenin had called a halt to any further retreat.[117] The Soviet delegation's basic guidelines, at least, were reasonably clear; only the conference itself would show if the concessions they provided for would be sufficient to satisfy the western powers and yet not so great as to prejudice the fundamental principles of which Chicherin had spoken.

6

The conference opens

The Genoa Conference began its formal proceedings on 10 April 1922.[1] Some thirty-four nations were present at its opening session, five of them representing the British empire (which sat as a single delegation). No fewer than 42 prime ministers were in attendance,[2] and a total of 216 other delegates or experts were listed in the official directory of delegations.[3] The 'Inviting powers', Britain, Belgium, France, Italy and Japan, as well as Russia and Germany, were allowed to nominate five principal delegates each; all the other powers were permitted two delegates each, apart from Luxemburg, which was limited to one. These norms of representation had been agreed at Cannes.[4] Apart from the diplomats, more than 800 journalists were present including Ernest Hemingway for the *Toronto Star*, Max Eastman for the *New York World*, J. L. Garvin for *The Observer*, Wickham Steed for *The Times*, Pietro Nenni for *Avanti*, and Edgar Mowrer for the *Chicago Daily News*. Frank Harris, then aged seventy-five, the literary critic and celebrated diarist, was present in a private capacity, and Maynard Keynes attended as a special correspondent for the *Manchester Guardian*.[5] All in all, more than 5,000 people with some relationship to the conference were in Genoa. It was, recalled the US ambassador to Italy, Richard Child, the 'largest international conference ever held in point of nations represented', larger even than the peace conference itself.[6] Lloyd George described it as the 'most important conference that has ever been held in Europe' in a speech to the British and American press;[7] the *Manchester Guardian*, rather more grandly, referred to it as the 'largest gathering of European statesmen since the Crusades'.[8] In terms of the tasks with which it was supposed to deal with the conference was in fact virtually without precedent.

The conference delegates assembled gradually, none more so than the Soviet delegation, which had admittedly the farthest to travel. After Riga and Berlin, the delegation made its way through Austria towards the Brenner pass. For security reasons as little as possible was divulged about the delegation's movements from this point onwards. Only a few senior officials and stationmasters knew in advance by what route the delegation would be proceeding to Genoa, and rumours were put about that it would be passing through Chiasso, 150 miles to the west. The delegation's three coaches were in fact attached to the 16.06 from Brenner station on 5 April and travelled onwards to the conference through Verona and Milan. The presence of the Soviet delegation in their three German railway coaches appears to have gone unnoticed, even by the other passengers on the train, but Italian security officials were stationed at each door and Soviet guards patrolled the corridors. The train was surrounded by security staff on its arrival at Verona, in the early hours of 6 April 1922, and again on its arrival at Milan, where a lady delegate was observed to make a rapid visit to the station buffet. The delegates were beginning to look out of the windows at this stage, and the train itself finally arrived at Genoa station at 9.45 the same morning. Chicherin, who had retired to bed rather late, had only just completed his toilet. Only one delegate left the train, to buy the morning papers; a number of local officials, however, boarded the train to convey the official greetings of the municipality. Chicherin, who received them, returned their good wishes and informed them that his father and mother had in fact been married at Genoa, on a Russian ship just off the coast. A member of the RCP Central Committee, the only one on the train who spoke Italian, added for the benefit of journalists that they were hoping for a 'good result from the conference'. The delegation left Genoa at 10.00 and arrived at Santa Margherita, near to their hotel, about half an hour later.[9]

A large crowd was at the station to greet the Soviet delegates, but there were no incidents. Cordons of *carabinieri* in black uniforms lined the station and the route to the delegation's hotel just in case. Chicherin was the first to descend from the train, followd by the other delegates, about forty in number; a fleet of ten cars then took them to the Imperial Hotel in Rapallo, where they were to be accommodated. The delegation was headed by Chicherin, Litvinov and Ioffe; Krasin and Radek were due to arrive two days later with the other members of the party. All were reported to be in good health, although somewhat tired after their long journey.[10] Chicherin and Erlikh, a security official who knew Italian, having studied at Milan Polytechnic, went out rather later for a short walk so that Chicherin could buy a scarf and more generally establish his presence. The delegation had already been suited by a Pole, 'the only tailor worthy of the name', in Moscow; Chicherin alone had been equipped more stylishly in Berlin.[11] Shortly afterwards, on 7 April, the delegation emerged for a photo session, and Chicherin gave his first interview to the Italian press. He emphasised that the sovereign rights of the Soviet government must be respected and that the economic independence of the Russian people must not be compromised. The international consortium proposals, he declared, had reduced Russia to the level of India, and had aroused great popular indignation; the Russian people would permit no proposal of such a character to be considered. The delegation itself would be 'conciliatory, but firm'.[12]

The Imperial Hotel was in fact by no means an ideal residence from the delegation's point of view. It was certainly sumptuous, and had accommodated members of the Italian royal family and of the Russian emigre nobility in the recent past;[13] on the other hand it was rather larger than the delegation required, and considerably more expensive than it would have wished. Erlikh, who made a preliminary visit to inspect it, eventually agreed to hire four of the five floors for the delegation's purposes (some elderly guests and children were allowed to remain in residence on the fifth floor), and reluctantly accepted the imposing tariff demanded.[14] The Soviet delegation had been lodged at Rapallo, according to the Italian authorities, 'so as both to avoid it becoming the object of favourable or hostile demonstrations, and for it to be better watched over and protected'. Only the British, French, Belgian, Italian and Japanese delegations were lodged in Genoa itself, the other delegations being accommodated in hotels throughout the length of the Italian riviera.[15] Chicherin complained to Arthur Ransome that the hotel was some thirty miles from the conference centre, and that it was reached by a road 'specially adapted for assassinations' (threats to the delegation's lives indeed, had already been received from Savinkov and from Russian monarchists in emigration).[16] The whole area was visited in advance by a detachment of the best members of the Cheka, disguised as 'honest civilians'; the Italian authorities for their part refused all Russian emigre organisations access to Genoa while the conference was in progress, and no Russians other than the delegation's members were allowed to take up residence.[17] An Italian warship was also stationed in Rapallo harbour with its guns pointing landwards, and 400 *carabinieri* as well as special and mounted police were attached to the delegation's headquarters.[18]

The Soviet delegates, for their own safety as well as for the protection of the local population from the Bolshevik bacillus, were kept in almost total isolation at their Rapallo headquarters. The Imperial Hotel, reported *The Times*, was the 'most strictly-guarded building in Europe'. The hotel staff had been issued with special passes to allow them to gain entrance, and journalists and spectators were able to come no closer to the hotel than the entrance to its gardens unless they had specifically been invited to enter by the delegation itself. The journalists had accordingly to 'satisfy their curiosity with occasional glimpses of very lightly dressed Bolshevik lady secretaries in the gardens and on the balconies'.[19] The gardens themselves were guarded by Cheka representatives as well as by the local *carabinieri*.[20] In fact it was 'easier to enter Paradise', reported the correspondent of *L'Humanité*, 'than the drawing room of the Imperial'. Inside the hotel itself Italian policemen, 'badly disguised', were stationed on all the corridors; they listened to all the conversations behind the doors they guarded, but to no avail as none of them knew Russian.[21] For their journeys to and from the conference centre the delegation was provided with a fleet of cars and a special railway line, which took it to the royal station at the back of the Royal Palace where all the commission sessions were to take place. The station itself was surrounded by a newly constructed wooden fence, which screened the Bolshevik delegates from public view as they made their way to and from the conference chambers. Despite every effort to facilitate the movement of delegates, not only between Rapallo and Genoa but between Nervi, Pegli and the other small resorts to the west of Genoa in which a number of the other delegations resided, the dispersion of delegates over such a large area remained a serious handicap for all the delegates concerned.[22]

Perhaps not surprisingly, the Soviet delegation was soon surrounded by a host of myths and rumours. There were repeated reports, for instance, that Lenin would after all be attending the conference, and some suggested that he was already on his way, travelling incognito as he had so frequently done in the pre-revolutionary period.[23] Chicherin, indeed, told journalists on his arrival that Lenin had hoped to attend the conference and meet

Lloyd George and that it was not impossible he would do so at a later stage.[24] The Italian police in fact believed that Lenin had been brought to the conference by the delegation in a large container, which they unloaded and brought to the delegation's hotel with particular care. It actually contained a large part of the NKID library, including original documents dating back to the early Tsarist period, which Chicherin had brought with him to consult as the conference proceeded.[25] The French ambassador in Copenhagen passed on a report that the head of the Soviet bureau at the conference, a certain Rosenberg, had half a million roubles with him for the purpose of buying up British, American and other western journalists, and that two specialist jewellers had been included among the secretaries in order to meet unexpected expenses and to subsidise Bolshevik propaganda in the locality. All of these operations were believed to come under the control of the Soviet mission in Rome.[26] Many other rumours about the delegation circulated. Lenin, it was reported, had shot Chicherin, and Chicherin had shot Vorovsky; and Bukharin was reported to have taken on the task of impersonating Lenin at workers' meetings in Russia.[27] The Soviet delegates, for their part, reported back to Moscow that the French were still trying to break up the conference and were threatening to withdraw unless the Cannes conditions were unconditionally accepted; Lloyd George and the Italians, however, were anxious to avoid a breakdown and were proposing a compromise, and towards this end had urged the Soviet delegates to avoid unduly controversial issues in their opening address.[28]

Arrangements were meanwhile proceeding among the inviting and other powers. The British delegation, Chamberlain informed the House of Commons on 16 March 1922, was not yet settled but would certainly include the prime minister and the Secretary of State for Foreign Affairs. On 21 March Chamberlain announced that the Chancellor of the Exchequer would also be included among the British delegates.[29] Curzon himself regarded the prospect of participation with no great enthusiasm. Political issues were likely to be raised and therefore 'I suppose I must go', he minuted on 1 February.[30] On 1 April he wrote to Hardinge in Paris, informing the ambassador that he had had a hard week in the Foreign Office and was resting in bed. 'I shudder at the prospect of Genoa a few days from now', he added.[31] A few days later the foreign secretary wrote to Lloyd George to be asked to be excused from setting off to Genoa with the rest of the delegation on 7 April. He was 'not fit to move yet as I still have the back pains', he explained, a recurrence of the complaint from which he had suffered for more than thirty years. The only cure was for him to lie flat on his back; he hoped, however, to be able to leave at the beginning of the following week.[32] In the event the illness persisted and Curzon was forced to miss the conference entirely (*pace* a Soviet historical source, which reports not simply that Curzon was a member of the British delegation but that he was among the bourgeois politicians who 'played the most active role' in its proceedings).[33] The British delegation was headed by Lloyd George (who was allocated the Villa d'Albertis, on the outskirts of Genoa); its other members were the Chancellor of the Exchequer, Sir Robert Horne, the Secretary of State for War, Sir Laming Worthington-Evans, and the Director of the Department of Overseas Trade, Sir Philip Lloyd-Greame. Five 'supplementary' delegates represented the British dominions, and there were seventy-five further members of staff in various capacities.[34]

On his journey to Genoa Lloyd George passed through Paris, where he took the opportunity to hold a short meeting with Poincaré. Because of President Millerand's imminent departure for Algeria, Tunis and Morocco the French premier's attendance was already doubtful; in addition he had been threatened by an anarchist attack, and had reportedly had 'cold feet'.[35] Poincaré formally declared his inability to participate in a message transmitted to the conference on 11 April, adding that he hoped the conference would nonetheless be successful in the great work of European reconstruction in which it would be engaging.[36] Poincaré had already told the French Chamber that the French delegation would permit no revision of the treaty of Versailles in any form at the conference, that the recognition of pre-war debts was 'in the first place' among the conditions on which it was to take place, and that the French government would not necessarily be bound by its decisions.[37] At his meeting with Lloyd George, which took place in a railway carriage travelling between the Gard du Nord and the Gare de Lyon on 7 April 1922, Poincaré assured the British premier that the French delegation would be taking a full and active part in the conference's proceedings, and that the French government was fully committed to its success. There were differences, however, about procedure, and both premiers drew attention to the strength of domestic opinion on the matters with which the conference would be dealing. Poincaré in particular argued that close collaboration with Germany would be 'premature' and that guarantees should be sought from Russia before trade was fully resumed.[38] The meeting, described by *The Times* as 'of the customary cordial character',[39] in fact served to identify once again the divergence of interest and attitude between the two premiers and, indeed, between the two countries they represented.

In Poincaré's absence, the French delegation to the conference was led by Louis Barthou, Keeper of the Seals and deputy premier. The other French delegates were Maurice Colrat, Under-Secretary of State in the premier's office, Camille Barrère, the French ambassador in Rome, Jacques Seydoux, Assistant Director of Commercial Affairs at the foreign ministry, and Ernest Picard, Assistant Director of the Banque de France.[40] The French delegates were empowered to deal with all the questions that would arise at the conference, but had no authority to conclude or sign any agreement which might bind the French government. As 'Pertinax' put it in the *Echo de Paris*, the French delegation would 'in reality . . . be directed from Paris by the Prime Minister', and its members would be 'observers and spokesmen rather than plenipotentiaries'.[41] The delegation's instructions, which were communicated by Poincaré to Barthou on 6 April 1922, gave the French delegates the authority to engage in discussions with the other powers on matters that had been covered in the Cannes resolutions, but not to commit the French government, whose position, and that of the French parliament, must be 'entirely reserved'. There could be no discussion of the peace treaties or of disarmament at the conference, as Lloyd George and Poincaré had agreed at Boulogne. The question of a treaty with the Russians would not arise until it had become clear that the Soviet delegation had accepted and was willing to implement the conditions that the other powers had laid down, and this stage would be reached only at the end of the conference. Both the British and French governments reserved full liberty of action for themselves at this point. The sincerity of the Soviet government's professions, Poincaré went on, could be judged only after a trial period; promises alone would not be enough. If despite French objections the conference proceeded to discuss such matters, the delegation should refer immediately to Paris, where it would be decided if it could remain; the delegation for its part should seek to ensure that such a course of action was not taken by France alone.

On economic and financial matters, Poincaré went on, the experts' report agreed in London could be accepted, provided that the conditions it contained were made more precise. Debts and private claims must be distinguished; and pre-war Russian debts and the claims of French nationals must be recognised and guaranteed. War debts must also be recognised by the Soviet government at least in principle, their full settlement being reserved for a later date when inter-Allied debts would also be regulated. If the Soviet delegation put forward a claim for damages suffered during the civil war, the French delegation should put forward claims of its own for damages suffered following the conclusion of the treaty of Brest-Litovsk and Russia's withdrawal from the war. The property of French nationals must be restored if that was possible; if not, because of land reform or other reasons, an appropriate indemnity should be sought. On the consortium, which appeared unlikely to materialise because of Soviet hostility and German indifference, the French delegates should agree to participate only to ensure that its operations were not directed against French interests. The question of Allied debts in general should be treated with care, and no formal discussion should be permitted; the reparations commission should rather be encouraged to establish a sub-committee to look into the matter further. There must be no derogation of the powers of the League of Nations, there must be no attempt to reconstruct the Supreme Council so as to include Germany, and there must be no attempt to establish a permanent body of any kind.[42] The document's uncompromising tone, sustained by Poincaré in a series of telegrams as the conference proceeded, made clear the difficulties that would have to be surmounted if a Soviet–Western or any other sort of agreement was to be successfully accomplished.

Inter-Allied differences, indeed, began to make themselves apparent at a series of meetings between the convening powers before the conference itself had opened. On 8 April 1922 Lloyd George met Facta, Schanzer and two other Italian representatives. In order to meet French objections it was agreed that the committees into which the conference would be divided should in the first instance consist of all the powers, but that each committee would have the right to form itself into a smaller bureau of the great powers whenever necessary. Disarmament could not be discussed in detail, but it would be difficult to avoid the subject altogether if peace and the reconstruction of Europe were to be considered. The guarantee of non-aggression which would be sought from all the powers should be a formal signed undertaking, not simply a resolution, but Lloyd George was particularly concerned that it should not, as the French were urging, be directly linked to the Covenant of the League of Nations. Russia, Lloyd George thought, should be recognised as soon as western parliaments had ratified the pact of non-aggression. The method of recognition should however be gradual, beginning with representation at the level of chargé d'affaires, and there should be no formal diplomatic recognition until it had become clear that the Soviet government was abiding by its undertakings to the other powers. Progress in this direction, it was agreed, would depend upon the behaviour of the Soviet delegates at the conference itself. Schanzer expressed himself delighted with the measure of agreement that had been reached between the two powers, and hoped the French would not break the Allied front. Lloyd George replied that he thought the French attitude would depend upon the support they were able to obtain for a negative attitude among the other powers, particularly the Little Entente. 'This was the crux of the conference.'[43]

A further meeting of the inviting powers took place the following day, Sunday 9 April 1922. After some discussion, the rules of procedure of the conference were finally agreed. Barthou made it clear that the French delegation would be reserving the right, if unforeseen circumstances arose, to seek further advice from the French government. Lloyd George remarked that it would be 'very serious if the representatives of a Great Power were only present as note-takers and had to refer everything to their Government' and hoped no questions of this kind would occur. Barthou explained that the French delegation 'was not at Genoa with its hands tied', but if a question of sufficient gravity arose the French delegation, which unlike others was not represented at the conference by its prime minister or foreign secretary, would have no alternative but to refer back to Paris. The delegation, however, shared Lloyd George's wish to deal speedily with the various items on the conference agenda.[44] The meeting reconvened later in the afternoon to give further consideration to the organisation of the conference. It was agreed, following French pressure, that the chairman should open the first session by noting that the conference had been convened on the basis of the Cannes resolutions and that all the powers present, by virtue of their attendance, would be deemed to have accepted them. The detailed examination of the implementation of the Cannes resolutions, however, would be a matter for commissions rather than for the conference as a whole. It was agreed that all the powers present should be represented on all the commissions; in the first or political commission, however, a smaller sub-committee would be formed, consisting of the inviting powers, Russia, Germany and four other powers, to engage in more detailed discussions.[45]

The conference formally opened its proceedings on Monday 10 April 1922 in the Palazzo San Giorgio, an impressive building constructed in 1260 which took its name from the bank which had established its headquarters there in the fifteenth century. Irreverent locals immediately dubbed it the 'Palazzo Lloyd Giorgio'.[46] The city itself had been carefully prepared for the occasion. Its 'Anglo-American bars' had been redecorated, and all the public seats had been repainted (the *Times* correspondent reported that it was dangerous to sit down anywhere).[47] A special series of performances at the local opera house had been arranged, and negotiations had been concluded with Toscanini, who agreed to give a performance at Genoa together with all the artists of La Scala of Milan.[48] Security arrangements had been given no less attention. About 1,500 special policemen were recruited from all over Italy and brought to Genoa for the conference; none of them was a native of the city so they could, as Hemingway reported, 'shoot either side without fear or favour'.[49] The full complement was in fact 1,000 *carabinieri*, 2,000 military police, 5,000 soldiers and 500 detectives. By the evening the conference opened they had already made 2,000 arrests.[50] The police kept a particularly close watch on the 'various taverns which suspicious characters are accustomed to frequent'; they also attempted to prevent any actions 'derogatory to Genoa's dignity', such as shaking carpets in the street or hanging up washing in public.[51] A fleet of 167 motor vehicles and over 500 special trains were placed at the disposal of delegates for the duration of the conference; a special telephone system was installed which handled more than six million words of telegrams over the same period, and about 50,000 pages of duplicated matter were produced daily by the Secretary-General's office, the paper for which filled five railway carriages.[52] The Italian government's costs for the conference came to over 30 million lire, despite attempts to put pressure on hoteliers and others to reduce their rates.[53]

The Palazzo San Giorgio was full to overflowing at 3 p.m. as the conference began. The conference hall itself contained about 2,000 spectators, the 'flower of the Italian bourgeoisie', as *Pravda* described them, with military and administrative circles predominating but also some ladies of fashion and the scarlet-costumed Cardinal of Genoa, who was representing the Pope. Several hundred journalists filled the gallery.[54] Heavy rain earlier in the day had been succeeded by sunshine, and the streets outside were crowded with local people eager to see the delegates and to welcome the conference's opening. Work was ended for the day in the town and in the port, and shops closed their doors. The tightest security was in force; the central part of the town was closed to public as well as private traffic, and all diplomats and journalists had their credentials carefully checked. Some 10,000 *carabinieri* surrounded the Palazzo San Giorgio itself. [55] Genoa was 'off its head with enthusiasm', Philip Lloyd-Greame wrote to his wife, and had a 'great feeling of faith that something is going to be done'. The scene inside the conference hall itself was 'amazing', with a 'great concourse of spectators beyond and in a gallery packed like sardines the Press of the world'.[56] At 3 p.m. precisely Lloyd George and the other British delegates entered the chamber, followed by an outburst of applause which was quickly silenced. The other delegates also took their places at the appointed time. At 3.05 p.m. a further five delegates, 'embarrassed and anxious', as *Le Matin* described them, and 'looking for all the world as though they had stepped out of a Drury Lane Panto', as J. D. Gregory put it, entered the hall and took their seats. Whistles of disapproval (according to French sources) or approval (according to Russian sources) burst forth as the Soviet delegation was identified.[57] A few minutes later Facta declared the conference open, welcomed the delegates, and read out messages of good will from King Victor Emmanuel and from Poincaré. On the proposal of Lloyd George, seconded by Barthou, he was duly elected chairman of the conference.[58]

Facta, in his opening address, reminded delegates of the importance of the tasks they confronted and added that the conference had been convened on the basis of the resolutions adopted at Cannes, which had been communicated to all the powers that had been invited to attend. The attendance of the powers present, he went on, would be taken to indicate the willingness of their governments to accept the principles contained in those resolutions. The floor was thereupon extended to the representatives of the inviting and other powers. Lloyd George, who was the first to speak, began by describing the conference as the greatest gathering of nations that had ever been held on the continent of Europe. Its results would be equally far-reaching in their significance. The states represented met on equal terms, but they must also accept equal conditions, conditions which were essential to day-to-day intercourse between nations. When a country entered into contractual relations with another country or its nationals, for instance, that contract could not be repudiated when the country concerned changed its government unless an appropriate amount of compensation was paid. Nor could any country be permitted to wage war upon the institutions of another country, or to attack its territory. The nationals of any country were also entitled to impartial treatment in the courts of any other country. These, the principles laid down at Cannes, were the fundamental basis of the conference's proceedings and must be regarded as having been accepted by all the powers that had accepted the invitation to attend. A joint effort was urgently needed to restore the devastation of the most destructive war the world had ever seen. There was unemployment in the West, famine and pestilence in the East. Unless a common effort was undertaken this suffering might deepen into despair. Peace, Lloyd George believed, was the essential condition for European recovery, and for the restoration of the exchanges, transport and credit. It would not be easy to reconcile their domestic publics to all the decisions that the conference might reach in this connection; but public opinion was amenable to guidance and direction, and would heed an appeal directed to it by the assembled statesmen of Europe. The United States government might also be persuaded to participate at a later stage.

Barthou, who followed him, promised the 'loyal co-operation' of his government in the conference proceedings. The French government had sought to have the conference postponed, not to be destructive, but so that it could be prepared more thoroughly, and the French delegation were present not as observers but as 'fellow workers' ready to play their full part in its proceedings. The conference was not, nor could it be, a court of appeal before which existing treaties could be brought up, judged and revised. On all financial and economic questions, however, which were central to the task of European reconstruction, discussion would be absolutely open and the French attitude would not be a negative one. Viscount Ishii, the head of the Japanese delegation, noted that his own country, although remote geographically from Europe's difficulties, was still affected by the collapse of the Russian market, the uncertainty of economic relations between nations and the instabililty of the exchanges. They would do all they could to help the conference overcome these problems. Theunis, the Belgian premier and chief delegate, conveyed his government's concern that remedies should be found to put an end to the economic depression from which all countries, and Belgium in particular, were suffering. Chancellor Wirth, for the German delegation, affirmed the willingness of his government to join with those of other nations in the task of economic reconstruction which lay before the conference. Germany's geographical position at the centre of the European continent and her central role in international economic relations meant that German economic problems were inseparably connected with those of other countries; Germany's own prosperity, in turn, would be the best guarantee of the economic prosperity of her neighbours.

At last it was the turn of the Soviet delegation. Chicherin, speaking in French, began by associating his government with the calls for the establishment of a secure peace which had been made by previous speakers. The Soviet delegation, he assured his audience, had come to the conference in the interests of peace and the general reconstruction of the economic life of Europe, which had been ruined by prolonged war and by post-war policies. While itself holding to communist principles, the delegation recognised that at least for the time being economic collaboration was necessary between countries representing two different systems of property. The first point of the Cannes principles, to which the delegation attached particular importance, provided for collaboration upon such a basis. The Soviet delegation had accordingly come to the conference, not for the purpose of making communist propaganda, but to engage in practical relations with the other governments concerned. The task of the economic reconstruction of Europe in general required the cooperation of all governments; the economic reconstruction of Russia in particular was necessary if this task was to be accomplished successfully. Towards this end, the Soviet government would be willing to facilitate the development of international trade, to open up millions of acres of fertile land for cultivation, and to grant forest, mining and other concessions. The delegation accepted the Cannes conditions in principle, while reserving the right to supplement or amend them at a later stage. The economic restoration of Russia and of Europe generally would, however, be impossible if the Soviet government was required to accept a series of obligations which were beyond its ability to discharge. These objects would also be prejudiced if the threat of further war continued to hang over the continent. The Soviet delegation would accordingly be proposing a general limitation of armaments and modifications to the rules of war, provided that this was on a reciprocal basis and that appropriate guarantees were provided. He repeated the whole speech, for the benefit of Lloyd George, in English.

The speech, according to *Pravda*, made a 'powerful impression';[59] other observers confessed to some disappointment, and some found Chicherin's high-pitched voice and curious pronunciation difficult to follow (the German diplomat Count Kessler found Chicherin's French so exotic that at first he thought he had been speaking Russian, and found his English still less intelligible).[60] The speech, however, particularly its reference to disarmament, immediately provoked Barthou. Chicherin, he charged, had suggested in his speech that a universal and still more comprehensive congress should be called, and that the question of disarmament should be raised. Nothing of the kind had been provided for in the Cannes conditions, on the basis of which the conference had been convened, and the French delegation would allow no discussion of such topics, either directly or indirectly. Chicherin replied mildly that the Soviet delegation had not been officially informed of the conference agenda, which was in any case provisional and included other questions not discussed at Cannes, and it had been Lloyd George himself, in one of his recent speeches, who had raised the idea of periodic gatherings of this kind. The Soviet delegation, however, would be prepared to accept the conference's decision if it was decided to exclude disarmament from its agenda. Lloyd George, who intervened at this point, remarked that all had heard this exchange with 'great interest'; his own view was that unless the conference led to disarmament it would have been a failure, but peace would have to be established first of all, and if disarmament was added both causes might well founder. Facta, as chairman, pointed out that the agenda, like the conference itself, had been based upon the Cannes resolutions; this had been announced at the opening of the session, and had not been contested. He would therefore regard the question as closed. The further work of the conference, he announced, would take place in commissions; the first commission, which would consider the first three points of the conference agenda, would hold its first meeting the following day.[61]

Commenting on the first session, Philip Lloyd-Greame wrote to his wife that the prime minister's speech had been a 'really fine effort – sincere, clear, tactful and smoothing while not ignoring any difficulties'. Chicherin's speech, by contrast, had been 'long, unsatisfactory, indeterminate, definitely trying to raise non-Cannes proposals'; Lloyd George, however, had countered it with a 'wonderful speech' which had been witty but 'absolutely damning to Chicherin'.[62] Writing to Austen Chamberlain, Hankey remarked that the French had 'not yet been able to divest themselves of the post-war idea of victors and vanquished'. They had sought to prevent the Russians and Germans from speaking at the opening session, but had been opposed by Facta and Schanzer with 'admirable firmness', and by Lloyd George. The Russians, Hankey reflected, 'do not lack ability, but they seem almost entirely devoid of tact'. This had been apparent in Chicherin's calls for disarmament and for economic reconstruction on a global scale; but such remarks, Hankey believed, had probably been designed to 'save his skin in Moscow'.[63] In the battle between the French and the Russians, Count Kessler commented, the Russians had definitely emerged the victors. Lloyd George's speech, however, had been the 'star attraction', with the whole conference, onlookers, journalists and all, applauding wildly for minutes when it had ended.[64] At the opening, André Siegfried wrote to Jean Gout, head of the League of Nations department at the French foreign ministry, Chicherin had mixed insolence with the appearance of good will in a very skilful manner. The Bolsheviks had exhibited a 'mixture of innocence, of flexibility, of politeness, of humorous fantasy, which astonishes, amuses, which disarms and cannot help but provoke a certain admiration'.[65] Another French representative commented frankly in a letter to François Charles-Roux, a counsellor at the French embassy in Rome, that the opening had 'not been good for us'. Barthou had been nervous and had not had the effect for which he had hoped, although his task was in any case a difficult and thankless one.[66] On all sides it was clear that a long and uncompromising struggle had begun.

Proceedings were resumed at a meeting of the first (political) commission the following day, 11 April 1922. The commission in turn elected a sub-commission on which Russia, Germany, each of the five inviting powers and four other states were to be represented.[67] The sub-commission met later the same afternoon. Schanzer, who presided, began by reminding the delegates present that the task of the sub-commission – which effectively became the focal point of East–West negotiations at the conference – was to determine the means by which the principles contained in the Cannes resolutions were to be applied. It was agreed that discussion should take place upon the basis of the experts' report prepared in London, although none of the governments concerned was necessarily bound by its provisions, and that the report should be distributed to all the delegations at the conference, with the Soviet delegation being allowed at least two days to study it before the sub-commission reconvened.[68] The Soviet delegation's preliminary response was considered by an Allied meeting on 13 April. The delegation, Schanzer reported, was prepared to accept pre-war debts, including railway, municipal and public utility loans. It was unlikely, however, to accept responsibility for war debts, and it was likely to insist upon a principle of reciprocity on the basis of which it would itself demand compensation for losses suffered during the period of intervention and civil war in which the Allies had been involved. So far as the claims of private citizens were concerned, the Soviet delegates had been willing to provide compensation for losses suffered during the period of intervention and civil war in which the Allies had been involved. So far as the claims of private citizens were concerned, the Soviet delegates had been willing to provide compensation in the form of treasury bonds for property which had been confiscated, but not to return it in its original form. There might also be difficulties with regard to mixed arbitral commissions and judicial matters. Lloyd George thought a formula could be agreed by which the Russian counterclaims might be set against war debts, but private pre-war debts could not be included in any such arrangement. He thought it might be best to explore the possibilities directly with the Soviet delegation before it was compelled to adopt a public stance at one of the commission meetings. At his suggestion it was agreed to postpone the next meeting of a sub-commission and to seek an informal meeting with the Soviet delegates themselves.[69]

The meeting with the Soviet delegates took place the following day, Good Friday, 14 April 1922. The Allies were represented by Belgium, Britain, France and Italy (the Japanese were to be kept informed of developments); the Soviet delegation, by Chicherin, Litvinov and Krasin. 'The Genoa Conference only begins today', Barthou is reported to have remarked as the delegates assembled.[70] Lloyd George began by asking Chicherin to indicate his delegation's atti-

tude to the London experts' report. Chicherin replied that the report
would place the Russian people in an impossible position if they
accepted it. It was universally believed in Russia that the old order
had been superseded, and it would be extremely difficult to convince
the mass of the people that they must nonetheless repay the pre-war
debts which that order had incurred. There had also been wide-
spread suffering during the intervention and civil war periods; people
felt that they should be entitled to substantial damages from the
Allies in this connection. The delegation could not resist the universal
will of workers and peasants on such matters. If the Allied experts'
report were accepted, moreover, an annual interest payment would
have to be made which was equal to the whole of Russia's pre-war
exports, at a time when a substantial part of the country's economic
capacity had been destroyed. A burden of this kind would make the
economic reconstruction of the country impossible and thereby frus-
trate the conference's declared objective. The proposed debt and
arbitral commissions appeared also to encroach upon Russian sovereignty, and the proposal to restore property *in natura* was often
impossible either because the property in question had been nationalised or else because the workers concerned would resist it. Anxious
as he was to reach an agreement, it would be impossible for the
Russian delegation to return home having agreed to pay the annual
interest demanded by the experts, having failed to secure recognition
of the principle of reciprocity, or having accepted the principle of the
restitution of private property. It was in fact faced by an 'enormous
historical problem' and its resolution would demand the most careful
consideration of all possible solutions.

Barthou, Schanzer and Jaspar, on behalf of Belgium, agreed that
there were difficulties and identified some of the most important
issues involved. Lloyd George, who followed them, reminded Chicherin that the Allies also had their domestic public opinion and the
'die-hards' in their own governments to consider. The general British
view was that the system of government in Russia was a matter for
the Russians themselves, but when trading and diplomatic relations
were concerned certain conditions, such as the recognition of private
and public debts, were held to be indispensable. Only if debts were
recognised would British industrialists be willing to take part in trade
between the two countries, and only if they were prepared to do so
would Russia recover economically. On war debts, all that was being
asked was that the Soviet government should adopt the same position

as that of other governments, which was that the debts should be acknowledged but that their settlement should be deferred to a later stage at which they would all be considered together. Compensation for private owners in the form of bonds of dubious value would not be acceptable, but a lease, with the option of renewal, might offer a satisfactory alternative. This would enable foreign owners, with their skill and capital, to return to Russia and resume their economic activities. So far as the Russian counterclaims were concerned, some adjustment of the total of Russian war debts might be possible, without necessarily raising the difficult issue of principle that was involved. Barthou agreed with Lloyd George that the discussion should centre upon the two key questions of debt and private property, leaving other matters for a later stage.

Chicherin, in reply, suggested that some of these difficult issues should in fact be left in abeyance for a number of years, by which time their resolution might be easier. Resistance to the recognition of private ownership and of debts other than on a reciprocal basis in Russia was a matter not just of a few 'die-hards' but of the great mass of the population, who would not permit such principles to be entertained. All debts contracted by the new regime would however be faithfully honoured. An arrangement analogous to that which Lloyd George had suggested was available in the form of concessional agreements, a number of which had been concluded with western interests. The 'Alabama' case of 1862, in which the United States government had secured compensation for the activities of a British-built ship operated by Confederate forces during the American civil war, appeared to provide a precedent for Russian claims for compensation arising out of the Allies' role in Russia after the revolution. Litvinov added that the Russian people, rightly or wrongly, would regard the recognition of previous obligations as new debts. The delegation could hardly return with a further and very substantial burden of debt, but with no assurance that any capital or a loan would be forthcoming. The discussion was adjourned at this point; over lunch, for which the Soviet delegation remained at Lloyd George's villa, the prime minister arranged for Litvinov to get together with Sir Sydney Chapman of the British delegation to try to find a formula on debts which would be acceptable to both sides. Krasin, meanwhile, explained the Soviet government's detailed requirements in terms of foreign assistance for the reorganisation of agriculture, transport and industry, and replied to a number of questions from the Allied representatives on these matters.

The meeting between Chapman and Litvinov, in the event, failed to produce a satisfactory settlement, Litvinov insisting on grouping all Russian debts within a single category and setting the Soviet counterclaims against them. Lloyd George, with the agreement of the other Allied representatives, insisted for his part that public and private debts must be kept separate. Nor, added Barthou, could discussions on the matter be referred to a separate committee which might continue to meet after the conference had ended. This would be contrary to the Cannes conditions. The principles involved would have to be settled first of all, Lloyd George continued. Private and public debts, in particular, could not be mixed up, for practical reasons if no other. Traders, he noted, would certainly refuse to do business if they thought their claims against the Soviet government might be confused with those of governments, and individuals owed money by the Russian government could not be held liable for any damage done by Wrangel, Denikin and others. They had had quite a pleasant day and got to know each other better, Barthou remarked, but they were not making progress. It was essential to come to some understanding. The Soviet delegates had had the experts' report for only two days, but they had had the Cannes resolutions for at least two months. The Soviet delegation now appeared to be acting contrary to those conditions. At Lloyd George's suggestion the French, British and Soviet experts again withdrew in order to attempt to reach agreement on the issues that still remained in dispute. This time there was some measure of accord and it was agreed that the experts should meet again the following morning to try to secure a closer understanding.[71]

The experts' meeting took place at 11.30 a.m. on the following day, Easter Saturday, 15 April 1922. At this meeting the Soviet representatives for the first time produced their detailed claims for damages as a result of the intervention and civil war.[72] The Soviet claims, Lloyd-Greame reported to an Allied meeting later the same day, had amounted to 12 or 13 milliard gold roubles, with further claims in more general terms which swelled the total to some 35 milliard gold roubles. Additional claims covering such matters as pogroms, the occupation of Bessarabia and Russian property abroad would bring the total to about one-third of the total wealth of Russia, or some 50 milliard gold roubles. The western experts present had refused to accept the Soviet figures, still less the principle of liability. The Soviet delegates had nonetheless pointed out that, even if the Allies agreed to set the total of Russian war debts against the Soviet counterclaims, there would still be a large balance in the Soviet favour which would have to be satisfied in some other manner. Lloyd George insisted that, whatever allowance was made for the devastation of Russia, the claims of private citizens must not be affected, nor their right to secure the restoration of their property or compensation for damages. The Allied governments might agree to accept some reduction of their own claims against the Soviet government, but they could accept no formal liability for damages, and any adjustment of claims must be limited to the war debts of the Soviet government towards its western counterparts.[73]

The meeting reconvened with Chicherin, Litvinov, Krasin and Lyubimov in attendance at 4.30 p.m. Lloyd George began by expressing incredulity at the extent of the Soviet counterclaims. Britain, he pointed out, had presented no bill to France in respect of that country's support of the British monarchical cause during the civil war in the seventeenth century, nor had Britain, Austria and other powers been presented with a bill for their support of the old regime during the French revolution. Countries which had experienced a revolution, he observed, could not send in the bill to other countries. The western powers for their part could put in a claim for damages arising out of the Soviet government's signature of the Brest-Litovsk treaty, as a result of which the war had been prolonged and nearly lost. The Allied powers were willing to take Russia's present economic difficulties into account, at least as far as intergovernmental debts were concerned; the total of war debt could be reduced by a percentage to be agreed, and not only the postponement but also the remission of part of the interest on these debts could be considered. No allowance could be made, however, in respect of the obligations of the Soviet government to foreign nationals, or the right of those nationals to the return of their property and to compensation for any loss or damage that they might have suffered.

Chicherin, in reply, disputed Lloyd George's historical parallels and insisted that the counter-revolutionary armies in Russia had arisen directly from the Allies' support and that they had been under the Allies' control. He also queried the Allies' specific proposals. The restoration of factories previously owned by foreign nationals, for instance, was an impossibility; the enterprises concerned had generally been absorbed into larger concerns, and in any case there would be resistance to such a move on the part of the workers involved. Litvinov added that the Soviet delegation had no intention of seeking payment for themselves of the 50 milliard gold roubles to which their counterclaims amounted; their idea was rather that the money should be used to reimburse the western creditors. After a short private discussion among the Allied representatives it was agreed that the Soviet delegation should be allowed some time to consult with its government on the question of the recognition of debts, and of private debts in particular. If the Soviet government were willing to recognise these debts in principle, Barthou explained, they could go on to consider the method of repayment, and the moratorium that the Allies proposed to grant; but if the debts were not recognised, then it would be pointless to discuss the matter further. The French delegation, he emphasised, would not be unnecessarily obstructive in this connection; but how, he asked, could they discuss new obligations unless the old ones had been acknowledged? And how could they discuss the administration of justice, or the position of foreigners in Russia, unless they knew that the Russians would keep their promises? The principle of the recognition of debts was in any case one of the Cannes conditions. Chicherin argued in reply that the fundamental difference was rather one of reciprocity; the Russian delegation had agreed to recognise the claims of the western powers, but the western powers were unwilling to accept the Soviet counterclaims. He would, however, communicate the Allied proposals to Moscow; and in the meantime it was agreed that the first commission should consider a number of less sensitive matters.[74]

The short break allowed all the parties to reflect on the position that had been reached. Writing to Moscow on 15 April 1922, Chicherin explained the circumstances in which the informal meeting with the Allies had taken place and noted that it had once again shown up the enormous differences between the Soviet delegates and their western counterparts. A large number of topics had been discussed, as the stenographic record would indicate. Lloyd George had insisted upon the Soviet delegates accepting the Allies' proposals; it had taken some time, however, to formulate those proposals precisely. Lloyd George's main concern seemed to be that private claims should not be considered in conjunction with intergovernmental claims. At the meeting of 15 April he had finally produced a formula to cover this point, the text of which had been sent to Moscow by cypher. The Allies, it appeared, would be prepared to write down a substantial part, in fact probably the whole, of Russia's wartime debts, and also to reduce and postpone the payment of interest on the pre-war debts, in view of Russia's economic difficulties. These concessions would be made in exchange for the abandonment of the Russian counterclaims. The Soviet delegates for their part had expressed their willingness to offer long-term concessions on their property to former western owners or, where this proved impossible, to provide a satisfactory form of compensation upon a basis to be agreed.[75]

After its dramatic opening, Hankey wrote to Austen Chamberlain on 16 April 1922, the conference was now 'following the ordinary course of conferences'. All the technical work had been delegated to commissions, while the more critical and delicate political negotiations were being dealt with behind the scenes by informal meetings between the representatives of the major powers. During the first day of such discussions at the Villa d'Albertis the Russians had kept trying to avoid the point; they had continually dragged in extraneous issues, and when they were asked specific questions they replied in generalities. The experts' meeting on the Saturday morning had been an 'absolute frost'; Litvinov, 'rather the villain of the piece', had withdrawn concessions previously agreed and had insisted on 'preposterous' counterclaims. The whole question had been thrashed out at great length in the afternoon session; Chicherin in his replies had shown himself 'no mean Parliamentarian, though the prime minister had distinctly the better of the encounter'. It had eventually been agreed to refer the Allied proposals to Moscow for consideration. They were rather curious as to what the Soviet reply would be; Hankey himself was inclined to put the odds at 6:4 in favour of acceptance, though he thought the delegation might begin with something 'more or less evasive'.[76] More generally, Gregory wrote to the Foreign Office on 13 April, the situation was 'very satisfactory' from the British point of view; the Russians had accepted the Cannes conditions at the opening session, and British delegates had established a 'remarkable ascendancy in all committees and international meetings'. The French had been left isolated, with the whole of Europe opposed to the attitude they were taking.[77]

The opening days had also given the Soviet and western diplomats the chance to make each other's acquaintance. At their meeting at the Villa d'Albertis, Hankey wrote to his wife on 15 April, they had for the first time been able to meet the Bolsheviks face to face. They had predictably found that the Soviet delegates were 'very much like other people. They did not have faces on both sides of their heads, nor club feet, nor even "the hairy paw of the baboon"', which Churchill had always refused to grasp. Because of the distances involved they had stayed at Lloyd George's villa for lunch on 15 April. Hankey himself had sat beside Litvinov, a 'horrible ruffian' with a 'fat puffy face'; Chicherin, however, appeared an 'intelligent cultured man'. In general he found the Russians very like Orientals to do business with; if they were asked a question they replied either in generalities, or else by raising something entirely different, and it was very difficult to pin them down. Hankey nonetheless believed that they would come to terms in the end.[78] Grigg, writing to Austen Chamberlain on 18 April, remarked that Chicherin improved upon acquaintance; he was far abler and more tactful than he had appeared to be at first, and both he and Krasin gave the impression of being authoritative and capable people who could see their way to a settlement. Litvinov, however, aroused no comparable enthusiasm (a 'revolting little bagman with a cruel, dirty face', and probably a permanent object of animosity to his colleagues for fear that he would go behind their backs and report their concessions to the extremists in the Soviet government). The Soviet delegates' main preoccupation, Grigg thought, was whether they could obtain any substantial assistance from the West in return for accepting their conditions; much would depend upon whether they could be given any credits for the restoration of their economy.[79]

The French position at the conference, as Gregory had indicated, was indeed an isolated one. The local press, in the first place, was generally hostile to them. The Italian press, Barthou complained to Poincaré on 16 April 1922, had in fact been hostile to the delegation since before its arrival. It was using old incidents to stir up public opinion and was attempting to misrepresent French action and to isolate the French delegates. He had complained to Schanzer about this campaign, which was 'far too disciplined to be spontaneous'. The Catholic press had also been hostile, as well as the Vatican and the Archbishop of Genoa. There had been no feeling of Latin affinity, and the Catholic press combined with Soviet and German propaganda had produced a very hostile atmosphere which it was difficult to combat. Barthou described Facta as a man of the 'second or third rank', while Schanzer, who represented Italian interests at the conference, hoped to further his own career by a successful meeting and was accordingly very friendly towards the Russians and anxious at all costs to avoid a breakdown. He was also personally subservient to Lloyd George and hostile towards France. The Little Entente, Barthou continued, had offered some support, but they were divided among themselves, particularly between Czechoslovakia and Poland; while the Belgian delegation, although generally sympathetic to the French position, had been cautious and taciturn.[80] The French counsellor in Rome wrote to Poincaré on 18 April in the same terms. The Italian press, he noted, was generally hostile, depicting the French position as nationalistic or egoistic, in contrast to that of Britain or of Italy herself. Italians were generally more interested in the development of trade, the relief of unemployment and European detente than in reparations and Russian debts, and some papers had gone so far as to suggest that Italy should pursue her own interests regardless of the French position.[81]

There was also dissatisfaction within the French delegation, and more particularly with its leader, Louis Barthou. Barrère, for instance, wrote to the French counsellor in Rome that he had known Barthou before but had not previously seen him in diplomatic action. Great had been his disenchantment. Barthou's desire to please, he told Charles-Roux on 12 April, his love of flattery and of applause stultified his actions.[82] Jean Roger, another member of the French delegation, had the same reaction. Barthou, he wrote to Charles-Roux, was too keen for compliments, and too concerned with what would be said about him in parliament and the press. He was nervous, gave insufficient attention to the problems of the minor states, and was irritated by Poincaré's numerous telegrams and yet fearful of him.[83] Poincaré's constant flow of directives certainly caused Barthou some difficulty. Poincaré's 'excessively restrictive instructions', Barthou complained to the French counsellor in Rome, had 'paralysed all diplomacy' and forced him to 'walk with a knife to his throat'.[84] Poincaré himself, according to Jean Roger, was unduly preoccupied with parliament and the press. Some of his telegrams had been received with 'real anger' in Genoa and had led to exchanges in 'very lively terms'. The French premier, Roger went on, spoke a lot, reflected little and spent a large part of his time in the company of journalists, whom he was constantly afraid of alienating. Poincaré's constant interventions and his ignorance of the detailed course of the negotiations had made it difficult for the delegates to make any progress; his telegrams, which contained more criticism than advice or instructions, were evidently designed at least as much to appease his parliamentary critics as to benefit the delegation itself.[85]

The messages that Barthou received from Poincaré certainly left him little room for manoeuvre. On 14 April, for instance, Barthou reported to Poincaré on the first day's informal discussion with the Russians, and noted that some progress had been made. Poincaré replied the following day approving Barthou's decision to take part in the discussions, but emphasising that there could be no concessions on Russia's pre-war debts and that the Russian claims in regard to war debts were unacceptable in the form in which they stood. The recognition of Russian debts and the certainty of their being paid, he wrote to Barthou on 16 April, were the 'essential and prior condition of any commercial entente with the Soviets'.[86] The same day Barthou wrote again to Poincaré to inform him of the outcome of the second day's negotiations with the Russians, whose decisions, he noted, were consistent with the Allied experts' report and with Poincaré's own instructions, and were being referred to Moscow for further consideration.[87] In a telegram to the Ministry of Finances of 17 April Barthou pointed out that a reduction in the Russian war debt might provide a useful precedent for France in her dealings with Britain and the United States, and he asked for a view on the acceptability of a reduction of Russia's war debts of about a third in view of that country's economic difficulties.[88] Poincaré replied the following day, insisting that there could be no reduction in French claims without the agreement, not just of the French Treasury and government, but of the French parliament itself. Such a step, he thought, would be inappropriate in view of the fact that British and American claims against France had remained unchanged, and any reduction in Russian debts should more generally be subordinated to a settlement of inter-Allied debts in their entirety. The Ministry of Finances later concurred in these views.[89]

The conference accordingly reached the end of its first stage precariously balanced between success and failure. French hostility to the Soviet position had been apparent at every point; indeed in their hatred of the Bolsheviks, Hankey wrote to his wife on 12 April, they seemed almost to have forgotten their hostility towards the Germans. On the other hand they were 'quite a nice lot individually';

Barthou in particular was 'quite a good fellow', and some of the delegates had not concealed the fact that they were acting under instructions from Poincaré and had been somewhat embarrassed by this.[90] The French position, at the same time, had not moved significantly towards that of Britain and Italy, and any reports of an accommodation tended to increase the fears of Poincaré in Paris and still more those of French parliamentary and public opinion, which remained steadfastly opposed to any agreement with the Soviet government which did not include the recognition of all debts and the restoration of nationalised property, not merely compensation for its confiscation. British parliamentary opinion was also becoming increasingly restive as the conference proceeded. All was still quiet, Austen Chamberlain reported to Lloyd George on 12 April, but opposition to the recognition of Russia, even in the strictly limited form that had been agreed, was tending to grow rather than to diminish.[91] The Soviet government had still to respond to the Allies' proposals of 15 April, and unless that response was an accommodating one the conference was unlikely to proceed further. The Soviet delegates themselves, moreover, had not been idle. On Easter Sunday, 16 April 1922, an astonished conference was informed that the Soviet and German delegations, early that morning, had concluded an agreement at the Soviet delegation's hotel in Rapallo which provided for the full restoration of diplomatic relations between the two states. The continuation of the conference itself, not simply the possibility of a Soviet–Western accord, was immediately placed in question.

7

Rapallo

A closer Soviet–German relationship had been developing for some time before Genoa, prompted (on the German side) by their wish to restore trade relations with a market in which they had traditionally held a dominant share, and (on the Soviet side) by the Russian government's wish to secure economic assistance and to break down its isolation among the outside powers.[1] As with other countries, the issues of propaganda, the return of prisoners of war and debts delayed the resumption of relations, but on 6 May 1921, a few weeks after the corresponding Anglo-Russian agreement, a provisional trade agreement was signed in Berlin which placed relations between the two countries on a new and more stable basis. The agreement extended the powers of the representatives responsible for prisoners of war in each country to all matters concerning their respective nationals, and provided for the appointment of trade representatives to each mission in order to facilitate the development of economic relations between the two countries. The RSFSR mission in Germany was acknowledged as the only recognised Russian mission in that country; the representatives of both countries, however, were required to limit themselves to the fulfilment of the agreement, and 'in particular ... to refrain from any agitation or propaganda against the government or state institutions of the country in which they [we]re located'. The agreement, like its British counterpart, signified the conferment of *de facto* diplomatic recognition by the German upon the Soviet government, although in both cases the agreements were stated to be provisional pending the conclusion of a further agreement which would finally establish full *de jure* diplomatic relations between the governments concerned.[2]

The further development of Soviet–German relations was influenced by a set of considerations more varied and numerous than in the case of Soviet relations with any other western country. As in some other western nations, particularly Britain, there were strong economic pressures in Germany to develop closer relations with the new Soviet government, the more so as German industrialists had traditionally held a major share of the Russian internal market (in 1913, for instance, Germany had been Russia's principal trading partner, accounting for more than 38 per cent of her total foreign trade turnover).[3] Major heavy industrial concerns, such as Siemens and Krupps, were naturally keen to revive this trade after the revolution, and they were willing, if necessary, to recognise the Soviet government in order to do so, particularly if German interests appeared likely to be granted a dominant or even monopolistic position in certain sectors. German light industry was generally less preoccupied with the Russian market, and more willing to explore whatever opportunities were available in association with other countries; its influence upon government policy, however, fell some distance short of that of its heavy industrial rivals.[4] Political and public opinion was similarly divided. A substantial segment, associated particularly with the Chancellor, Joseph Wirth of the Centre party, favoured closer relations with the Soviet government as a means of circumventing the restrictions imposed upon Germany by the Treaty of Versailles, and there was some sympathy for this policy among trade union and working-class opinion and particularly among German Communists. The Social Democrats, however, were less favourably disposed towards a government which was so closely associated with their domestic political opponents, and more conservative political and diplomatic circles objected to closer relations with a power which had sequestered the private property of German nationals and was actively promoting communist propaganda.[5]

In the German case more particularly a further element was involved in the equation: this was the policy of the German military, which had a tradition of corporate exclusiveness, a feeling of professional community with their counterparts in the Red Army, and an obvious practical need to find a means of escaping the restrictions upon German military power which had been imposed by the Treaty of Versailles.[6] The German General Staff appears to have taken an interest in the opportunities that Russia might provide in this connection as early as 1919. It was not until the spring of 1921, however, that negotiations began to make real progress. By early 1921 a special section devoted to Russian affairs, 'Sondergruppe R', had been established in the German war ministry, and in the spring of the same year discussions were begun between German military and Soviet representatives with a view to the conclusion of an agreement by which Germany would assist the development of the Russian armaments industry in return for the provision of artillery ammunition which Germany was prohibited from manufacturing under the Versailles treaty. A special mission was despatched to Moscow in December 1921 and then, with Wirth's knowledge and approval, a more far-reaching arrangement was made in the summer of 1922 for the provision of German tank and aviation training schools on Soviet territory and for the production of German war materials. General Hans von Seeckt, Chief of the Army High Command, supported to a considerable extent by Wirth, favoured an active eastern policy in association with Soviet Russia and directed against Poland, France's principal ally in the east and a pillar of the Versailles settlement. As Wirth told him, 'In times when our policy in the West has been blocked, it has always been right to be active in the East.'[7] The divisions and lack of communication between military and political leaders, between 'easterners' such as von Seeckt and 'westerners' such as President Ebert, and between different sections of industry, the political parties and public opinion, made Soviet–German relations more ambiguous and unpredictable than Soviet relations with any of the other major powers.

On the Soviet side the position was hardly less complicated. In the first place, Germany, as the country with the strongest communist party and the country in which the revolution had been most confidently predicted, exposed at its sharpest the disjunction between a revolutionary and an orthodox foreign policy which also applied, to a greater or lesser extent, to Soviet relations with other countries. Communist-led risings in Germany in the spring of 1921, and again in the autumn of 1923, found Zinoviev and the Comintern seriously at odds with Chicherin and conventional diplomatic opinion, which saw the development of closer and more friendly relations with the German government as a means of undermining Allied unity and the Versailles settlement. The issue of nationalised property was a less important one in Soviet–German relations than in Soviet relations with either Britain or France, but another legacy of the revolution, the assassination of the German ambassador, Count Mirbach, by Left Socialist Revolutionaries in Moscow in July 1918, still awaited settlement. The allocation of a substantial part of Upper Silesia to Poland in October 1921, however, following a plebiscite in which a majority had opted for unification with Germany, strengthened Russophil tendencies in German government and diplomatic circles. 'Better late than never', remarked *Izvestiya* on 9 November 1921, commenting upon the German government's new interest in the East. If they really wished to adopt a new policy towards Soviet Russia there would be no objection; the Soviet point of view had 'always been that the resumption of normal political and economic relations between Germany and Soviet Russia would be in the interests of both countries'.[8] The British ambassador, Lord d'Abernon, commented from Berlin that there was now 'considerable ground for the opinion that German government circles are more inclined than ever before to cooperate with the Soviet'.[9]

Influenced by these various considerations, Soviet–German relations advanced slowly and irregularly over the latter part of 1921 and early 1922. Commercial relations between the two countries, on the whole, advanced more rapidly than relations at a political or diplomatic level. On 13 May 1921, just a week after the provisional Soviet–German agreement had been concluded, a Soviet–German Transport Company was set up in Berlin, directed jointly by the RSFSR trade mission and by the Hamburg–Amerika line, with the aim of providing land and sea transport between the two countries.[10] Analogous arrangements were made later in the year with other German commercial firms to establish a joint Russo-German company for scrap metal (Derumetall) and a Russo-German company for air transport (Derulyuft), and credit facilities were arranged with a German bank.[11] Chicherin, in a letter to Lenin on 14 June 1921, pointed out the importance of developing such relations in order to prevent the formation of a united front of German, French and British interests for the exploitation of Russia along the lines suggested by Stinnes.[12] The German representative in Moscow, however, in a lengthy report to the German foreign ministry in December 1921, noted that trade was still developing rather slowly, despite the interest that had been shown in it, and that there were many obstacles still to overcome.[13] So far, Lenin complained in a letter of 30 November 1921, there had been 'only words' from the Germans.[14]

Wirth generally inclined towards a policy of 'fulfilment' of the Versailles treaty and had therefore favoured a relatively slow

resumption of relations with the Soviet government, although this
was the policy that he himself supported. The partitioning of Upper
Silesia, however, appears to have suggested to him that little would
be gained from the continued pursuit of concessions from the Allies.
In the same month (October 1921) he dismissed his anti-Russian
foreign minister, Friedrich Rosen, and recalled the strongly pro-
Soviet Baron Ago von Maltzan from Athens, where Rosen had
banished him. Maltzen became head of the Eastern Department in
the German foreign ministry, and 'easterners' generally gained in
influence at all levels.[15] Formal discussions with Soviet representatives began soon afterwards. In January 1922 Radek arrived in
Berlin, remaining there until the end of April; and on 16 January
1922 negotiations began between Wirth, Rathenau, Maltzan,
Stinnes, the director of AEG (the General Electric Company) Felix
Deutsch, and representatives of Krupps and other German banking
and industrial interests, and Krasin, the Soviet representative in
Germany N. N. Krestinsky, and B. S. Stomonyakov, who was
attached to the Russian trade mission in Berlin. The negotiations
continued intermittently for about a month.[16]

The discussions were by no means easy or straightforward. At a
meeting in the Auswärtiges Amt on 25 January 1922, for instance, the
Soviet representatives were invited to explain the nature of the
assistance they required from German industry. The Soviet government, they explained, was against a single consortium for the
economic development of Russia, but was not opposed to the establishment of several consortia for this purpose. They would have to
bear in mind that, for instance, it would be dangerous to collaborate
with Britain in the Caucasus while Britain was still a major Asian
power. Russo-German relations, they insisted, must also be clarified before the Genoa conference assembled, and defined in a formal
treaty. The Germans demurred, arguing that the issue of article 116
of the Versailles treaty (covering the Russian right to reparations)
must be included in any such agreement.[17] Further discussions
concerned the full normalisation of diplomatic relations between the
two countries and the provision of a major Russian loan.[18] On 16
February Maltzan presented a German draft of a provisional agreement, which however retained for Germany the right to present
claims against Russia for nationalised German property, while the
Soviet government was required to surrender its right to reparations
under article 116 of the Versailles treaty.[19] Rathenau, Chicherin

complained in a letter to Moscow of 8 February, had evidently decided that general reparations policy and relations with France were more important than the development of closer economic relations with Soviet Russia; Litvinov, in a letter of 16 February, added that the Germans appeared also to be hoping they would secure more advantageous conditions for economic activity in Russia by joint action with Britain and France rather than by direct negotiations with the Soviet government.[20] Wirth, influenced by Rathenau and Stinnes, ultimately decided to await the outcome of the conference rather than to conclude a separate agreement before it, and the negotiations concluded without result on 17 February 1922.[21]

The development of Soviet–German relations, although not widely reported in the German press, was known to and commented upon by other diplomatic representatives in the German capital. Charles Laurent, the French ambassador, reported to Paris on 21 January 1922 that the Soviet representatives in the negotiations were proposing to extend the Soviet–German commercial agreement of 6 May 1921 and to consider the full restoration of diplomatic relations between the two countries. They would, he believed, be prepared to make concessions on the issue of private property, and even to restore to foreign owners their previous possessions. The foreign trade monopoly would probably be abandoned in June.[22] The British ambassador, Lord d'Abernon, reported for his part that the Soviet representatives (particularly Radek) had been seeking to put pressure upon the Germans by comparing their offer with one allegedly received from France under which that country would assist the Soviet government to recover reparations from Germany under article 116 of the Versailles treaty, the proceeds being used to repay Russia's debts to France. Radek (whose discussions proceeded in parallel with those conducted by Krasin and his colleagues) had also proposed the re-establishment of full Soviet–German diplomatic relations before the conference began, although the point had not been pressed.[23] The Germans, d'Abernon added on 28 January, had however taken the view that the full resumption of diplomatic relations would be difficult so long as the issue of the murder of Count Mirbach had not been satisfactorily resolved; they had also no resources of their own to devote to Russian reconstruction, and had warned that the provision of a large loan by German industrialists would antagonise the Allies, as such resources were supposed to be devoted to the repayment of

reparations. In general, d'Abernon thought, the German government was anxious to take no step in regard to Russia which might
conflict with the views of the British government.[24]

The Soviet–German negotiations had in fact been 'stormy', the
French ambassador reported to Paris on 20 February 1922, according to what appeared to be reliable sources. The Soviet representatives had opposed the international consortium and had insisted on
the conclusion of a Soviet–German agreement before the Genoa
conference took place. They had also demanded a loan of 1 milliard
marks, a sum that had astonished Rathenau, who had pointed out
the impossibility of obtaining such a sum while Germany remained
committed to the payment of reparations. The Soviet delegates'
references to parallel negotiations with France had also annoyed the
foreign minister and German public opinion generally.[25] Speaking to
the Reichstag committee on foreign affairs on 21 February, Rathenau
expressed doubts about Russia's economic potential, at least in the
short term, and urged participation in the international consortium
so that German interests could be adequately protected. The Soviet–
German negotiations that had been taking place, he reported, had
mainly concerned the question of German diplomatic recognition of
the Soviet government and economic assistance. Rathenau himself
believed that Russia and Germany should cooperate at Genoa, but
that the German representatives at the conference should not orient
themselves exclusively towards Russia nor seek a monopoly for their
economic activities in that country.[26] Private trading companies
should go into Russia individually, Rathenau suggested to Lord
d'Abernon; once a sufficient number of contracts had been obtained,
the Soviet system would fall. Rathenau reported himself impressed
by the moderation of the British representatives with whom he had
come in contact at London and Cannes; and he had become conver-
ted to the idea of international conferences, though with a limited
number of participating powers in each case. He had great hopes of
Genoa in particular.[27] The Russians, Rathenau told d'Abernon,
were simply trying to create a rift between Britain and France in
order to create competition for closer relations with their own
country.[28]

Matters were taken further when the Soviet delegation stopped
over at Berlin on their way to Genoa. The Germans, Chicherin
complained to Moscow on 4 April 1922, had been unwilling to come
to terms before the conference began, and the formula they had

proposed to cover compensation for private citizens whose property had been nationalised had been worse than the formula they had proposed in the earlier negotiations.[29] In a further telegram of 8 April Evgeny Pashukanis, at this time a legal counsellor at the Soviet mission in Berlin, filled in the background in more detail. The delegation, he reported, had arrived at Berlin on 1 April. They had had a private meeting that evening together with Radek, Stomonyakov and Pashukanis himself. It had been decided that the negotiations should be conducted in two parts: Stomonyakov was to discuss the proposed loan with the Germans, where neither the conditions nor the sum so far suggested had been satisfactory, while negotiations towards a separate political agreement were to concentrate upon the renewal of full diplomatic relations and the complete renunciation of all claims, including private ones, by both parties. Maltzan had earlier been prepared to cover these matters in a secret protocol, effectively reducing the right of compensation to negligible proportions, but this was unacceptable to the Soviet delegates, as their object was to secure the formal renunciation of claims for compensation by at least one of the major powers. This, the delegation believed, would prove to be the most difficult proposition for the Germans to accept, and they would hardly come to a satisfactory agreement on this before Genoa.[30] This indeed proved to be the case.

Formal negotiations began the day after the delegation's arrival, Sunday 2 April 1922. Wirth and Rathenau were unavailable until the Monday, and Maltzan was accordingly invited to Chicherin's hotel, the Estland, for preliminary discussions. The main item of controversy, as expected, was the question of the compensation of private citizens for the loss of their nationalised property. Maltzan pointed out that no German government could appear in the Reichstag having surrendered the rights of its citizens to compensation for their losses, but had nonetheless indicated some willingness to seek a compromise. The following day, Monday 3 April 1922, Chicherin and Litvinov were received by Wirth and Rathenau and spent almost the whole day engaged in discussions with them. A compromise formula began to emerge to the effect that Germany would renounce her claim arising from the nationalisation provided the Soviet government announced it would refuse to accept the claims of any other power. If any such claims were in fact accepted, then a further agreement would be negotiated. The same evening the Soviet delegates prepared a draft agreement along these lines, basing themselves upon Maltzan's proposals of the previous February but incorporating several necessary amendments. The German representatives were also to be required to state that they would be willing to take part in the operations of the proposed international consortium, provided the Soviet government gave its consent, but they were to be encouraged to declare that they would equally be willing to take part in economic activities in Russia on an independent basis.

On the Tuesday, 4 April 1922, Maltzan and Chicherin held a further meeting to agree upon a final text of the proposed agreement. Maltzan, however, appeared with his own and, from the Soviet point of view, less satisfactory version. On the issue of private claims for compensation arising from nationalisation, Maltzan now proposed that Germany should reserve her right to claim damages, but be prepared to renounce any such claims if other powers did likewise. He insisted that the meaning of the clause was the same, but the effect, from the Soviet point of view, was very different: Germany, rather than renouncing her claims, was now insisting upon them. Maltzan added that Rathenau, after discussions with other members of the German Cabinet, had committed himself to this new formula and would accept no change in it. The German draft agreement, moreover, could be initialled but not signed, as it had not been discussed by the Cabinet. When Litvinov asked if the Cabinet could not be convened before the delegation left for Genoa, Maltzan evaded and then replied that the agreement involved such serious financial sacrifices for Germany that its consideration would take a long time. It was, Pashukanis believed, quite clear that the Germans were resolved to conclude no agreement of any kind with the Soviet delegation before Genoa, and that they intended to create no more than the appearance of a Soviet–German understanding at this stage.[31] Later the same day the Soviet delegation left for Genoa.

Allied representatives in Berlin were well aware, at least in general terms, that Soviet–German negotiations of some sort were taking place. The French, who had perhaps the most reason to be concerned, were informed by their ambassador in Stockholm on 2 April 1922 that the Soviet–German talks had led to a decision to cooperate in all matters of common interest at the conference, and that Germany would support the full diplomatic recognition of the Soviet government.[32] The French minister in Berlin, Saint-Quentin, added that agreement had been reached that the Russians would not exercise their rights under article 116 of the Versailles treaty, and that the Germans would not assist the establishment of the proposed international consortium. No understanding had however been reached regarding the claims of the former owners of nationalised private property.[33] Rathenau, although warning against 'exaggerated optimism' in relation to the conference, was reported also to have taken part in discussions between the Soviet delegation and German industrial interests, including AEG (of which he had until recently been president), Stinnes and Krupps, although no agreement had as yet been reached.[34] The Germans, the Italian ambassador, Frassati, reported to Rome, were reluctant to renounce their property rights in Russia as this might be taken as a precedent by Latvia, Lithuania and Estonia, and they believed that they would in fact be unlikely ever to be required to pay obligations under article 116 of the Versailles treaty. They were therefore following a temporising policy towards the Soviet delegates.[35] The Belgian ambassador confirmed that there might be joint Soviet–German action at Genoa on certain questions, but he added on 12 April that 'fairly serious differences of opinion' had emerged on Chicherin's last day in Berlin, and that the delegates had parted on worse terms than they had met. This appeared to be the general view of the Berlin diplomatic community.[36]

Early Soviet–German dealings at the conference certainly gave few grounds for believing that an agreement was imminent. According to Maltzan's subsequent account, the German delegates first became seriously concerned when they read the text of the experts' report, which was made available to them on 11 April. The report explicitly confirmed Russia's right to reparations under article 116 of the Versailles treaty but excluded any possibility that Germany might make claims of a reciprocal nature against Russia. Maltzan explained the German delegation's concern to J. D. Gregory and other members of the British delegation, who promised that Lloyd George would be informed. Maltzan pointed out that the Russians, in their negotiations in Berlin, had shown themselves rather more accommodating in relation to article 116; he also expressed his concern to a member of the Belgian delegation. Meanwhile reports began to reach the German delegation that far-reaching conversations (the discussions at the Villa d'Albertis) were proceeding between the inviting powers and the Russians. At 11 p.m. on Friday 14 April Francesco Giannini of the Italian delegation reported to it that the discussions were continuing and that they would probably lead to an agreement. The Russians, it was believed, would probably be willing to recognise their pre-war debts in the form of long-term obligations. Leases or concessions for ninety-nine-year periods were being considered as a form of compensation for nationalised property; and war debts would so far as possible be settled with regard to Russia's counterclaims, though these could not be accepted formally. Rathenau, in reply, expressed the German delegates' reservations about the Allied experts' report and added that they would have to reserve their position and accept concessions in regard to article 116 wherever they could find them.[37]

The following day, Saturday 15 April 1922, the press secretary of the German delegation, Oscar Müller, reported to Berlin that the Allied powers and the Russians were meeting and that an agreement between them, without Germany, was definitely in prospect.[38] The same day Maltzan met Ioffe and Rakovsky and was given a more precise account of the Allied–Soviet negotiations. Maltzan offered to be more forthcoming with regard to economic assistance if the Russians were willing to provide guarantees in respect of article 116 of the Versailles treaty and also to give the Germans most-favoured-nation status. Ioffe and Rakovsky were receptive but argued that the best course in the circumstances was to sign the agreement already negotiated in Berlin, which they were still prepared to accept. Maltzan immediately tried to contact the British delegation, but failed to do so. In the afternoon, however, he saw Frank Wise and informed him of the Russians' renewed offers and that further negotiations would be proceeding. Wise expressed no surprise and noted that the difficulties of the German position were well understood; he added that the Allied negotiations with the Russians in Lloyd George's villa were themselves taking a more favourable course. That evening the rumours of a French–British–Russian understanding continued to accumulate.[39]

At about 1 a.m. on the following day, Easter Sunday, 16 April 1922, Ioffe telephoned the German delegation to report that the Russians were ready to resume negotiations that day and would be glad if the Germans would come to their hotel in Rapallo at about 11 a.m. for this purpose. Maltzan tried to contact Wise at 8 a.m. and again at 9 a.m. but was unable to reach him. The German delegation then set out for Rapallo, arriving at 11.30 a.m. After lengthy negotiations, centring particularly upon the need for better guarantees that Germany would obtain no less favourable treatment than other states if compensation was eventually paid for nationalised property, the treaty was finally signed at 7 p.m. Allied delegates were informed later that evening and a press statement was released the following morning.[40] Maltzan later informed d'Abernon that a variety of sources, Dutch and Italian among them, had reported to the German delegation on the Saturday evening that an Allied–Russian agreement had in fact been signed, leaving Germany alone and isolated. They had gone to bed gloomy and depressed, having decided that there was nothing they could do about it. Maltzan had been woken in the early hours by the hotel porter, who told him that a 'man with a queer name' (Chicherin) wanted to speak to him on the telephone.[41] Sensing that the Russians must have failed to come to an agreement with the Allies, Maltzan had temporised, explaining that the German delegation had organised a picnic for the following day and that he himself had to go to church. Eventually, however, on the express condition that most-favoured-nation status would be granted, Maltzan agreed to sacrifice his religious duties and make the trip to Rapallo.[42]

Maltzan then went to Rathenau, who had been pacing his room anxiously in mauve pyjamas, and persuaded him to attend. Maltzan, it appears, may not himself have believed in the danger of German isolation at the conference, and may have used this argument to persuade the generally more reluctant foreign minister.[43] Slow progress had been made at the meeting until a telephone message had arrived for Rathenau from Lloyd George, seeking a meeting at the earliest opportunity. The Soviet delegates had thereupon become more conciliatory and the agreement was signed shortly afterwards.[44] The Soviet delegation's hotel was in fact in Santa Margherita, rather than in Rapallo proper; the two localities were connected by a large park in which the Imperial Palace, the hotel in which the Soviet delegation were staying, was located. It was unclear, two members of the Soviet delegation later recalled, why it had been called the Rapallo rather than the Santa Margherita treaty; perhaps Rapallo was easier to pronounce, or perhaps it was because Santa Margherita was administratively subordinate to its larger neighbour.[45] At any rate it was as the Rapallo Treaty that the Soviet–German agreement subsequently became known.

The Rapallo Treaty, signed on 16 April 1922, was a short and, on the face of it, unremarkable document. Its first article covered the state of war which had previously existed between the two powers;

under its provisions both parties agreed to renounce all claims for compensation against the other in respect of the costs of the war and war losses, including costs incurred on behalf of prisoners of war. This effectively disposed of Russian rights under article 116 of the Versailles treaty. The second article covered the rather more sensitive area of compensation for nationalised property; under its terms the German government agreed to renounce all public and private claims arising out of the legislative acts of the Soviet government, provided that Soviet government gave no satisfaction to similar claims by other states. A secret exchange of notes contained an assurance that if any claims in respect of nationalised property by third parties were accepted by the Soviet government, then German claims would be treated upon the same basis. The Germans also undertook not to participate in the proposed international consortium without the prior agreement of the Soviet government.[46] The other articles of the agreement provided for the immediate resumption of full diplomatic and consular relations between the two countries, for the application of most-favoured-nation principles to their commercial and economic relations, and for the consideration of the economic needs of the other party (in other words Russia) in an 'accommodating spirit'.[47] A further letter from Maltzan to Litvinov confirmed that the German authorities would henceforth undertake no official dealings with the white Russian diplomatic mission in Berlin.[48]

The news that the treaty had been concluded not surprisingly caused a convulsion in the conference's proceedings. The meeting of the first commission which had been due to take place on 17 April was cancelled, and the Allies instead held an informal meeting in Schanzer's residence to consider what their response should be. Lloyd George began by remarking that, although he had no idea that the agreement was imminent, he had indicated to Schanzer that some such arrangement was obvious conceivable. Schanzer added that the Germans had feared they would be excluded from a general Soviet–Allied agreement, although he regretted that they should have found it necessary to conclude the peace treaty during the conference itself. Barthou, who followed him, thought the situation was not simply serious, but extremely grave. The agreement, he believed, was contrary to the provisions of the Versailles treaty, which required the reparations commission to approve any transfer of German assets to other nations, and also to the Cannes conditions.

The French delegation, he announced, would be unable to continue negotiations with either the Soviet or the German delegation until it had been repudiated. Schanzer, however, pointed out that if the conference failed the consequences would be very serious indeed. Bolshevik propaganda would be resumed with even more vigour, and an outburst of military hostilities between Russia and Poland was quite likely. If there was no agreement with the Allies, moreover, Russia would be thrown back entirely into the arms of Germany. He was also doubtful if the treaty was necessarily a violation of Versailles or of the Cannes conditions. Lloyd George urged Barthou not to be hasty; a French withdrawal would mean either the expulsion of Germany and Russia from the conference or else the isolation of France. He thought an Allied communication of some sort might perhaps be sent to the Soviet and German delegations, drawing attention to their breach of diplomatic courtesy; in the meantime lawyers could study the relationship between their agreement and the Versailles treaty. Barthou eventually agreed to postpone a final decision, although he insisted he could enter no more private negotiations with the Soviet delegates because of their lack of good faith.[49]

At a further meeting on 18 April 1922, with Czech, Polish, Romanian and Yugoslav delegates also in attendance, Lloyd George's proposed communication to the German delegation was discussed in more detail.[50] The letter, which was despatched to Wirth later the same day, expressed its signatories' 'astonishment' that Germany, during the first stages of the conference and without reference to the other powers, should secretly have concluded a separate agreement with the Soviet government. The questions covered by the treaty were precisely those on which all the powers had been invited to confer, and its conclusion, behind the backs of the other delegates, was a violation of the conditions to which the German delegation had pledged itself by its acceptance of the invitation to the conference. The German delegates had thereby destroyed the spirit of mutual confidence which was indispensable for international cooperation and which it was the principal object of the conference to establish. The Russo-German treaty was not, apparently, open to examination or amendment by the other powers represented at the conference, and was, in fact, a 'violation of some of the principles upon which the conference was based'. In the circumstances the signatories – the inviting powers, together with Czechoslovakia, Poland, Romania, Yugoslavia and Spain – thought it neither fair nor equitable that the

German delegates, having reached a separate agreement of their own with the Russians, should be involved in further discussions between their own countries and the Soviet delegates. By their own actions, therefore, the German delegation would be assumed to have renounced further participation in the discussion of the conditions of an agreement between Russia and the other powers represented at the conference (in effect, the German delegates were to be excluded from further meetings of the first or political commission).[51]

Lloyd George held a private meeting with Rathenau and Wirth the following day, Wednesday 19 April 1922, to discuss the matter further. The whole incident, he remarked, had been 'very unfortunate'. Since arriving at Genoa he had had many talks with Barthou, who had gradually been brought round to a much more accommodating frame of mind than he had been in when the conference began. Now, however, all this had been prejudiced by the Germans, who, whatever the merits of their action, had gone behind the backs of the other delegates on the very matters with which the conference was dealing. Barthou was threatening to leave, and the situation could only be retrieved by a bold step. Lloyd George suggested that the treaty should in fact be withdrawn for the time being, allowing more general negotiations to proceed; if these failed to cover all questions of interest to both powers it would be possible to deal with them in a subsequent agreement. He could see no other way out. Rathenau, in reply, drew attention to the Germans' difficult position at the conference, their fears concerning article 116 of the Versailles treaty, and his own unsuccessful attempts to contact Lloyd George during the earlier stages of the conference. The treaty could not be withdrawn, but it might perhaps be held in suspense and inserted later into the conference's proceedings. Lloyd George again urged the German delegates to withdraw from the treaty, reserving the right to engage in subsequent negotiations on any matters that might not be covered in a more general agreement. Rathenau, however, insisted that they could not withdraw from the treaty, not, at least, without the agreement of the Russians, who were its other signatories.[52] The Soviet delegates, in the event, refused to contemplate the cancellation of the agreement, although they were prepared to postpone its implementation until the conference had ended,[53] and the German delegates accordingly withdrew from further meetings of the first commission which were concerned with Russia. They were, however, permitted to remain at the conference for the discussion of other matters.[54]

The news of the conclusion of the Rapallo treaty caused consternation not only at the conference but also among European governments and publics more generally. It had been a 'crisis of the first magnitude', Hankey wrote to his wife on 18 April 1922, although if they kept calm they might still be able to put matters right.[55] Writing to Austen Chamberlain on the same date Hankey noted that rumours of discussions between the Russians and the Germans had been current for some time, but news of the conclusion of the treaty had reached them only the previous day, together with a not entirely accurate copy of the treaty itself. Rathenau had sent a message to Lloyd George to the effect that the treaty was 'really quite harmless', and that the Germans had every intention of cooperating in a more general agreement with the Russians. In the long run, Hankey believed, a Russo-German alliance was 'horrible to contemplate', but the Germans would be unable to give the Russians what they wanted for some time to come, and the two powers were very likely to quarrel before their association reached this point.[56] Two days later he wrote to Chamberlain that the prospects were 'a little brighter', although he would 'not like to say that we are quite out of the wood'. The Germans had let it be known that they had no wish to break with the conference altogether, and they were quite willing for the Allies to put pressure on the Russians to release them from the treaty, in which case they would be able to denounce it and rejoin the discussions.[57] The Germans seemed to have concluded the treaty in a mood of panic, Grigg wrote to Chamberlain, believing that arrangements being made by the Allies with Russia would ignore Germany's special difficulties in regard to Russian claims to reparations under article 116. 'Even so', he added, 'the stupidity of [their] action is unintelligible; only the Hun can do these things.'[58]

J. D. Gregory, who represented the Foreign Office within the British delegation, reported similarly that the whole situation had been 'transformed' by the Russo-German treaty.[59] Rex Leeper of the Northern Department of the Foreign Office minuted on Gregory's despatch that he had heard from a good source that the Russians and Germans had practically concluded, though not yet signed, a military convention which was believed to cover reciprocal assistance in the event of an attack by Poland. Curzon asked Gregory to investigate the matter further.[60] Gregory replied on 20 April that the rumours could not be confirmed, and questioned the authenticity of the source.[61] The Secret Intelligence Service, however, reported on

21 April that the French secret service believed that a secret military convention had indeed accompanied the treaty, and on 22 April the *Daily Mail* published what purported to be the text of such a convention.[62] The War Office reported to the Foreign Office on 21 April that, according to information supplied by its representatives in Berlin who in turn had received it from senior German officers, a military agreement had indeed been concluded.[63] Hodgson added from Moscow that he had been given the most authoritative assurances that the Russo-German agreement contained no clauses other than those which had been published. Conventions had however been concluded covering matters such as military and naval cooperation, and the 'general tendency', Hodgson concluded, was 'certainly towards closer relations with Germany'.[64]

Lord d'Abernon, in Berlin, visited von Haniel, Under-Secretary of State at the Auswärtiges Amt, on 26 April 1922, and showed him a copy of the *Daily Mail* allegations. After consultation with the head of the Russian department, von Haniel assured the ambassador formally that the subject of military cooperation had never been mentioned in the negotiations that had taken place with the Russians, and that the Russians had made no proposal of the kind indicated. D'Abernon pointed out that clauses similar to those published by the *Daily Mail* had been proposed by the Soviet government in other treaties they had concluded, notably that with Czechoslovakia. Von Haniel, however, maintained his denial, and showed d'Abernon a copy of a statement in which Krupps had officially denied the existence of a contract for the construction of an arms factory in Russia.[65] D'Abernon himself was generally sceptical of the possibility of a close military understanding or a substantial increase in trade between the two countries, and in a series of further reports he sought both to explain the German delegation's conduct and to explore the implications of their action. The treaty had been signed in a panic, he wrote to London on 23 April, the German delegates finding themselves isolated and imagining non-existent dangers.[66] His own confidence in Wirth and Rathenau had not been shaken, despite the conclusion of the treaty; provided close liaison was maintained with them they would 'run straight enough'.[67] It was a misconception to suppose that any dominant section in Germany really wanted to cooperate closely with the Bolsheviks or to form an alliance with them, the ambassador wrote to Curzon on 24 April. For different reasons all the parties (other than a few extremists) feared them, and the public too was generally hostile. He thought no extravagant deductions as to the future should be drawn from the treaty; it was a warning, rather than a revelation.[68]

D'Abernon's comments were received with no great sympathy in London. Sir William Tyrrell, Assistant Under-Secretary of State at the Foreign Office, suggested in a note to Curzon on 24 April that d'Abernon had seriously underestimated the importance of the Rapallo Treaty. It seemed to Tyrrell himself the most important event that had taken place since the armistice. It would weaken the ability of the French to impose sanctions upon Germany; the Poles would be forced to keep up their military preparations, and economic recovery would be further delayed.[69] Leeper similarly believed that d'Abernon had failed to appreciate the real importance of the treaty, or indeed to warn London that something of this kind was imminent. Whether there was a secret military convention or not, Germany and Russia had been thrown into each other's arms; and if the French looked like marching into the Ruhr to enforce sanctions upon Germany, the Russians would probably make threatening moves towards Poland and the Little Entente would appeal to Paris for protection. Curzon added that he did not know whether to be more surprised by d'Abernon's apparently casual attitude towards the treaty or by the 'cynical duplicity' of the German government. All the great continental powers, he believed, were now 'relapsing into the deepest slime of pre-war treachery and intrigue'.[70] The only benefit, he remarked to the French ambassador, was that everyone, including Lloyd George, had now been taught a lesson.[71] The press was equally outraged. The treaty had come as a 'bomshell', wrote *The Times* in a reasonably representative report; it had been a studied insult to the conference, a 'stab in the back', and the Allies had been 'duped'.[72] Keynes wrote rather more temperately in the *Manchester Guardian* that the Germans undoubtedly had excuses for the conclusion of the treaty, but that did not justify the signing of such a document without prior notification of the other powers.[73]

Opinion in Paris was even more outraged. Writing to Barthou on 18 April, Poincaré described the treaty as a defiance of all loyal collaboration, which had evidently been prepared over a long period and whose published articles were unlikely to be the only ones it contained. It was also an audacious violation of at least two articles of the Treaty of Versailles, and it diminished the guarantees that had been given in regard to the payment of reparations. On the Russian side it represented an attempt to put pressure upon the Allies, and was a clear violation of the Cannes conditions and of the Anglo-French agreement at Boulogne. A government meeting would be held in the very near future to consider the matter further. Poincaré's own view was that a joint Allied protest should be sent to the delegations concerned; if not, the French delegation should declare that it was impossible to continue to take part in the work of the conference without referring to its government for instructions.[74] Poincaré wrote to Barthou again on 19 April after the French Cabinet had met. He conveyed the government's view that the Russo-German treaty created a new and 'extremely grave' political situation in Europe, and instructed Barthou to yield no point of the French position as it had been set out in the memorandum of 31 January 1922. If discussions with the Soviet delegates continued, the government counted upon Barthou to maintain the French position even 'at the risk of a rupture, which opinion [here] would certainly prefer to any kind of capitulation'.[75]

Barthou sent Poincaré the text of the Allied note of protest on 18 April.[76] The note, Poincaré complained the following day, should have made reference to the violations of the treaty of Versailles, and it should have rebuked the Soviet delegates for their part in the affair. If Lloyd George and Schanzer persisted in seeking an accord with the Russians at all costs, the French parliament would probably have to be recalled.[77] Speaking to the Italian ambassador on 20 April, Poincaré, evidently under strong parliamentary and public pressure, went so far as to insist that the treaty must be annulled. The agreement, he thought, was 'insignificant in itself', but it was likely to have been associated with a politico-military accord.[78] Charles Laurent, from Berlin, wrote to Poincaré on 21 April to point out that the German secret service had for a long time been in contact with Moscow and that military contacts had already been established. A few days later he was prepared to state that a formal military agreement had probably been concluded between the Russian and German governments, or at least between the Soviet government and German industrialists.[79] A secret report of a meeting of the RCP Central Committee to discuss the Rapallo treaty, which was sent to Poincaré by the French minister in Riga, noted that Zinoviev had not denied the existence of military clauses attached to the treaty; he had argued rather that the treaty would compel Poland and Romania to abandon their attacks upon Soviet territory, and that it could anyway be repudiated.[80] Saint-Aulaire reported to the same effect from London.[81] A purported military convention between the Soviet and German general staffs, dated 3 April 1922, was in fact published in early May by the Brussels paper *Nation Belge* and by *L'Eclair* in Paris; the authenticity of the document was immediately denied,[82] but similar information was received from Berlin emigre, Latvian and other sources.[83] Individual reports were often of doubtful authenticity, but it was difficult in Allied capitals, despite persistent German denials, to believe that some sort of Russo-German military understanding had not been concluded or was not at least under active consideration.

At Genoa itself Lloyd George held a press conference on 20 April 1922 at which he insisted that the conference was still going strong, despite the difficulties it had encountered, and that the Russo-German incident had been 'satisfactorily disposed of'.[84] Poincaré, however, still believed that the Allied response to the treaty had been insufficient. Writing to President Millerand on 20 April, he complained that the Allied note had been 'much too feeble for French public opinion' and that it had 'even produced, by its excessive moderation, a very profound reaction in all parliamentary circles'. The French premier believed it would be dangerous to allow Germany's violation of the Treaty of Versailles to pass without protest, by France alone if necessary.[85] On 21 April, accordingly, Barthou wrote to Facta, as chairman of the conference, to complain that the text of the German reply to the Allied note, a version of which had been given to the press by Rathenau, was entirely unacceptable. The German delegation, he pointed out, had presented the Rapallo treaty as a legitimate act; the French delegation, on the contrary, believed that it violated the Cannes conditions, to speak of no other formal engagements of the German government, and that it also destroyed the spirit of mutual confidence which was indispensable for the development of international cooperation, and which it was the object of the conference to establish. He urged Facta to call a formal meeting of the heads of the delegations which had signed the Allied note at the earliest opportunity.[86]

The Allied meeting took place on the afternoon of 22 April 1922. The German reply of 21 April, defending the conclusion of the Rapallo Treaty and indicating the delegation's wish to include it within the framework of a more general settlement, had meanwhile been received.[87] The general tone of the German reply, Barthou complained, was 'intentionally disagreeable', and it contained a number of false assertions. It was untrue, for instance, that negotiations had taken place with the Russians without German participation; there had only been semi-official conversations, intended to prepare the way for a subsequent agreement, and it had clearly been understood that all final decisions would have to be made by the first commission and by the conference as a whole. Lloyd George agreed that the German letter was inaccurate in these respects, but he doubted if the falsehoods were intentional. It was eventually agreed to consider a draft Allied reply to the German note at a meeting of the sub-committee of the first commission the following day.[88] The Allied letter, which was adopted on 23 April, noted with satisfaction the Germans' agreement that, having made a separate treaty of their own with the Russians, they should take no part in the continuing discussions towards a more general agreement with the Soviet delegation. The signatories, the note went on, also wished to correct a number of misstatements in the German reply. In their dealings with Allied representatives the German delegates had not suggested that the experts' report provided no basis for further consideration by the conference, nor had they indicated that a separate treaty with the Russians was about to be concluded. There had, in fact, been no danger that the Germans would be confronted with a previously agreed scheme for the resumption of relations with Russia without the opportunity to discuss it further; misunderstandings of this kind could in any case provide no justification for the action that the German delegation had taken, which was entirely contrary to the spirit of loyal cooperation which was essential to the restoration of Europe. They now regarded the incident as closed.[89]

The implications of the Rapallo Treaty have reverberated down subsequent decades and have generated a substantial academic literature of their own.[90] Its direct contribution to events, in particular to the development of economic relations between the two countries, was perhaps rather less than its symbolic importance, as an indirect attack upon the Versailles settlement and a model for what later became known as 'peaceful coexistence'; but in both respects the treaty probably disappointed both the hopes of its supporters and the fears of its opponents. German–Soviet trade developed steadily, but by the end of the 1920s it still fell far short of the massive volumes of pre-war years; and both French and British diplomatic sources, later in 1922, indicated that the initial enthusi-

asm aroused by the treaty had been replaced by disappointment and
pessimism as the limited opportunities provided by the Russian
market became apparent and as the monopoly of foreign trade
remained intact (German traders, d'Abernon reported, had found
that their Soviet counterparts were 'jews in making a contract, and
Russians in carrying a contract out').[91] There was no greater
rapprochement in political or diplomatic terms as Stresemann's
government continued the policy of 'fulfilment' of the Versailles
treaty, joining the other western powers in 1925 in the Locarno Pact
and entering the League of Nations a year later. For the moment,
however, the crisis had been overcome; there was no German reply to
the Allied note of 23 April, and the conference was able, although
without German participation, to return to the central issues of
East–West relations with which it had previously been concerned. It
soon became apparent that the Russians, who had undertaken to
consult their government further at the end of the discussions in the
Villa d'Albertis, were prepared to move at least some distance to
accommodate the Allies' pressure. Their response, and the negotiations that followed it, were the matters to which the remainder of
the conference was devoted.

8

Closing stages

The Allied initiative of 15 April 1922 had in fact been shrewdly judged. After consultation with Moscow, Chicherin returned to the discussions with a more accommodating response. He saw Wise on 19 April and gave a verbal outline of the Soviet reply,[1] and then on 20 April, together with Litvinov and Krasin, he brought the draft reply to Lloyd George's private residence. The Soviet note, Lloyd George commented, was unacceptable in a number of respects: war debts would have to be 'written down' rather than 'written off', and there would have to be some provision for the restitution of private property or for an appropriate form of compensation. It was essential, the prime minister pointed out, to get the City of London to support them; otherwise credits would not be forthcoming. He understood the delegation's political difficulties; all that was asked for, however, was that compensation should be paid if restitution was impossible. This would not interfere with the principles upon which the Soviet system was based. Apart from the United States, there were three countries in which a Russian loan could be raised. The first was Britain, where government guarantees for foreign trade and exports were available. Belgium, a very rich country with no war debts and flourishing industries, would certainly assist, and perhaps also France, provided some method of restitution or compensation was agreed. The more countries that were involved, the less the loan would cost. Chicherin replied that the subject of restitution of property or compensation had been left out because the prime minister had indicated that it was to be reserved for future discussion. They would be very sorry to break on a small point, but nationalisation was a point of principle to which the Russian people were firmly committed, and on which the delegation's instructions were very clear.

Some slight modifications were made to the letter following more detailed discussions with Worthington-Evans, and the Soviet delegation then took their leave.[2]

The Soviet reply of 20 April, as amended, was distributed to the other delegates the following day. The letter began by remarking that Russia's present economic position and the circumstances that were responsible for it should justify the release of Russia from all Allied claims in return for the abandonment of the Russian counterclaims. In order to make some contribution towards a satisfactory settlement, however, the delegation were prepared to accept points 1, 2 and 3(a) of the Allies' proposals; in other words, they would accept that the Allied creditor governments represented at the conference could acknowledge no liabilities towards the Soviet government and that no allowance could be made in respect of the claims of private citizens, although in view of Russia's economic situation the country's war debts would be written down and some part of the arrears remitted. Not only war debts, however, but interest payments on all debts would have to be written down, and adequate financial help would be necessary to assist Russia to recover from her present economic state in the shortest possible time. Foreign economic assistance, the delegation maintained, was 'absolutely essential' for the economic reconstruction of their country, and if there was no prospect of such assistance there would be little point in the delegation assuming obligations it would be unable to discharge. On the question of nationalised property, the other element in the Allies' proposals of 15 April, the Soviet government would be prepared to give former owners the use of their property, or where this was impossible to satisfy legitimate claims either by mutual agreement or in accordance with arrangements which could be determined at a later stage. The Soviet government would also be unable to admit any liability for the obligations of its predecessors until it had secured full *de jure* recognition from the other powers. The delegation hoped that this response would provide a sufficient basis for the resumption of negotiations.[3]

The Russian reply was considered at an informal meeting of members of the sub-committee of the first commission on the morning of 21 April 1922. Lloyd George began by remarking that there was a good deal in the Russian reply which could not be accepted, and a good deal that required further explanation. Further inquiry was particularly necessary on the question of compensation and on the terms of the proposed *de jure* recognition. He thought himself, however, that the document as it stood did not justify a rupture in the negotiations, and he suggested that a committee of experts be appointed to examine it more closely together with a number of experts from the Soviet delegation. Barthou more cautiously agreed that the Russian reply was not such as to justify a breaking off of the negotiations, but he disagreed about the proposed procedure, suggesting that the Allied experts should meet together beforehand to determine their response. He also insisted on reserving the French position with regard to *de jure* recognition. The five inviting powers thereupon nominated an expert each; experts were also appointed by the Romanian and Dutch delegations to represent the Little Entente and the neutrals respectively. The experts, it was agreed, should not engage in general discussion, but should simply indicate the points on which there was disagreement and those on which further clarification was required.[4] These areas of disagreement and the procedure for resolving them were considered further at a meeting of the sub-committee the same afternoon with Chicherin in attendance. The Soviet foreign minister accepted the establishment of a committee of experts for a further consideration of the Russian reply; the composition of the committee was also agreed, and its first meeting was set for the following morning, Saturday 22 April 1922.[5]

The British representative, Sir Laming Worthington-Evans, took the chair at the meeting of the committee of experts; France was represented by Seydoux, Italy by Giannini, and Russia by Rakovsky, assisted by Litvinov, Krasin and Rudzutak. Rakovsky began by remarking that the text of the Russian reply which had been circulated the previous day contained an error; all war debts and interest payments were to be annulled, rather than simply reduced (as Chicherin's letter to Lloyd George had originally provided).[6] At a further meeting later the same day Seydoux, for the French delegation, objected to a memorandum that had been made available by the Soviet delegates earlier in the day which, he believed, reopened matters already settled, particularly the Cannes conditions. So great was the importance of this document that he would have to withdraw from the proceedings until further instructions had been received from the French government.[7] The Soviet memorandum, dated 20 April 1922, was certainly a more uncompromising document than Chicherin's letter of the same date. Commenting on the London experts' report, the memorandum charged that, despite the Cannes conditions, it represented nothing less than the 'complete enslavement of the Russian working people by foreign capital', while completely ignoring the means by which the Russian economy was to be revived. Faced by the huge task of European economic reconstruction, the memorandum argued, the claims of private citizens, however legitimate, should take second place. The economic restoration of Russia in particular required a substantial long-term loan from the other European powers, the necessary security for which could be provided only if the Soviet government was recognised *de jure*.[8] Rakovsky, however, explained to Worthington-Evans that the document had set out the Soviet delegation's reply to the London experts' report, and that it had been superseded by Chicherin's letter of 20 April. It was agreed that the memorandum should be disregarded.[9]

The committee of experts held a further meeting the following day, Sunday 23 April 1922. Worthington-Evans, who again presided, suggested that the committee might best proceed by discussing the London experts' report, article by article; Rakovsky, for the Soviet delegation, argued that debts could not be considered before the Soviet delegates knew what financial assistance would be made available by foreign governments, as distinct from private citizens. They also wanted to know if the Soviet government was going to be granted full *de jure* recognition. After some procedural wrangling, it was eventually agreed that the Soviet delegates could reserve their position on each of the articles of the experts' report, which would nonetheless be taken as the basis of discussion. Rakovsky continued to insist that war debts and interest must be cancelled, not simply written down; there was some discussion, however, as to whether municipal and other debts contracted during the war were to be placed in the same category, whether charities were to be considered on the same basis as public utilities, and by what means compensation was to be determined.[10] At a further meeting the following day Rakovsky presented the Soviet delegation's counter-proposals to articles 1–7 of the London experts' report, and expanded upon various points in response to the queries of other delegates.[11] The Soviet counter-proposals, dated 24 April 1922, accepted the financial obligations of the Russian imperial government towards foreign states and their nationals which had been contracted before 1 August 1914, provided that immediate and adequate financial assistance and full diplomatic recognition were extended to the Soviet government.

The obligations of local authorities and public utilities would be recognised upon the same basis. Foreigners would be granted the use of their former property, or, where this was not possible, priority in obtaining a concession or lease to the property concerned. All arrears of interest on war debts would however have to be cancelled, and the payment of interest on other debts would have to be postponed for several years.[12]

The Soviet proposals were considered by the other members of the committee of experts later the same day and again on the following day, 25 April 1922. It was agreed that the Soviet proposals as they stood were unacceptable, and that a document containing the Allies' minimum conditions should be presented to them.[13] The political work of the conference was 'rather stuck' at the moment, Hankey wrote to Austen Chamberlain, although he believed they were now 'in a position to start on the real business'. The 'real difficulty', he added, was that there was a 'clash of fundamental principle. We, of the West, simply cannot deal with people who don't recognise their debts, and who sequestrate private property. The Russians of the East have as their slogan sequestration without compensation. Their delegates probably fear their throats will be cut if they break their principles. Statesmanship has not had an easy task to reconcile these two principles. So great, however, is the need for the Russians and so ingenious is the Prime Minister, that I cannot but think that some way will be found by which business can be done without raising the question of principle too acutely.'[14]

Despite Hankey's optimism, Allied unity was in fact already beginning to crumble. Poincaré, writing to Barthou on 21 April 1922, pointed out that the Soviet memorandum of 20 April, if accepted as a basis for discussion, appeared to include a number of principles which the French government could not accept: that Russian war debts should be reduced independently of a general settlement of such matters; that interest payments on all debts should be reduced; that Russia should receive financial support from the French budget; and that *de jure* recognition of the Soviet government should precede that government's recognition of its debts.[15] On 23 April he wrote again to inform Barthou that French public opinion was 'very anxious' about the conference, and that he had conveyed these views to the Italian ambassador.[16] The French premier added that he could not himself leave France for the time being, but if Barthou could visit Paris the following week the government would be able to discuss the situation with him in more detail.[17] Barthou, in reply, urged Poincaré not to judge the conference by the articles of 'Pertinax' and others in the French press, which were often inaccurate.[18] Poincaré's attitude was in fact influenced, not simply by the French press, but also by the reports he was receiving that Lloyd George's position was less than secure within the British delegation. He had been informed by Leslie Urquhart, the president of the Association of British Creditors of Russia, that Lloyd George's policy was not acceptable to the members of his Association. Horne and Lloyd-Greame were also believed to take a different view from that of the prime minister, and Horne in particular was believed to be totally opposed to a bill that Lloyd George intended to introduce to provide for a state loan to Russia.[19] Most of the French press, the Belgian ambassador in Paris reported, were in fact in favour of breaking off the conference at this point.[20]

Poincaré made his misgivings public in a speech to the Conseil Général de la Meuse at Bar-le-Duc on 24 April 1922. The French premier began by referring to the Rapallo Treaty, which, he pointed out, made it impossible for France to disarm as rapidly as she might have wished. French public opinion, he added, would have found it entirely natural if the conference had been dissolved after the treaty had been published; the Allies, however, had shown studied moderation in their response. Germany, he went on, had not really been disarmed, and the German authorities appeared to be unwilling to pay France the reparations that were due to her. If this proved to be the case the French government would be prepared to take whatever action was necessary to enforce payment, together with the other Allies or even independently, as the Versailles treaty permitted them to do. Nor would the French delegation remain at the conference if any further concessions were made to the Soviet or German representatives.[21] It had been a 'strong, not to say violent' speech, Sir Maurice Cheetham reported to the Foreign Office from the British embassy in Paris, and yet it appeared to have been well received by French public opinion.[22] With a few exceptions, he added, all sections of the press, with 'remarkable unanimity', condemned the attitude the British government had been taking at the conference.[23] The new firmness of the French government was soon apparent at Genoa itself. On 25 April Seydoux reported at a meeting of the committee of experts that, following instructions from Paris, the French delegation could no longer support the Allied proposals of 15

April under which Russian war debts could be written down in exchange for Russia's withdrawal of her counterclaims;[24] the following day Poincaré telegraphed Barthou to urge him to resist Lloyd George's reported insinuations of French bad faith and to prepare if necessary to leave the conference.[25]

On 26 April 1922 Barthou met Lloyd George to consider more closely the situation arising from Poincaré's speech. Barthou thought Lloyd George might have provoked Poincaré by a speech he had made the previous Sunday, 23 April, in which the prime minister had said that Britain must proceed along the path of peace, if necessary in opposition to the views of chauvinists of all countries. His remarks had been taken as directed against France. Lloyd George disputed this view, but agreed to make a statement at an early opportunity on the need for a closer understanding with France. He pointed out, however, that Poincaré had apparently committed himself to taking action against Germany, if necessary without the Allies, in order to enforce the payment of reparations. Could he not have consulted the other Allies before making such a speech? Barthou, in reply, suggested that Poincaré had in fact been operating upon the assumption of Allied support in maintaining the peace treaties and enforcing the payment of reparations, but he undertook to convey Lloyd George's views to the French premier. Poincaré, Lloyd George went on, had also indicated that the French delegation would withdraw from the conference if French policies did not prevail. He suggested, with Barthou's agreement, that there should be a meeting of the signatories of the Treaty of Versailles to consider the issues that might arise in the event of German non-payment of the next instalment of reparations, due on 31 May.[26] Barthou, Hankey reported to Austen Chamberlain, was a 'decent fellow, and I think really anxious to help matters along'. Poincaré, however, had 'deluged him with telegrams and injunctions'.[27] A lunch between the prime minister and Barthou had been a 'great success', Barthou being 'extremely frank about the difficulties imposed upon him by Paris'; his remarks about his relations with the French government on 26 April had in fact been so frank that he had asked that no notes be taken of them. The difficulties between Barthou and Paris were nonetheless the source of much delay.[28]

The Allies' draft ultimatum to the Soviet delegates was considered further at a series of meetings of the first commission and of individual delegations. Lloyd George explained to Barthou, at their meeting on 26 April, that his aim was to avoid bringing the Russians and Germans still closer together and to keep the restoration of Russia in the hands of the other powers, and at the same time to go as far as possible to accommodate the Russians so that a break, if it came, would appear to be the responsibility of the Soviet delegation not only in the West but also in Russia itself. Barthou expressed general agreement with these sentiments, although it would be impossible, he believed, to concede *de jure* recognition before the Cannes conditions had been accepted and implemented, as the Soviet delegation had been demanding. Worthington-Evans then read out a British draft of the proposed memorandum to the Russians, incorporating a writing down of Russian war debts by 50 per cent and also an undertaking to refrain from subversive propaganda in other states. It was agreed that the draft should be discussed further by representatives of both countries and the same afternoon.[29] The British draft was also discussed by an informal inter-Allied meeting on the evening of 26 April. Seydoux, for the French delegation, raised objections to the proposed moratorium on interest payments; this would require the agreement of French bondholders, he insisted, and the French government could not act without their permission. The French delegates also objected to the proposal to substitute leases for freehold property in Russia. M. Cattier, the Belgian delegate, pointed out that on the continent, unlike Britain, there was only one recognised form of property, and that to substitute leases for freehold could not be done without serious implications for the whole notion of private property, in their own countries as well as Russia.[30]

The discussion continued on 27 April 1922, first between British, Belgian and Italian representatives, and then between British, Italian and Japanese delegates.[31] A formal meeting of the subcommittee of the first commission followed on 28 April, at which both a British and French draft of the proposed Allied communication were considered. The French draft, unlike the British, did not provide specifically for the reduction of war debts; it provided for a moratorium on interest payments only after negotiations had taken place with the bondholders; and it took a very much more uncompromising position on the restitution of nationalised property. Schanzer remarked that the French draft represented a step backwards as compared with the Allied note of 15 April; Barthou replied that the Soviet–German treaty had altered the basis of their earlier understanding, so that France could no longer be bound by it, and he drew attention to Rakovsky's provocative presentation of the Soviet viewpoint at the meeting of the committee of experts on 24 April. Lloyd George observed that it was a question, at bottom, of whether they sincerely wanted to reach an agreement with the Soviet government or not. He also deplored the withdrawal of concessions that had earlier been agreed, in particular that Russian war debts should be reduced and that interest payments should be remitted. The French draft, unlike the British, also gave little attention to the economic assistance that could be offered to the Soviet government, and there were several references to the needs of Russia that were unnecessarily provocative.[32]

An attempt was made to reconcile the British and French viewpoints by the establishment of a small drafting committee, and this formed the basis of renewed discussions at a further meeting on 29 April 1922. The Polish, Japanese and Swedish representatives present indicated what their governments could offer towards the economic restoration of Russia, and there was an extended discussion of the related issues of propaganda, frontiers, public and private debts, and *de jure* recognition.[33] Barthou, for the French delegation, continued to insist that no reduction of war debts could be considered, although various means might be found of easing the burden of repayments. Lloyd George, supported by the Italians, maintained that the principle of reduction in war debts had been presented to the Russians as an Allied proposal and could not now be withdrawn.[34] At a further meeting on 1 May the Belgian delegate, Jaspar, raised additional difficulties by insisting upon the principle of restoration of nationalised property wherever this was physically possible, not simply the principle of restoration or compensation. This, Schanzer remarked, was hardly consistent with the Cannes conditions, which had allowed compensation as an alternative to restitution.[35] Further discussions dealt with arrangements for arbitration and judicial reform.[36] At a final meeting on 2 May the text of the Allied memorandum was approved, the French delegates abstaining until Barthou (who had returned to Paris) had been able to discuss the matter with the French government. The Belgians also withheld their support, their proposals concerning the restitution of private property having found no support among the other delegations.[37]

The Allied memorandum of 2 May 1922, endorsed by the representatives of Italy, Britain, Japan, Poland, Romania, Switzerland

and Sweden, was despatched to the Soviet delegates the same evening. The memorandum began by assuring the Russian delegates of the other powers' concern that their country's economy should be restored and with it a genuine peace throughout the continent. The prosperity of Russia, however, could not be restored without the capital and commercial experience of the West; and western capital and experience, in turn, would not be available until the necessary guarantees of security had been established and debts had been recognised. Western governments could also help, either through the international corporation, or else through loans and credits to private traders who wished to do business with Russia or to settle there. The Soviet government, for its part, would be required to refrain from propaganda or other actions subversive of the established order in foreign states. It would also have to recognise all public debts and obligations contracted by itself or its predecessors (although no repayment of capital or interest would be demanded for the time being), and it would be required to recognise the claims of foreign nationals. The financial obligations of all municipal authorities and public utilities would also have to be acknowledged. A separate agreement was to be concluded between the Soviet government and foreign bondholders covering the repayment of interest and of the bonds themselves, although account would be taken of Russia's economic condition and of her need for economic reconstruction. In the event of disagreement a mixed arbitral commission would adjudicate the claims involved.

So far as private property was concerned, the memorandum went on, the Soviet government would be required, without prejudice to its rights under the Cannes conditions, to restore it or to compensate foreign claimants for any loss or damage they might have suffered through the confiscation or withholding of their property. Where the foreign owner was not enabled to resume possession of the property concerned, an offer of compensation would have to be made, any disagreements on which would be referred to a mixed arbitral commission. Provision would also have to be made for foreign nationals to enforce their claims against individual Soviet citizens. Compensation would be awarded in the form of new 5 per cent bonds, the terms for the payment of interest and amortisation of which would be the same as for existing bonds, as determined by the mixed arbitral commission. In the interests of the most rapid possible resumption of new and existing undertakings by foreign nationals, all necessary measures would have to be taken by the Soviet government to ensure the protection of the person, the property and the labour of foreigners. Further arrangements were to be made to cover the liquidation of pre-war contracts between Russian nationals and foreigners and the Romanian valuables held by the Soviet government.[38] All now depended, Hankey wrote to Curzon, on the reply the Russians gave to the Allied memorandum. At times it had needed great optimism to see the possibility of a successful conclusion to the conference; personally, however, he had 'never lost hope', and he put the 'odds at 5 to 3 on a settlement of some sort'. There seemed to be 'some possibility of an acceptance', he wrote to Chamberlain two days later.[39]

Not simply, however, had the French and Belgian positions hardened since the discussions in the Villa d'Albertis; perhaps more crucially, the Soviet position had also become less accommodating since Chicherin's letter of 20 April. The Soviet delegation, it emerged, was in fact a less than united one, both in relation to Chicherin's *démarche* and in other respects. There were differences, for instance, about whether the delegation should attend a reception given by the King of Italy; the senior Soviet delegates were in favour of doing so, describing the occasion as a 'capitulation to us by monarchy', but Rudzutak and some other delegates, according to an intercepted telegram, were against it.[40] Reports by the Italian police, who followed the delegation's movements with close attention if not always skill or discretion, also indicated that there were differences among the Soviet delegates. Preobrazhensky, they reported, had the personal trust of Lenin and had taken up an extreme 'left' position within the delegation, supported by Litvinov; Vorovsky and some other delegates, however, appeared to have taken a much more moderate line. Chicherin was attempting to manoeuvre between these two extremes.[41] Other reports suggested that Rakovsky was also one of the delegation's more intransigent members and that he and other delegates were constantly in touch with Moscow and with Lenin personally.[42] Further police reports spoke of 'strong disagreements' and 'lively discussions' between the two tendencies in the delegation, representing a policy of conciliation and intransigence respectively.[43] According to other sources, Preobrazhensky was in fact attending the conference to keep an eye on the senior Soviet diplomats, who were not entirely trusted by the party authorities; and there were reported to be rivalries between Chicherin and

Litvinov, the latter apparently aspiring to Chicherin's job and willing to conspire with the French and other delegations in order to obtain it.[44]

Lenin, in a telegram of 19 April to Chicherin and L. S. Sosnovsky (the editor of the peasant paper *Bednota*), had already expressed concern about the delegation's position at Genoa. 'All the information from Genoa', he wrote, 'shows that we are being taken in by deception.' Lloyd George, by his attacks on France, was in fact concealing his main objective, which was to force the Soviet government to repay foreign debts and private debts in particular. This effort must be systematically exposed in the Soviet and foreign communist press.[45] Two days later he urged Chicherin to resist the recognition of private debts at all costs, even if it meant the breakdown of the conference.[46] A majority of the members of the Soviet delegation in fact regarded Chicherin's amended letter of 20 April as a violation of party directives, and on 22 April Rudzutak reported their misgivings in a telegram to Narkomindel in Moscow.[47] Lenin, responding to the telegram in a letter to Stalin and other members of the Politburo, remarked that Chicherin had either made or was about to make an undoubted mistake and to depart from Central Committee directives. His mistake was that, obtaining very little of value in return, he might surrender their only basic means of explaining the breakdown of the conference: that the Soviet delegates had refused to restore the private property of foreign capitalists.[48] On 25 April a telegram was sent to Chicherin and the delegation generally endorsing the objections of Rudzutak and urging that no concessions be made on this crucial issue. Chicherin had been advised of the maximum that could be permitted, and no further retreat could be contemplated. If no agreement was possible on this basis the conference should be allowed to collapse, leaving Soviet diplomats with two points of departure for future negotiations: the Russo-German treaty, and their refusal to restore the private property of foreign capitalists.[49]

On 30 April Lenin renewed his warnings. Chicherin had conveyed Krasin's belief that the conference had ceased to make progress and that significant departures from Central Committee directives would be necessary if an agreement and a major foreign loan were to be secured. Krasin had suggested in this connection that pre-war debts should be recognised, but without interest payments, and that compensation should be paid to former foreign owners, the sums involved being covered by a loan which in turn would be secured by the issuing of bonds to the foreign owners concerned. The Soviet government would also have to be given a *de jure* recognition and economic assistance. Chicherin himself added that the Allies would grant economic assistance of this kind only after the Soviet government had agreed to compensate all the former owners.[50] Lenin, in reply, insisted that a reconvened conference at a later stage would not be disadvantageous from the Soviet point of view, and he urged the delegation to resist any financial obligations and even partial recognition of the Russian debts. Krasin's arguments in particular were 'absolutely wrong and unacceptable'.[51] Litvinov had also indicated in telegrams to Moscow that a western loan was unlikely to be obtained unless there had been some agreement to compensate the former owners, and that the Allies would refuse even to discuss such an arrangement unless private claims had been recognised.[52] Ioffe, in telegrams of 1 and 2 May, suggested that financial compensation could be paid, without conceding the right to expropriate private property, by issuing Soviet state bonds which would mature over a ten-year period.[53]

Lenin, in response to what he described as the 'unspeakable shameful and *dangerous* vacillations of Chicherin and *Litvinov* (not to speak of Krasin)',[54] obtained Politburo approval for a telegram to the delegation on 2 May 1922 which insisted that they maintain their refusal to restore private property and agree to concessions only on condition that a satisfactory loan was obtained. In the event of the slightest hesitation, he warned, Chicherin would be publicly disowned and relieved of his responsibilities. Three members of the delegation, Lenin added, should be sent to attend the forthcoming session of the Central Executive Committee; Chicherin should stay in Germany after the conference and have a good rest. The Politburo decided to remove the reference to disavowal, but otherwise approved Lenin's draft, and added in conclusion that the party 'categorically insisted on the fulfilment of this directive'.[55] The Allied memorandum of 2 May, Lenin complained three days later, must be unequivocally rejected, although the delegation might make cautious overtones towards Italy individually.[56] The general unacceptability of the Allied memorandum, he wrote to Litvinov on 8 May, appeared to offer a suitable opportunity to break off the conference, which was bound to collapse in any case.[57] The Russo-German treaty, he wrote to Chicherin, should serve as the only model of an international agreement acceptable to the Soviet government.[58] Chicherin, in a letter to Facta of 28 April complaining about the delay in the resumption of negotiations with the other powers, in turn advised the conference chairman that if the western powers were no longer prepared to regard his letter of 20 April as a basis for continuing their discussions, the Soviet delegation would for its part have to withdraw the concessions set out in the letter and would revert to the position set out in the Soviet memorandum of the same date.[59]

Despite Facta's conciliatory reply,[60] the Soviet delegation's response to the Allied memorandum was a much more uncompromising document than Chicherin's earlier communication. The Russian memorandum, which was distributed on 11 May, began by regretting that the Allied proposals of 2 May had represented a step backwards from the basis of agreement that had earlier been envisaged, and even from the London experts' report. Their detailed proposals for the economic restoration of Russia, the memorandum went on, and thereby of Europe generally, had not even been discussed. Many foreign capitalists had already begun to invest in Russia despite the fact that no agreement had yet been reached on the recognition of debts. Far more important, the memorandum suggested, were the guarantees that the Soviet government could give for the future, and the international consolidation that would result from the *de jure* recognition of the Soviet government by the other powers. There were precedents among the states represented at the conference for the repudiation of debts and the nationalisation of the property of foreign citizens, yet they had not led to the same ostracism to which the Soviet government had been subjected. The interests of the bondholders and former owners themselves were hardly the explanation; much more to the point were the political objectives of the powers represented at the conference, which were seeking, in Soviet Russia, to defeat collectivism and to defend the interests of capitalist individualism. Unilateral demands in regard to propaganda, the support of revolutionary movements in other countries and relations with Romania and Turkey provided evidence of this.

More generally, the memorandum continued, governments which emerged from revolutions carried with them new juridicial relations and could not be bound by the obligations of their predecessors. The French revolutionary government, and that of the United States, had followed this principle. Nor did revolution, akin in this respect to *force majeure*, confer any right to indemnity upon those who had suffered from it. The Soviet government, in a spirit of conciliation, was nonetheless prepared to accept liability for pre-war public debts, provided that its counterclaims were recognised. The counterclaims would in turn be renounced if a number of concessions were made by the other powers, the most important of which was that a substantial loan should be made available to the Soviet government. The Allied memorandum provided no satisfactory response on this, and deferred the question of a moratorium and the cancellation of interest on pre-war debts to an arbitral commission. Any arrangement of this kind as between two forms of property would place Soviet sovereignty in jeopardy and could not possibly be accepted. The Soviet government would, however, be prepared to grant previous owners a preferential right to their former property either in the form of a lease or share in a mixed company or in some other manner. The Soviet government was still prepared, the memorandum concluded, to make important concessions with a view to achieving an agreement, but only on condition that the other powers made concessions of comparable significance. The negotiations that had taken place did appear to open the way to a *rapprochement* between Russia and the western powers; the differences that had arisen in the resolution of their financial claims against each other should not prevent a measure of agreement being reached on the other matters with which the conference was concerned, especially the economic reconstruction of Russia and the consolidation of peace in Europe.[61]

Relations between the principal Allied powers had meanwhile deteriorated further. French public opinion, already hostile to the conference, was not reassured by reports at the beginning of May that a separate Soviet–British agreement was in prospect and that the Soviet delegation had reached an understanding with British, Dutch, Belgian and German oil interests giving them a monopoly of the production and sale of Russian oil and extensive leases in the areas of Baku and Grozny.[62] Reports from the French delegation itself suggested that the British were definitely contemplating the *de jure* recognition of the Soviet government if the Allied memorandum of 2 May was accepted.[63] The representatives of former French interests in Russia and the main French economic associations had already written to complain about the provisions of the Allied memorandum in respect of private property, which, they maintained, effectively gave the Soviet government the right to confiscate the property of foreign nationals in return for bonds of very little value.[64] Barthou, who arrived in Paris on 3 May, gave the Cabinet an account of the state of negotiations at Genoa later the same day. The government was unanimous in instructing the delegation not to adhere to the Allied memorandum of 2 May unless the Belgian delegation did likewise, even if this meant not acting jointly with the British delegation.[65] Poincaré informed Barrère in addition of a variety of more detailed objections to the Allied memorandum, which he should seek to incorporate if the discussions proceeded further.[66] The French government did agree to support the pact of non-aggression already under consideration at Genoa, but only if French rights under the Treaty of Versailles were not affected; French liberty of action in relation to the recognition of the Soviet government must also be entirely reserved.[67]

On 5 May 1922 Poincaré set out these new guidelines in a set of revised instructions to the French delegation at Genoa and secured formal government approval for them. If, the instructions began, Lloyd George agreed to insert a clause on private property into the Allied memorandum which satisfied the Belgians, and if they could therefore resume negotiations, it would be essential to ensure as a minimum that the conditions put to the Soviet government allowed for no discussion or modification of the Cannes conditions or of the principles set out in the French memorandum of 31 January, which had been approved by the Chamber of Deputies. The French delegates were to enter no further negotiations unless the Belgians were present, and were to remain associated with the Belgians in the defence of private property. The proposed non-aggression pact was of interest only if the Soviet delegation signed it; it would then require amendment so as, for instance, to exclude any reference to disarmament, which was properly the responsibility of the League of Nations. French rights under the Treaty of Versailles must also remain unaffected. No decision could be made and no document could be signed in any case without further consultation with the French government.[68] Hardinge, disgusted by these manoeuvres, wrote to Curzon on 5 May describing Poincaré as a 'dirty dog, a man of very mean character'; he had made no friendly gesture towards Britain but had rather done his best, and 'very successfully', to destroy the Entente which it had taken so many years to establish. Hardinge had met Barthou that morning and had remarked that he appeared to have got on well with Lloyd George; Barthou had replied that he 'got on much too well with him for Poincaré, but mind you do not tell him so'. Curzon, in reply, remarked how tired he was of the continuing crisis in relations with France, and added that he wished Poincaré, with his meticulous lawyer's brain, was 'at the bottom of the sea for ever'.[69]

Barthou returned to Genoa on 6 May 1922 and met Lloyd George the same afternoon. The atmosphere in Paris, he explained to the prime minister, had been very anxious; the Soviet–German treaty had aroused great emotion, and there were fears of mobilisation or even war. Public opinion had also been very impressed by the Belgian stand on the issue of private property. He thought himself, however, that it would not be impossible to find a formula which would satisfy the Russians and which would also be acceptable to France and Belgium, as well as to the other Allies. Lloyd George replied that the Soviet delegates were in any case likely to reject the terms that had been put to them, in which case the issue would not arise. Krasin, whom the prime minister had seen the previous day and who was more anxious to come to an agreement than the other Soviet delegates, had been very gloomy and had held out little hope of a settlement. Public demonstrations in Moscow on 1 May appeared to have impressed the Soviet delegates, who would otherwise have been more inclined to seek an understanding with the other powers. Barthou remarked that if the conference failed, the greater part of French public opinion would still regard it as a misfortune. Lloyd George observed that the implications of a failure for Franco-British relations would be serious: the French, a nation of small proprietors, had been thinking of their property, while the British, an industrial nation, had been thinking of trade and business. There was 'no use in concealing', the prime minister remarked, 'that this might prove a turning-point in Anglo-French relations'.[70] Grigg, writing to Austen Chamberlain on 7 May, remarked that Barthou appeared to have thrown in his lot with Poincaré for the time being; the atmosphere at the meeting, Hankey added, had been one of 'great depression and sadness'.[71]

Nor was this the only area in which the prime minister's proposals had been losing ground. The international corporation, for instance, the *deus ex machina* which was supposed to undertake the practical side of the economic restoration of Russia and eastern Europe, had scarcely advanced beyond the broad agreement in principle that had been concluded earlier in the year. A meeting of the consortium's

Organising Committee was held at Genoa on 29 April 1922. Eighteen countries were represented, the French as observers. The representatives present reported the sums they proposed to make available to the corporation; the secretary of the Organising Committee in London was to be notified thirty days after the conference had concluded as to whether the countries concerned would definitely participate in its operations.[72] Lord Inverforth, who presided over the meeting on behalf of the British delegation, informed Sir Robert Horne subsequently that the provisional agreement of the previous February had largely been confirmed, and that the meeting itself had been 'unanimous and friendly'.[73] Matters, however, proceeded little further. The French expressed reservations about the composition of the corporation's new executive committee, and observed that parliamentary approval and a Treasury guarantee would be needed before the necessary capital for the French corporation could be subscribed. A period of thirty days for a definitive decision was in any case manifestly too short.[74] B. H. Binder, the secretary of the Organising Committee, explained on 3 July that it had been decided that the thirty-day period should begin after the conclusion of the Hague Conference, to which the Genoa Conference had agreed to transfer its unfinished business. Rather later, however, he wrote to inform the governments concerned that the consortium was not after all to be established; the Organising Committee was to be dissolved and unspent cash balances would be returned (because of exchange rate fluctuations the French in fact received back more than they had originally subscribed).[75]

Rather more serious, from Lloyd George's point of view, was the increasing discontent in Britain among his Cabinet colleagues. Indeed, the King himself was among those who were expressing misgivings about the course the negotiations at Genoa appeared to be taking. As Horne put it to Worthington-Evans on 23 April 1922, the King was 'very anxious about all we are doing at Genoa' and was strongly of the view that the Soviet delegates should be pressed to give definite assurances on the matter of propaganda.[76] Churchill, predictably, was also concerned; Sir Philip Sassoon found him lying in bed with bruised ribs but '*fulminating* against Genoa' and insisting that there was 'seething public indignation' about the matter.[77] Sassoon himself thought that parliamentary and public opinion was rather one of irritation and impatience with the position the French delegates had been adopting.[78] Austen Chamberlain wrote to

Hankey to remind him that any aid for Russia would have to conform with the conditions of the Trade Facilities Act, most of the credit available under which had already been allocated.[79] Curzon wrote to Hardinge to express his concern about the trend of discussions at Genoa; the prime minister, he remarked, meant to have some sort of agreement at any price with those 'pestilential ruffians from Moscow'.[80] Chamberlain also wrote to Worthington-Evans to urge 'great caution' upon the prime minister. In the atmosphere of the conference there was a danger that he might lose touch with British domestic opinion. Chamberlain was particularly concerned about the premier's treatment of the issue of private property; public opinion, he pointed out, would not support him in obtaining compensation in the form of bonds of little value if the French and Belgians were opposed to such a settlement.[81] He repeated his worries in a further telegram of 4 May to the other British ministers at Genoa.[82]

The British delegation itself had differing views about some of these issues, in particular the question of credits for the Soviet government. Lloyd George, supported by Worthington-Evans, was anxious to provide them; Horne and Lloyd-Greame, however, took the view that they could do no more than extend the same terms that were available to other countries under the Trade Facilities Act and other legislation. They were supported by the Lord Chancellor, Lord Birkenhead, who had paid a brief visit to the conference. The prime minister, Lloyd-Greame wrote to his wife, was 'so anxious to settle that it makes him lose all sense of proportion in relation to domestic politics – particularly our [Unionist] party'.[83] Lloyd-Greame himself favoured a special allocation of capital, he wrote to Baldwin, but it should not be offered on terms different from those of existing schemes, other than perhaps in an extension of the period of repayment.[84] The clause on private property in the Allied memorandum of 2 May, Lloyd George pointed out to Chamberlain, had in fact been approved by the Association of British Creditors of Russia and by other representatives of the business and financial world.[85] Chamberlain replied on 9 May that the president of the Association of British Chambers of Commerce had obtained the support of his committee for the article on private property, but there was concern lest its provisions be diluted in any way. Chamberlain added that this clause was the 'absolute minimum acceptable here' and that it must on no account be weakened.[86] The negotiations with Soviet Russia were not popular with their supporters, he wrote to Lloyd George on

10 May, but he felt the prime minister would be on safe ground if he retained the support of Urquhart's association and of the Chambers of Commerce. Public opinion, however, would not understand a break with France for the sake of Russia.[87]

The scope for an agreement had thus decreased substantially by the time Lloyd George and Schanzer met to consider what they both agreed to be a 'bad document', the Russian memorandum of 11 May. The Soviet government's political difficulties, Lloyd George believed, had made it impossible for them to accept the Allied proposals of 2 May. Other governments also faced political difficulties of some sort. What Lloyd George suggested was that a memorandum should be prepared which would begin by reaffirming the Cannes conditions, and then delegate the matters of credits, debts and private property for further investigation to separate commissions which the conference itself would appoint. The prime minister had already outlined a scheme of this kind to the British empire delegation on 10 May.[88] There should also be a pact of non-aggression which should remain in operation for as long as the commissions continued their deliberations. Individual governments might make their own separate arrangements in the meantime, as the Italian government, for instance, clearly wished to do.[89] Barthou, who met Lloyd George and Schanzer later the same day, also agreed that the Soviet reply was a bad one. It was in fact a 'very clever propagandist document and very dangerous'. Any agreement with the Russians was not 'quite impossible'. Schanzer pointed out that the Russian reply did, at least, appear to hold out the prospect of further discussions along the lines that Lloyd George had indicated, and he thought such a proposal could hardly be rejected out of hand.[90] Lloyd George discussed the proposal further with representatives of the neutral and Little Entente powers, and again with the Italian delegation the following day, 12 May.[91]

A formal meeting to consider the Allies' reply to the Soviet memorandum was held on 13 May 1922. Barthou had meanwhile been instructed by Poincaré not to associate himself with an Allied reply and to reserve the full liberty of action of the French government in relation to any further meeting with Soviet representatives; he was also urged to resist the conclusion of a pact of non-aggression, as this would weaken the French right to impose sanctions upon Germany under the provisions of the Versailles treaty.[92] Lloyd George, who opened the Allied discussion, thought it generally agreed that the

Soviet reply had been a provocative and unsatisfactory one. A complete rupture should, however, be avoided, as it would deprive the starving Russian people of hope and reopen the floodgates of war and anarchy. In the end, if they were to obtain the economic assistance they clearly needed, the Soviet authorities would have to acknowledge their debts and restore nationalised private property or at least provide satisfactory compensation for it. He suggested that the most important matters remaining at issue – debts, private property and credits – should be remitted to a commission or commissions for further investigation. These commissions would have Soviet participation. In the meantime there should be a pact of non-aggression and a collective understanding to refrain from propaganda subversive of the established order in other countries. Barthou was doubtful if an agreement on these issues would be possible after further discussion, the Russians having shown little inclination to compromise at Genoa, and France could certainly not be associated with such a proposal. Schanzer, however, thought that five weeks was not a very long time in which to resolve the serious matters with which the conference had been confronted. If they really wanted to achieve results, months and months of negotiation would be necessary. The Italian government, at least, favoured Lloyd George's suggestion.[93]

Discussion continued later the same day and over the two following days in an attempt to reconcile the French and British positions and to clarify the points that still remained at issue. It was eventually agreed that the proposed commissions should meet at The Hague, and that they should begin their work on 15 June (the Soviet delegates would be invited to join them on 20 June). The United States government should also be invited to participate. The proposed invitation to the Soviet government did not, however, imply *de jure* recognition, which would not be accorded until a final agreement had been reached. The list of countries to be invited to The Hague was also agreed; Germany, having made a separate agreement with the Russians, was to be excluded. The French and Belgian delegations, which had not endorsed the Allied memorandum of 2 May, explained that they would be unable to take part in the presentation of these proposals to the Soviet delegation, but undertook to recommend them to their own governments. The Japanese delegates expressed their particular concern that the pact of non-aggression should not be held to apply to the Japanese troops in eastern Siberia, where they were engaged (it was represented) in tasks of a purely defensive nature.[94] These proposals were discussed further with the Soviet delegation on 16 May. Chicherin queried the exclusion of Germany, since matters not covered by the Rapallo Treaty were to be discussed, and drew attention to the absence of any reference to *de jure* recognition. There was also a vigorous exchange of views with Viscount Ishii on the subject of the Japanese troops in Siberia and the status of the Soviet Far Eastern Republic.[95] Chicherin protested at the manner in which the proposals had been prepared and objected to the choice of The Hague as a location, as the Soviet government had not established even *de facto* relations with its Dutch counterpart. These matters notwithstanding, the Soviet government would nonetheless be willing to participate.[96]

These agreements were duly ratified by the third and final plenary session of the conference, which took place on 19 May 1922. The resolutions prepared by the economic commission were adopted, those of the financial and transport commissions having been adopted on 3 May, and discussion then moved to the report of the political commission. Schanzer, who presided, began by reviewing the commission's discussion of the Russian question, and then explained the proposal to resume negotiations with the Soviet delegates on debts, private property and credits at The Hague. A pact of non-aggression, based on the existing status quo, was also proposed, which, although temporary, might ultimately contribute towards the conclusion of a firmer and more general peace settlement. The proposal to continue discussion at The Hague was formally accepted by M. Plantin of the Dutch delegation, and the resolutions were then endorsed by the Soviet, British and other delegations. The French and Belgian delegations reserved their positions but undertook to recommend the adoption of the resolutions to their governments. Lloyd George, in a more general contribution, called the conference 'one of the most remarkable ever held in the history of the world'. He thanked the Italian government and people for their skilful guidance of the conference and for their hospitality. The work of the financial, economic and transport commissions alone, he believed, would have justified the conference's existence. The real excitement, however, had centred upon the issue of the relations between Soviet Russia and the outside world. Considerable progress had been made in this connection and he hoped that further progress would be made at The Hague, particularly if the Soviet delegation avoided offending the susceptibilities of the other powers as its memorandum of 11 May had done. The prime minister had a word of advice for anyone who was trying to obtain credits: they should not, in their application, enter upon an elaborate defence of the doctrine of the repudiation of debts.

Barthou, who followed the British premier, associated himself with Lloyd George's remarks concerning the Italian government and its hospitality. Great progress, he believed, had been made at the conference. The French government had every intention of putting its resolutions into effect, and of strengthening a genuine European peace. Chicherin, for the Soviet delegation, did not attempt to disguise the fact that the conference had not realised the great hopes that it had aroused among the peoples of all nations; this was partly, he thought, because certain questions, such as disarmament, had been excluded from its proceedings, and partly because the nations represented, despite the Cannes conditions, had not in fact been treated upon an equal basis. Debts must indeed be repaid, but damages for unprovoked attack had also to be taken into account. Despite these differences, the conference, he thought, would be a 'milestone of the greatest significance along the road to peace'. Facta, who replied to the debate, thanked the delegates for their kind words for the Italian government and people, and affirmed that remarkable results had been obtained in a relatively short period of time. Even in the difficult area of relations between Russia and the outside world some measure of agreement had been achieved, and the issues on which disagreement still remained had been defined more precisely. Although no final agreement had been reached, the continuation of their labours at The Hague would, he believed, allow them ultimately to come to a complete and satisfactory solution of the problems that still remained before them. On this the conference concluded.[97]

9

Genoa and after

The conference and its achievements were subject to a close scrutiny in press, parliamentary and political circles over the months that followed. It was impossible to disguise the fact that its direct results had been distinctly modest, at least when set against the aspirations of those who had inspired it. Even Lloyd George, addressing the British House of Commons on 25 May 1922, was unable to go so far as to pronounce the conference a success. It had been probably the largest gathering of nations that had ever assembled in the history of the world, he told the House, and despite their previous differences, the thirty-four nations represented had met in perfect calm and in perfect harmony. Their aim had been to restore financial and trade relations, to improve diplomatic contacts, and to remove the disputes which were threatening the peace of Europe. The problem that had aroused the most controversy in this connection had been the Russian question. There were three possible courses of action in relation to Russia, the prime minister suggested. The first of these, force, had been tried and failed, and had not been suggested at Genoa by even the most anti-Soviet delegations. Another possibility was to leave Russia to her own devices until a more acceptable form of government had emerged, and to ignore her vast and destitute population. The third possibility was what Lloyd George called the 'Pitt policy', in other words that abhorrence of the principles on which a foreign government might stand should not preclude relations with it and thereby with the people over whom it ruled. The prime minister and the Dominions had all favoured some attempt to establish relations of this kind with the Soviet government, allowing the conditions of life of the Russian population to be alleviated, facilitating the revival of international trade on which many millions depended for their livelihood, and reducing the risk of political instability throughout the continent.

What means could be found, the prime minister asked, to bring the Russians' need to purchase and the West's need to produce into association? Large-scale revolutions, he pointed out, always carried with them the confiscation of property without compensation; this had been true of both the English religious revolution and the French revolution, where the land had been confiscated without any attempt to compensate. Russia, however, unlike France, was seeking credits from the other powers, and these would be forthcoming only if the necessary confidence was created. The Soviet leaders, if not their followers, knew this well. The cancellation of interest and some reduction of their outstanding debt appeared to raise no insuperable difficulties of principle. The Russian counterclaims were quite unacceptable in general terms; there was however no doubt that damage had been caused by the civil war, and this could be taken into account in considering the Soviet government's liabilities. The question of private property had been more complicated. Property in countries like Czechoslovakia and Romania had been confiscated with a minimum of compensation; complaints had been received from British nationals about this, but the government had been unable to intervene. The third Cannes condition had stated that, in such cases, the government concerned must either restore the property concerned or else provide satisfactory compensation. There had been no disagreement between Britain and France about this; the Belgians, however, had insisted that property must be restored if this was materially possible. This went beyond the Cannes conditions and had prompted the Russians to issue their memorandum of 11 May, which had retracted some earlier concessions.

A great struggle was taking place in Russia, Lloyd George believed, between the 'practical statesmen of the Soviet system' and 'extreme theorists'. Theorists were unfortunately unable to realise the difference between a logical proposition and a business one, such as the question of raising credits. Before 1 May they had been having a businesslike discussion on matters such as debts, bonds and interest; afterwards, however, the Soviet delegates had 'nailed their flag to that barren fig tree of Communism under which millions are dying of pestilence'. The vast majority of properties could in fact be restored, as the Russians were unable to run them themselves; for the rest, they were prepared to consider compensation in some form, such as concessions or bonds. All these questions would be discussed further at The Hague, where the prime minister was 'very hopeful that when we come to an examination of the practical details, something may be achieved'. A pact of peace had meanwhile been concluded among the nations represented at the conference, which he hoped might ultimately become a more formal and permanent arrangement. Lloyd George was not prepared to say that the conference had achieved all its objectives, but it had at least 'accomplished great things already'. If it failed, the consequences for Europe and the world generally would be tragic.[1]

Domestic commentary on the prime minister's achievements was generally unsympathetic. Asquith, who replied to Lloyd George's statement in the House of Commons for the Liberals, complained that the results of the conference had been 'depressingly and even distressingly meagre'. The pact of peace, its one substantial achievement, was in practice of little value, as Germany was excluded from it.[2] J. R. Clynes, for the Labour party, welcomed the conference's aspirations but pointed out that no solution could be achieved so long as the Versailles treaty was regarded as sacrosanct.[3] Press comment was equally unfavourable. The Genoa Conference, declared *The Times*, had just 'crumbled away, without any definite conclusions, without any conspicuous achievements'. It had been a 'painful object lesson in the way not to do things'. The conference might have achieved something if it had dissipated the 'unfortunate illusions' in which its origins and procedure had been enshrouded. There was now a clear need, the paper thought, for the entente with France to be revived and consolidated, and for relations with the United States to be improved.[4] *The Economist* thought the conference 'almost entirely barren of results, except for the Russo-German Treaty, which is, if anything, a retrograde step'.[5] The *Glasgow Herald*, more temperately, remarked that solid achievements had been recorded in fields other than the political, which by themselves would have justified the holding of the conference. So far as relations with Russia were concerned, Lloyd George had simply failed to achieve the impossible.[6]

The results of the conference were considered at some length in a debate in the French Chamber on 1 June 1922. Marcel Cachin, a Communist deputy and editor of *L'Humanité*, pointed out in opening the debate that the French revolution itself had led to the expropriation of private property, as had occurred in Russia. Poincaré, in reply, explained the French government's reservations about the conference and outlined the discussions that had taken place with the British and other governments with a view to limiting its scope. He had not gone to the conference himself because it had been necessary for him to be in Paris while President Millerand was in North Africa. The delegation had in any case received detailed instructions, to which he had had every confidence they would loyally adhere at all stages of the conference's proceedings. He paid tribute to the extent to which the delegation had in fact done so. If the conference had not in the end produced the results for which some had hoped, this was no the fault of France. The transport and economic committees had, he thought, achieved some useful results. The Rapallo Treaty, however, appeared to be in contradiction with the Treaty of Versailles, which the Allies were pledged at all costs to uphold. The French delegation had at the time urged stronger measures than Germany's expulsion from the first (political) commission, but Poincaré did not now regret that the delegation had taken no more extreme steps. It could, for instance, have left the conference, but it would have been isolated in doing so and would have been criticised for its lack of patience and good faith. The French delegation, rather, had done everything possible to prevent the failure of the conference, which had in the end been due to the extreme nature of the Soviet government's demands. The French government was not bound by the conference's final decisions, and had not undertaken to send delegates to The Hague.[7] His gloomy verdict on the conference was generally shared by other deputies and by the French press.[8]

Among the minor and neutral powers opinions were more varied. Henri Jaspar, for instance, the Belgian foreign minister, was personally opposed to the policies Lloyd George was pursuing, but he yielded to no one in his admiration of the prime minister's performance. Lloyd George's talents, flexibility, persuasiveness and authority, Jaspar told the French ambassador, had given him a preeminence at the conference which could not be challenged. He had influenced the minor powers and the neutrals, had a high standing among the journalists, and was popular with the Italian public. His departure from Genoa station had been 'triumphal, the departure of a sovereign'.[9] Addressing the Belgian parliament on 23 May 1922, Jaspar emphasised that although the achievements on finance, economic and transport matters contained little that was new, they nonetheless represented a programme for the alleviation of the

economic distress of Europe which it was now the duty of governments to implement. The Rapallo Treaty was to blame if the conference's political discussions had been less successful.[10] The Dutch
foreign minister Van Karnebeek also emphasised that the conference's achievements were not to be measured in terms of its final
resolutions; other and important results had been achieved, such as a
greater awareness of the dangerous tensions in Europe and the
non-aggression pact.[11] Edward Beneš, addressing the Czech parliament, argued that the conference had been premature and insufficiently prepared, and thought it would have been better if it had
been postponed, as the French had originally suggested. Yet he, like
others, had to admire the 'persistence, breadth of vision and optimism' with which Lloyd George had attempted to overcome the
various obstacles they had encountered. The conference, he thought,
was the first sign that an international community of nations was
coming into existence after the war, and it had brought Russia out of
her previous isolation and clarified many of the difficulties of re-
establishing relations between the Soviet government and its foreign
counterparts.[12]

Italian opinion, perhaps predictably, was still more inclined to
argue that the conference had been a success. Addressing the
Chamber of Deputies on 7 June 1922, Schanzer drew attention to the
rapprochement between Russia and the other European nations that
had taken place, and to the closer understanding that had developed
between Italy and the other governments represented at the conference. The Italian delegation had followed the policies that the Italian
government had followed since the war, in other words a policy
which sought peace and the re-establishment of confidence among
nations so that a greater degree of economic cooperation between
them could take place. Genoa, he admitted, 'could not work mira-
cles', but it had opened the way to further and more favourable
developments in European politics. In particular, the basis of an
agreement between Russia and the West had been 'solidly laid'. It
was also wrong to underestimate the message of peace to the nations
of Europe which was represented by the pact of non-aggression. By
'universal consent', Schanzer concluded, the Italian delegation at
Genoa had rendered a major service to Europe and to the cause of
peace.[13] The government's policy statement was approved by a large
majority, and press commentary on its position was generally favourable.[14] The *Corriere della Sera*, for instance, drew particular attention

to the 'italobritannic intimacy' which had been apparent at all stages of the conference's proceedings, and which had served both as the foundation of the conference and as an example to other nations.[15] Technically, the paper conceded, the conference had made limited progress, but politically and morally a great deal had been achieved. Italian opinion appeared generally to agree that the conference had been a definite if limited success, and that the international standing of the country had been substantially enhanced.[16]

German responses to the conference were understandably concerned above all with the Rapallo Treaty as well as with the achievements of the conference more generally. Rathenau, interviewed in the *Daily Mail* after the conference had concluded, thought that Genoa would be useful if it served as the prelude to a series of similar gatherings. At least five such conferences had been found necessary to re-establish the political order in Europe after the Napoleonic wars. The Genoa Conference, Rathenau thought, would rank in history beside the Congress of Vienna; its main result had been the recognition that international indebtedness was a single problem which could be dealt with only on an international basis.[17] Speaking to the foreign affairs commission in the Reichstag on 28 May 1922, the foreign minister again characterised the Rapallo Treaty as a treaty of peace, or even friendship, which did not obstruct but rather facilitated a more general understanding between Russia and the western powers. It might also offer economic opportunities for German businessmen, at least in the longer term. The conference had in the end been unable to resolve the differences with which it had been confronted; the first steps, however, had been taken towards a satisfactory settlement, and even if the Hague conference concluded with less than a complete agreement, the restoration of relations between East and West would nonetheless continue and Russia would again be included among the nations which were taking part in trading and other economic activities with other nations. For Germany the unspoken but near-universal recognition that the reparations question had still to be resolved, and that it was intimately connected with the economic restoration of the continent generally, had been particularly welcome. Friendly relations on a personal level had also been re-established with the other European nations, with the single exception of France.[18]

Wirth, addressing the Reichstag itself, argued that the idea of the conference had been 'bold, great and noble', but perhaps too ambitious to be realised in the atmosphere that still existed in Europe and in the world generally. Its value had been reduced by the non-participation of the United States, and by the exclusion from formal discussion (although not from private conversation) of such subjects as reparations. It had been a 'singular and great advance', however, for Germany to appear at an international conference on the same basis as the other powers. The German delegation had sought a general European understanding; the western powers, unfortunately, had constituted, if not a Supreme Council, then at least a union of the inviting powers from which Germany had been excluded. This grouping had conducted negotiations with the Russians directly, with no guarantee that German interests would be safeguarded, and the German delegates had accordingly had no alternative but themselves to negotiate with the Russians and eventually to conclude an agreement. Wirth believed the Rapallo Treaty, despite much ill-informed commentary, was in fact an honourable and genuine, even exemplary, peace treaty, which liquidated the consequences of war on both sides and might serve as a model of relations between East and West for other nations as well. Reports of a secret military convention were described as 'evil-minded slander'. The conference's own achievements had been 'small and modest', but an 'important step forward' had nonetheless been taken.[19] The Rapallo Treaty was duly ratified by the Reichstag on 4 July 1922, and in November 1922 its provisions were extended to the other Soviet republics.[20]

Reactions to the conference in Moscow were perhaps the most favourable of all. In part this reflected the fact that the Soviet delegates, on their first extended visit to an international conference in the capitalist world, had been received with great interest and sympathy both within the conference and more particularly outside it. Rakovsky, for instance, used the opportunity provided by the conference to give a series of lectures on current developments in Russia under the guise of informing journalist about the intentions of the Soviet delegation. The lectures had to be transferred from a hotel room to a large hall in the university, so great was the demand to attend them.[21] Chicherin, according to contemporary reports, met with 'loud ovations' on the street and in other public places. Even fascists were reported to take a friendly attitude towards the Soviet delegates.[22] According to other reports, the appearance of the Soviet delegates on the screen in cinemas, even in the 'most fashionable, smart cinemas where a far more democratic public was represented', met with great approval: the 'whole audience, to a man, rose in their seats and unitedly applauded', while the appearance of the French representatives led to a 'deafening whistle'.[23] The Soviet delegates were heard in the conference itself with great attention. Ernest Hemingway, who reported the proceedings for the *Toronto Daily Star*, noted that when Chicherin was speaking not a sound could be heard except the 'chink of the mass of decorations on an Italian general's chest as he shifted from one foot to another'. The Russian secretaries were also 'far and away the best-looking girls in the conference hall'.[24] 'Approved below, feted above, received by prelates and felicitated by kings', wrote a contemporary French observer, 'Chicherin sits enthroned and reigns.'[25]

More important, from the Soviet point of view, was the fact that the delegation had secured considerable advantages from the conference but made very few concessions in return. Although the delegation, as Preobrazhensky put it, had 'made a mistake' in accepting an 'elastic formula' on compensation in Chicherin's letter of 20 April,[26] the concession had been retracted and in any case had not been invoked because of a hardening in the Allied position over the period that followed. Rudzutak, who returned to Moscow with two other members of the delegation to report to the Central Executive Committee, told the Bolshevik fraction of the CEC on 12 May that however the conference concluded, it had yielded definite advantages for the Soviet participants. European public opinion was becoming more favourable to them, and the German treaty had been concluded, with others to come.[27] Ioffe, who returned at the same time and who also reported to the CEC, drew particular attention to the enormous significance of the conference, not so much in terms of its decisions, but in its destruction of the Entente and its political isolation of France. The conference had also done much for the moral prestige of the Soviet government (the British agent in Moscow, R. M. Hodgson, who was sitting in the gallery, remarked that on the whole this was quite correct).[28] The following day the CEC adopted a resolution affirming that the delegation had 'correctly carried out its tasks', preserving the full independence and integrity of the RSFSR and repudiating foreign attempts to re-establish private property in Russia and to enslave Russian workers and peasants. The resolution particularly approved the conclusion of the Rapallo treaty with Germany and the attempt, albeit an unsuccessful one, to raise the issue of disarmament.[29]

Later reflections, after the conference had formally concluded and the other delegates had returned to Moscow, were generally similar in character. Krasin, for instance, interviewed in Berlin on his return journey by *Nakanune*, remarked that the conference had completely failed to deal with Russia, as the credits issue had not been seriously considered. So long, he declared, as the capitalist states regarded the credits question exclusively from the point of view of guaranteeing their own profits, the Soviet government would continue to conclude separate treaties, and if necessary rely on its own resources.[30] Lyubimov, in an interview with *Izvestiya*, drew attention to the peace pact, the treaty with Germany, the work of the financial commission and the 'high moral authority' of Soviet Russia at the conference.[31] Radek, writing in *Pravda* on the results of Genoa, emphasised some of the tactical advantages that had been gained, such as the emergence of serious differences between the United Kingdom and France.[32] Ivan Maisky, at this time an NKID press officer, argued that the Soviet government had in fact been recognised – for how otherwise could a month of negotiations with thirty-three other states be interpreted? – and hailed the Rapallo Treaty as an 'immense achievement' which would undoubtedly be followed by others.[33] There was less praise for Chicherin's personal performance; Trotsky was reported to have sent him a 'very sharp note' proposing that Radek should replace him as foreign minister, as he had not defended Soviet interests with sufficient determination at Genoa,[34] and Litvinov led the Soviet delegation to The Hague. The Foreign Affairs Commissariat, reviewing the developments of the year as a whole, commented that if 1921 had been the year of diplomatic recognition, 1922 had been the year of the 'entry of Soviet Russia into the world arena'. After Genoa, it added, it had become clear to all that no major international problem could be resolved without Soviet participation.[35]

The report devoted less attention to the Hague Conference, called to complete the business of the Genoa Conference, and in which a Soviet delegation also participated.[36] The Hague Conference's achievements were, indeed, if anything more modest than those of Genoa; it certainly failed to resolve the issues of debts, credits and private property with which the Genoa Conference had entrusted it. The United States government once again declined to participate; Japan and Germany were not invited; and an elaborate memorandum from Poincaré on the 'conditions which are necessary, in the opinion of the French government, in order that the meetings of the Experts at The Hague may lead to practical results' made it clear that French participation would be no more likely to contribute towards a solution than had been the case at Genoa.[37] The western powers met first of all by themselves, on 15 June 1922; the Soviet delegation arrived on 26 June, and negotiations between the two sides began two days later. Few powers, certainly not the Soviet government, appear to have had substantial expectations that the conference would resolve the differences that had not been dealt with at Genoa.[38] Discussions took place in three sub-committees, which dealt with property, debts and credits respectively. Once again the Soviet delegates argued that recognition and credits must be dealt with before any repayment of debts could be considered; the western delegates responded with the equally familiar line that only when debts had been recognised could recognition and credits be discussed. Credits, in any case, were to be essentially a matter for private citizens and not for governments, and the leasehold concessions that the Soviet delegates had offered were regarded as no substitute for restitution or compensation. The conference concluded on 20 July 1922 having achieved little more than a restatement of these familiar positions.

In the absence of a general agreement, either at Genoa or The Hague, Soviet–Western relations developed further on the largely bilateral basis for which the Rapallo Treaty had provided a precedent. Negotiations towards a bilateral Soviet–Italian treaty in fact began the day after the conference had terminated, on 20 May 1922.[39] Four days later a new Soviet–Italian commercial treaty had been concluded and signed, replacing and extending the provisional agreement of 26 December 1921. The treaty envisaged 'equitable and proportionate' compensation for private property which had been nationalised, and otherwise provided for most-favoured-nation treatment in relations between the two powers. A general agreement covering other matters was to be signed by the end of the year.[40] The Soviet government, however, did not ratify the treaty, as it did not provide for full *de jure* recognition, and relations between the two powers continued to be based upon the earlier agreement, whose validity was extended for this purpose. Soviet–Italian relations were fully restored only in February 1924 when Mussolini's government conferred full diplomatic recognition upon the Soviet government, shortly after a similar move by the newly formed Labour government in Britain.[41] A Soviet–Czech commercial agreement was also signed in Prague on 5 June 1922, shortly after the Genoa Conference had concluded, and was duly ratified later in the same month. Its basis had been worked out during the conference by Litvinov and Dr Vatslav Giess, one of the Czech delegates.[42] Under its provisions the two powers agreed to exchange diplomatic representatives and to make every effort to facilitate bilateral trade; other issues, such as claims for compensation and the restoration of rights, were reserved for subsequent discussion.[43]

Franco–Soviet relations had advanced little further by the end of the year, but an exploratory visit in September 1922 by Edouard Herriot, the Socialist mayor of Lyons, apparently with the tacit approval of the French government, indicated that even Poincaré might not be indifferent to the commercial and other advantages of a closer relationship with Moscow.[44] Full diplomatic recognition was eventually conferred upon the Soviet government by France in October 1924, after a new Socialist government headed by Herriot had come to power.[45] Soviet–German relations continued to develop along the lines that the Rapallo Treaty had foreshadowed, although not as rapidly as either its supporters or opponents had originally expected. A further trading agreement was signed in October 1925, and a more formal treaty of neutrality followed in April 1926; but relations between the two countries lost some of their intimacy when Maltzan left the foreign ministry to become German ambassador to the USA. Under the chancellorship of Gustav Stresemann and after, German policy was oriented more towards a closer relationship with the West than with the socialist East.[46] Only much later, in November 1933, were full diplomatic relations restored with the United States; the agreement concluded at that time provided for the resumption of normal relations between the two countries and for a variety of religious and legal matters, but specifically reserved the question of claims and debts for subsequent discussion, as the agreements with other countries had done.[47] The USSR itself, denied western economic assistance on terms the Soviet government could accept, turned inwards and by the late 1920s had come to place much greater emphasis upon internal issues and upon a strategy of economic development that relied primarily upon the development of indigenous resources.

The recognition agreements into which the USSR had entered by this time generally made specific provision (as the Rapallo Treaty had done) for the cessation of propaganda subversive of the established order in other countries. The agreement with Britain, for instance, bound both parties to 'refrain from hostile action or undertakings against the other' and from 'any official propaganda direct or indirect' against the institutions of the other party; and the exchange of notes with France made it clear that henceforward the principle of non-interference in internal affairs would be a 'rule, regulating relations between our two countries'.[48] In the case of the USA, Litvinov sent to President Roosevelt, at the same time as the re-establishment of diplomatic relations, a note formally assuring him that the Soviet government would 'respect scrupulously the indisputable right of the United States to order its own life within its own jurisdiction in its own way' and refrain from any sort of interference in the internal affairs of that country; in particular, a commitment was made to provide no direct or indirect assistance to any organisations liable in any way to disturb the prosperity or public order of the United States, or engaging in agitation and propaganda designed to bring about a change by force in the social or political order in the United States.[49] Warnings could be issued and expulsions could be ordered if it appeared that any of these provisions were being violated, and indeed diplomatic relations could be broken off altogether; they were, for instance, suspended by the British government in 1927, after a police raid on the Soviet trading mission 'Arcos' had produced a number of mildly inflammatory documents, and were restored again only in 1929 after a new Labour government had been elected. Surveillance of domestic communist movements, which in fact rarely posed a serious threat to western governments, was a further means by which the 'Soviet threat' could be controlled. Debts, private property and credits, however, the matters over which both Genoa and The Hague had foundered, were not so easily settled; the agreements on recognition generally reserved them for subsequent discussion, and these in turn made little progress. Many of the issues involved indeed remain unresolved up to the present time.

It is difficult in retrospect, therefore, to resist the conventional verdict that the Genoa Conference was 'a failure', at least in terms of its immediate results. Indeed, given the circumstances of the time, it is perhaps surprising that it made as much progress as it did. In part this was because of insufficient preparation, a matter to which the French government had repeatedly, although not always disinterestedly, drawn attention. Partly also it was a result of the generally low level of information among the western powers about developments in Soviet Russia, and about the Soviet government's likely position on international issues in particular. The British government could rely upon its Moscow agent, R. M. Hodgson, and the staff of his mission; the German government had an official trade representative in Russia under the terms of the May 1921 agreement; and the governments of most of the limitrophe states, such as Poland, Czechoslovakia and the Baltic states, were generally well informed about the state of affairs in their more powerful neighbour. Most other western governments, however, had few first-hand sources of information about Soviet developments, and the French government, in particular, had to rely almost exclusively upon reports, many of them of doubtful authenticity, that reached it from its representatives in Warsaw, Riga, Stockholm and Copenhagen. Few western newspapers at this time had permanent correspondents or even regular visiting correspondents in Moscow, which might have repaired some of these deficiencies. The result was that the Soviet willingness to compromise was generally exaggerated, or seen as no more than a matter of persuading a few extreme theorists, and the extent of the changes introduced by the revolution was seriously underestimated.

The method of work that the conference adopted was a further source of difficulties. Lloyd George had hoped to use the conference to mobilise world, or at least European, public opinion towards the tasks of economic reconstruction and political stabilisation. The methods that were adopted, however, aroused considerable resentment, particularly the practice of discussing the most important questions in private sessions among the great powers, leading to accusations of 'Supreme Council methods'. The diaries of the Dutch foreign minister Van Karnebeek, for instance, contain repeated criticisms of the management of the conference by a small clique who took little notice of outsiders, and of meetings which were effectively 'gatherings of the Supreme Council with a few other states around it'.[50] In a very large conference there were obviously reasons for attempting to accelerate agreement by bringing the larger powers together for preliminary consultations. The exclusion or marginalisation of other powers, however, had serious consequences for the work of the conference: the Rapallo Treaty was concluded, at least in part, because the Germans had not been party to the Allies' direct negotiations with the Russians, and the composition of the conference's committees was a constant source of disagreement. The practice of secret or informal meetings outside the conference's framework also encouraged the spread of rumours, some of them of a most unlikely kind. A report went round, for instance, to the effect that 'France had been beaten by Germany'. On what issue, however, remained unclear. It later emerged that a women's boxing match had been taking place at a music hall in Genoa, and that this had been the occasion for the defeat in question.[51] The large number of reporters present, about 700 in all, helped to give currency to rumours of this kind, particularly when (as was often the case) there was little of interest taking place in the conference's formal proceedings.

Beyond this again, few of the governments represented at Genoa – at least of the major powers – were in a position of sufficient strength to allow them to make substantial concessions or to take initiatives that might have broken the impasse. Lloyd George's own position was highly precarious, as the leader of a coalition government within which his own supporters were heavily outnumbered by Unionists, and he was widely suspected of promoting the conference in order to secure a quick but illusory triumph in the foreign policy field which would enable him to appeal to the electorate for a renewal of his mandate. His relations were particularly poor with the Foreign Office, which was virtually unrepresented in the British delegation at Genoa and which he tended in any case to bypass through the use of his own private secretaries and trusted intermediaries, such as E. F. Wise. The Italian government, also a coalition, had been formed with a great deal of difficulty in February 1922 and survived only until the following October. Its head, Luigi Facta, was described by the French minister in Rome as a 'man of the second rank, if not of the third', and by Barrère, one of the French delegates at Genoa, as 'in politics, what one calls a utility actor in the theatre'.[52] Schanzer, the foreign minister, aroused no more enthusiasm, and the government had little domestic authority. The French government was certainly a strong one and apparently close to its own domestic public opinion, but no love was lost between Poincaré and the head of the French delegation, Barthou, who appears to have nourished an ambition to succeed Poincaré as premier and who was therefore eager to seize any opportunity to undermine his position.[53] The German government, although not a central participant in the conference, was also a notably unstable one.

Perhaps most fundamentally of all, an agreement at Genoa was frustrated by the fact that the interests of the parties concerned were far from identical, not simply between Soviet Russia and the West but among the western powers themselves. Some powers, such as Britain and Italy, attached more importance to the development of trade and industry than did other powers, such as France. France and Belgium, on the other hand, were more concerned than other powers to defend the payment of debts and the rights of private property, in Soviet Russia and elsewhere; this reflected the fact that they held a high proportion of the total Russian debt and particularly of the debts due to private citizens, whose interests weighed more heavily in their domestic political processes. The question of Russian debt was in turn related to international indebtedness, in which the powers had again a variety of different interests. Britain, as a net creditor, could afford to take a reasonably flexible attitude towards the matter, but France, as the largest net debtor, had every reason to press for the full payment of what appeared to be her due from other nations. The German government could obtain no adjustment of its international indebtedness at Genoa, given the exclusion of the reparations issue, but it had an obvious interest in reaching a private agreement with the Soviet government to cover its liabilities under article 116 of the Versailles treaty. The United States, which, as the largest net creditor, could make the greatest potential contribution to the economic reconstruction of Europe and to the readjustment of debts, stood outside the conference framework altogether: a sharp contrast to the position of that country after the Second World War, when its support was basic to the reconstruction programme embodied in the Marshall Plan.

The conference, then, might have seemed doomed to failure from the outset, given these various circumstances; and yet this would be altogether too gloomy and determinist a view. In fact, in the exchanges of 15 and 20 April 1922, a substantial step had been taken towards the general agreement between Russia and the West that Lloyd George and his associates had been seeking. Helped, perhaps, by the 'conference atmosphere' to which many memoirs have drawn attention (and into which Lloyd George had wished to draw Poincaré and Lenin), the basis of an agreement had indeed begun to emerge. The issue of propaganda, it was generally accepted, was to be covered by bilateral agreements, and by the pact of non-aggression to which the conference eventually agreed at its final session. War debts and arrears of interest would be reduced, and repaid after a lengthy moratorium (it was in any case understood that the whole question of international debt had still to be resolved and that no government was likely to discharge its obligations in the near future). In return, the Russian counterclaims were to be dropped, and pre-war debts, both public and private, were to be recognised, provided adequate assistance was given to the Soviet government so that their repayment became a practical possibility. Former property-owners would have their property restored to them *de facto* in the form of long-term concessions, and the remainder (on some accounts, less than 10 per cent of the total)[54] would be covered by compensation either in bonds or in some other form. The Soviet government would meanwhile be given diplomatic recognition on a probationary basis, which would become definitive when the guarantees given had been seen to be observed. An agreement of this kind would have secured some recognition of Russia's wartime debts, which would otherwise remain repudiated, and it would also have secured the use of their property or at least substantial compensation for a variety of private claimants who would otherwise have obtained nothing.

In the end, as we have seen, it proved impossible to secure a general agreement upon this basis. Several issues proved particularly intractable. Perhaps most crucially, the Belgian insistence that private property must be restored where it was physically possible to do so was a principle quite unacceptable to the Soviet delegates and more far-reaching even than the Cannes conditions, which had spoken of restitution or compensation as equally valid alternatives. The French delegates, bound by their instructions to stand beside Belgium, accordingly withdrew their support from the Allied memorandum of 2 May. That memorandum, at the French delegates' insistence, had already incorporated more uncompromising terms on private property than the British delegation's original proposals, which the Soviet delegates (according, at least, to the German delegation) might in fact have accepted.[55] There were other difficulties as well. In particular, there was substantial opposition within the British delegation, and more especially within the Cabinet, to the kind of government guarantees of Russian credits that the Soviet delegates were seeking, and without which they argued there could be no serious prospect of an economic recovery which would enable them to repay their debts. The reduction of Russian war debts was also a particularly difficult proposition for the French to accept in the absence of a more general readjustment of inter-Allied debts, which was in any case an issue excluded from the conference agenda. The continental powers were generally less willing than Britain to accept restitution in the form of long-term concessions rather than the restoration of full ownership, and some former owners, particularly in France, had understandably little interest in the conversion of their rights into bonds whose value had still to be determined. The Soviet delegates, for their part, were divided on the wisdom of the offer of 20 April and in the end were compelled by Moscow to withdraw it.

The evidence suggests, then, that a Soviet–Western agreement at Genoa, although certainly not achieved, may not have been beyond conclusion had a series of largely circumstantial factors been different. It was at least the view of some of those most immediately concerned in the negotiations that a Soviet–Western agreement at this time was not inconceivable in principle, but simply premature. Sir Sydney Chapman, for instance, who had taken charge of the earlier inter-Allied discussions and was one of the British delegates at the conference, concluded later that Europe was simply 'not yet ready for what was being attempted', whether the Rapallo Treaty had been concluded or not. 'Circumstances', Chapman believed, 'were too strong for us.'[56] Maynard Keynes, who attended the conference as a journalist and met many of its leading participants, including Chicherin, had in fact specifically urged a closer Soviet–German understanding as early as 1919, in order that German organising power could be allowed to assist the restoration of normal food supplies in Russia and central Europe.[57] Keynes contributed a series of articles to the *Manchester Guardian* which were widely syndicated, suggesting a scheme for the stabilisation of European currencies and exchanges.[58] He also argued that it was in Britain's as well as the general interest to provide a substantial loan to Russia, although a majority in the government were understood to oppose it. The conference, Keynes suggested, was therefore probably premature.[59] He met Chicherin at Genoa on 13 April 1922, just after the conference had begun: 'the old boy is an amazing [*sic*] good diplomat, and I must say that I like him personally', Keynes wrote to Arthur Ransome a few days later.[60]

Keynes dealt specifically with the problem of Russian reconstruction in his article in the *Manchester Guardian* on 19 April 1922. He proposed that (i) Russian war debts should be set off against the Russian counterclaims; (ii) Russian pre-war debts should be recognised, but covered by the issue of new bonds bearing interest at 2½ per cent after five years (lending money to foreign governments, he commented, was always risky); (iii) the property of foreign nationals should where possible be restored upon a partnership of profit-sharing basis, cases of disagreement being covered by the issue of bonds to the full value of the property which would earn 5 per cent after five years (otherwise, he remarked, the former property-owners would get nothing at all); (iv) the Soviet government should be recognised *de jure*; and (v) it should also be accorded a substantial loan, both in order to achieve a general settlement and the economic reconstruction of Russia and so as to benefit the western powers themselves through the restoration of Russian agricultural exports at lower prices than those that were then prevailing. Keynes suggested that to start this revival the United Kingdom should grant the Soviet government a credit of £50 million over two years, which should be spent on British goods that could be used to promote agricultural production in Russia.[61]

Keynes had little sympathy with the Allied memorandum of 2 May. Export credit guarantees and other schemes, he pointed out, were quite insufficient by themselves to bring about an economic recovery in Russia, and *de jure* recognition of the Soviet government had not been mentioned. If no government credits were made available Chicherin would retire with dignity and many gains, and there would be more separate agreements in future years along the lines of the treaty that had been concluded with Germany.[62] Keynes complained that the Soviet–Western negotiations on debts and repayments had been a 'miserable repetition of reparations and inter-Allied debt', which there was in fact no prospect of repaying. The conference, he wrote later, had been successful in terms of propaganda and in bringing about a change of atmosphere, but not in drawing up a plan for economic reconstruction. It had been too preoccupied with formulas and diplomacy, and not enough with on-the-ground realities; its closest parallel, he thought, was the Councils of the early church. Keynes himself remained, as in later years, in favour of a public initiative to restore trade and to raise levels of employment and prosperity.[63] In the event, it took the economic slump of the late 1920s and 1930s and the dislocation of another world war before such an initiative, on the scale of the European continent as a whole, could be put into operation; and even then it was conceived as (or at least became) a means of resisting Soviet or communist influence, rather than as a framework within which East and West could cooperate to their mutual advantage.[64]

The contending approaches to East–West relations apparent at the time of the Genoa Conference have much in common with the various approaches to East–West relations that have been evident over subsequent decades. One approach, more intransigent and generally associated with parties of the right and with the interests of banking and finance, has generally emphasised a limited role for state initiative and lower levels of public spending in domestic affairs, and a firm or even confrontationist attitude towards the Soviet Union and the other communist countries internationally. Soviet-type systems are held, then as now, to lack popular legitimacy and support, to be founded upon economic principles which are irrational if not unworkable, and to be aggressive and dishonest by their very nature. The appropriate strategy, from this point of view, must be to decline to enter into closer economic or other relations with a power which can have no respect for the norms of international diplomacy, whose long-term viability is doubtful, and whose domestic resources are disproportionately devoted to military preparations which represent a serious and immediate threat to western interests. Another approach, associated more closely with parties of the left and with organised labour and manufacturing industry, has generally placed less emphasis upon the repayment of debts and the restitution of property and rather more upon the revival of trade and the raising of living standards and levels of employment. This approach, in turn, has generally interpreted Soviet international behaviour in terms of security rather than expansionism; it has generally accepted the legitimacy of international boundaries, if not of communist rule as such; and it has typically favoured the regulation of East–West differences by negotiation, in what has subsequently become known as detente.[65]

The Genoa Conference, in the end, may perhaps best be regarded as a paradigm case of this second approach to international affairs. It failed to resolve the issues by which it was confronted; but it failed, perhaps, less because of the inherent impossibility of the objectives that had been set before it and rather more because the political forces committed to achieve them were weaker than the political forces that opposed them. Over subsequent decades the balance of these political forces has varied, and a 'Genoa' approach in East–West relations has sometimes tended to gain ground rather than to lose it. The Nazi menace during the 1930s, for instance, led to attempts to develop collective security on an East–West basis, and the Second World War led to the formation of an East–West alliance which was ultimately responsible for the defeat of Hitler. In the late 1960s and early 1970s the development of West Germany's *Ostpolitik* and a greater awareness of the threat to all nations represented by atomic weapons led to the full flowering of detente, and to formal East–West agreements such as the Final Act of the Helsinki Conference on Security and Cooperation in Europe, which was signed in 1975. These ideas in turn lost ground during the later 1970s and early 1980s as several western countries, particularly Britain and the USA, came under the influence of politicians of a more conservative disposition and with a generally more intransigent attitude towards the USSR and the other communist countries.[66] By the mid-1980s some moderation of these earlier attitudes was already discernible, at least in western Europe. The immediate objectives of the Genoa Conference, then, may not have been achieved; but its ultimate goal – a collaborative relationship between East and West, respecting the sovereignty of all parties, while stimulating trade and strengthening political stability and peace – has arguably remained at the centre of international politics from that time up to the present.

Notes

I EUROPE AND RUSSIA AFTER THE WAR

1 A. J. Toynbee, *Survey of International Affairs 1920–23* (London 1925) pp. 7–8. Modern accounts of inter-war diplomacy include Pierre Renouvin, *Histoire des relations internationales*, vol. 7 (Paris 1969), Raymond J. Sontag, *A Broken World 1919–39* (New York 1971), Sally Marks, *The Illusion of Peace: International Relations in Europe 1918–1933* (London, 1976), Jean-Baptist Duroselle, *Histoire diplomatique de 1919 à nos jours*, 8th ed. (Paris 1981), and Graham Ross, *The Great Powers and the Decline of the European States System 1914–45* (London 1983). The fullest Soviet accounts are A. A. Gromyko et al., eds., *Istoriya diplomatii*, 2nd ed., vol. 3 (M. 1965) and A. O. Chubar'yan et al., *Evropa v mezhdunarodnykh otnosheniyakh 1917–1939* (M. 1979).
2 Quoted in Marks, *Illusion*, p. 36.
3 See Derek McKay and H. M. Scott, *The Rise of the Great Powers 1648–1815* (London 1983), and Roy Bridge and Roger Bullen, *The Great Powers and the European States System 1815–1914* (London 1980).
4 See Derek H. Aldercroft, *From Versailles to Wall Street 1919–1929* (London 1977) and idem, *The European Economy 1914–1970* (London 1978), to which this account is much indebted.
5 David Thomson, *Europe since Napoleon* (London 1957), p. 537.
6 A. Sauvy, *Histoire économique de la France entre les deux guerres*, vol. 1 (Paris 1965), pp. 26, 31.
7 Aldcroft, *European Economy*, pp. 18–19, and *From Versailles*, pp. 20, 106.
8 Aldcroft, *European Economy*, p. 19.
9 Ibid., pp. 20, 33.
10 The most authoritative general account is still H. W. V. Temperley, *A History of the Peace Conference of Paris*, 6 vols. (London 1920–4); see also Harold Nicolson's irreverent *Peacemaking 1919* (London 1933).
11 C. L. Mowat, ed., *New Cambridge Modern History*, 2nd ed., vol. 12 (Cambridge 1968), p. 220.
12 FRUS: PPC, XIII, pp. 371–80; Marks, *Illusion*, p. 12n.
13 FRUS: PPC, XIII, p. 413.
14 Marks, *Illusion*, pp. 13, 38, 39; the definitive account is still Etienne Weill-Raynall, *Les réparations allemandes et la France*, 3 vols. (Paris 1947).

15 Marks, *Illusion*, pp. 19, 21. For a more general treatment, see Alfred Cobban, *The Nation State and Self-Determination* (London 1969), chaps. 4 and 5.
16 Marks, *Illusion*, p. 18.
17 Aldcroft, *European Economy*, pp. 30–2.
18 Aldcroft, *From Versailles*, pp. 23, 28; Sontag, *Broken World*, p. 12.
19 FRUS: PPC, XIII, p. 83.
20 Ibid., p. 88; for the Covenant as a whole, see pp. 69–122.
21 See further F. P. Walters, *A History of the League of Nations* (London 1952).
22 Aldcroft, *European Economy*, pp. 33–4.
23 Ibid., pp. 35–6.
24 Elizabeth Johnson, ed., *The Collected Works of J. M. Keynes*, vol. 17 (London 1977), pp. 50–1.
25 J. M. Keynes, *The Economic Consequences of the Peace* (London 1919), pp. 23, 57–8, 79–82, 86–91, 93–4, 105–13.
26 Ibid., p. 143.
27 Ibid., pp. 146, 162–87, 188.
28 *Statistical Abstract for the United Kingdom*, 71st ed., Cmd. 3084 (London 1928), p. 106.
29 *Statesman's Yearbook 1920* (London 1920), p. 840.
30 See Harold Nicolson, *The Evolution of Diplomatic Method* (London 1954), chap. 4, and idem, *Diplomacy*, 3rd ed. (London 1969), pp. 28–40; and more generally Arno J. Mayer, *Political Origins of the New Diplomacy, 1917–1918* (New Haven 1959).
31 Sontag, *Broken World*, pp. 17–18; full details in FRUS: PPC, XIII, pp. 9–21.
32 FRUS: PPC, XIII, pp. 22–5; Sontag, *Broken World*, p. 18; Marks, *Illusion*, p. 24.
33 *New Cambridge Modern History*, XII, pp. 230–1; Sontag, *Broken World*, p. 21.
34 *Documents relatifs aux négociations concernant les guaranties de sécurité contre une aggression de l'Allemagne (10 janvier 1919–7 décembre 1923)* (Paris 1924), nos. 14 and 15, pp. 56–8 and 58–60.
35 French foreign policy in the post-war period is conveniently surveyed in J. Néré, *The Foreign Policy of France from 1914 to 1945* (London 1975).
36 General accounts of French domestic politics in the early 1920s include Edouard Bonnefous, *Histoire politique de la IIIe République*, 2nd ed., vol. 3 (Paris 1968), Theodore Zeldin, *France 1848–1945*, 2 vols. (Oxford 1973–7), Jacques Chastenet, *Histoire de la Troisième République*, new ed., vol. 3 (1974), and Gordon Wright, *Modern France*, 3rd ed. (London 1981).
37 B. R. Mitchell, *European Historical Statistics 1750–1970* (London 1975), pp. 20, 362, 365–6, 399–40.
38 Marks, *Illusion*, p. 44. General accounts of post-war British foreign policy include F. S. Northedge, *The Troubled Giant: Britain among the Great Powers 1916–1939* (London 1966), W. N. Medlicott, *British Foreign Policy since Versailles, 1919–1963*, 2nd ed. (London 1968), and C. J. Lowe and M. L. Dockrill, *The Mirage of Power: British Foreign Policy 1902–1922*, 3 vols. (London 1972).
39 British domestic politics in the early 1920s are surveyed in A. J. P. Taylor, *England 1914–1945* (Oxford 1965), C. L. Mowat, *Britain between the Wars*

1918–1940, new ed. (London 1966), and Kenneth O. Morgan, *Consensus and Disunity: The Lloyd George Coalition Government 1918–1922* (Oxford 1979).

40 General accounts of Italian domestic politics during this period include Christopher Seton-Watson, *Italy from Liberalism to Fascism 1870–1925* (London 1967) and Renzo de Felice, ed., *Storia d'Italia contemporanea*, vol. 3 (Naples 1978); on foreign policy, see C. J. Lowe and F. Marzari, *Italian Foreign Policy 1870–1940* (London 1975).

41 Sontag, *Broken World*, p. 97; *New Cambridge Modern History*, XII, pp. 350–2. See also more generally Ian Nish, *Japanese Foreign Policy 1869–1942* (London 1977).

42 A good general account is available in E. H. Kossman, *The Low Countries 1780–1940* (Oxford 1978). On Dutch–Soviet relations more particularly, see Richard K. Debo, 'Dutch–Soviet relations 1917–1924: the role of finance and commerce in the foreign policy of Soviet Russia and the Netherlands', *Canadian Slavic Studies*, 4, no. 2 (Summer 1970), pp. 199–217.

43 German domestic politics during the early 1920s are surveyed in Erich Eyck, *A History of the Weimar Republic*, 2 vols. (London 1962–4), Gordon A. Craig, *Germany 1866–1945* (Oxford 1978), and V. R. Berghahn, *Modern Germany* (Cambridge 1982); on foreign policy, see particularly John W. Hiden, *Germany and Europe 1919–1939* (London 1977).

44 Cab 1/28/15, 24 March 1919.

45 C. E. Callwell, *Field-Marshal Sir Henry Wilson: His Life and Diaries*, 2 vols. (London 1927), II, p. 148.

46 See for instance Richard H. Ullman, *Intervention and the War* (London 1961), p. 3.

47 DVP, I, no. 2, pp. 11–14.

48 See for instance ibid., pp. 16–17, 28–30, 41–2.

49 Text in ibid., no. 78, pp. 119–66; a further accord was concluded on 27 August 1918 (ibid., no. 319, pp. 437–45). General accounts of early Soviet foreign policy include Louis Fischer, *The Soviets in World Affairs*, 2 vols. (London 1930), Teddy J. Uldricks, *Diplomacy and Ideology* (London 1979), and Richard K. Debo, *Revolution and Survival* (Liverpool 1979); the standard Soviet account is A. A. Gromyko and B. N. Ponomarev, eds., *Istoriya vneshnei politiki SSSR*, 4th ed., vol. 1 (M. 1980).

50 The fullest accounts of Allied intervention include Ullman, *Intervention*, and idem, *British and the Russian Civil War* (London 1968); United States intervention is covered in George Kennan, *Soviet–American Relations 1917–1920*, 2 vols. (London 1956–8), and that of other powers in John Bradley, *Allied Intervention in Russia* (London 1968).

51 See Richard H. Ullman, *The Anglo-Soviet Accord* (London 1972), and Stephen White, *Britain and the Bolshevik Revolution* (London 1980), chap. 1.

52 Text in Cmd. 1207 (London 1921) and in DVP, III, no. 344, pp. 607–14.

53 See DVP, II, no. 299, pp. 339–54, III, no. 12, pp. 28–42, III, no. 53, pp. 101–16, and III, no. 137, pp. 265–80.

54 See DVP, III, nos. 305, 309 and 342, pp. 536–44, 550–3, 597–604.

55 DVP, III, no. 350, pp. 618–58, IV, no. 203, pp. 298–303, and IV, no. 322, pp. 562–7.
56 Text in DVP, IV, no. 72, pp. 99–105; on German–Soviet relations more generally, see above, Chapter 7.
57 See ASD, AP: Russia, 1921, vol. 1529, file 6884 (Accordo commerciale con la Russia), and DVP, IV, no. 336, pp. 596–602. On Italian–Soviet relations more generally, see Giorgio Petracchi, *La Russia revoluzionaria nella politica italiana 1917–1925* (Bari 1982), and Matteo Pizzigallo, *Mediterraneo e Russia nella politica italiana (1922–1924)* (Milan 1983).
58 See Robert Paul Browder, *The Origins of Soviet–American Diplomacy* (Princeton 1953), chap. 1; Soviet accounts include V. K. Furaev, *Sovetsko-amerikanskie otnosheniya 1917–1939* (M. 1964), esp. pp. 21–61, and Lyudmila Gvishiani, *Sovetskaya Rossiya i SShA 1917–1920* (M. 1970).
59 FRUS: 1919: Russia, p. 120.
60 DVP, III, no. 225, pp. 388–90; FRUS: 1919: Russia, p. 144.
61 FRUS: 1919: Russia, p. 120.
62 General accounts include Maxime Mourin, *Les relations franco-soviétiques 1917–1967* (Paris 1967), and Anne Hogenhuis-Seliverstoff, *Les relations franco-soviétiques 1917–1924* (Paris 1981).
63 Mourin, *Relations*, pp. 125–6, 128.
64 See DVP, IV, no. 162, pp. 233–41, and ibid., no. 245, pp. 384–5.
65 For the agreements with France and the USA, see DVP, II, nos. 310 and 311, pp. 462–7, and FRUS 1921, II, pp. 813–17, respectively; the texts of other agreements are in *Sbornik deistvuyushchikh dogovorov, soglashenii i konventsii zaklyuchennykh RSFSR s inostrannymi gosudarstvami*, vyp. 1 (Moscow 1921), nos. 18–32, pp. 117–64.
66 See for instance DVP, IV, nos. 38, 73, 118, and V, no. 30.
67 See DVP, V, no. 264, pp. 593–5, and IV, no. 302, pp. 494–5.
68 See for instance DVP, IV, nos. 75, 128, 256 and 288.
69 See for instance Yu. V. Klyuchnikov and A. Sabanin, eds., *Mezhdunarodnaya politika noveishego vremeni v dogovorakh, notakh i deklaratsiyakh*, 3 vols., (M. 1925–8), II, no. 83, p. 100 (not in DVP), and DVP, II, no. 89, pp. 135–40, and no. 136, pp. 208–12.
70 *PSS*, vol. 41, pp. 124–8, and vol. 37, pp. 48–64.
71 See Ullman, *Anglo-Soviet Accord*, pp. 270–3.
72 DVP, IV, p. 375.
73 See DVP, III, p. 608, IV, p. 104, and IV, p. 596.
74 G. V. Chicherin, *Motsart: issledovatel'skii etyud* (Leningrad 1970).
75 See I. M. Gorokhov et al., *G. V. Chicherin: diplomat leninskoi shkoly*, 2nd ed. (M. 1974), and I. M. Maisky, *Lyudi, sobytiya, fakty* (M. 1973), pp. 118–29.
76 See N. I. Rogovsky, ed., *Resheniya partii i pravitel'stva po khozyaistvennym voprosam*, vol. 1 (M. 1967), pp. 15–17, 28, 33–45, 94–5.
77 Ibid., pp. 31–2.
78 DVP, I, p. 98.
79 Maurice Herbette and Charles Alphand, 'Rapport à M. le Président du Conseil', n.d. (1920), Alphand papers.
80 Noulens to Briand, 2 January 1922, Millerand papers, vol. 81.
81 Calculated from figures in Zeldin, *France*, II, p. 119.

82 P. V. Ol', *Inostrannye kapitaly v Rossii* (Petrograd 1922), p. 9.

83 *H.C. Debs.*, 5 ser., vol. 151, cols. 258 and 1962 (14 March 1922).

84 Georges Hersent, 'Note sur la dette russe', February 1922, MAE: R.C., vol. 105.

85 ICP 247C, 26 April 1922, Cab 29/96; Foreign Office memorandum, 4 November 1921, FO 371/6933/N12254; Petracchi, *Russia revoluzionaria*, p. 216.

86 According to the *Revue économique internationale*, 25 May 1922, in BFM 10.991, 15 May 1922, state debts represented only 18.3 per cent of total Belgian Russian debts; on Italian debts, see Petracchi, *Russia revoluzionaria*, p. 216.

87 For a good general account of this matter, see Harold G. Moulton and Leo Pasvolsky, *World War Debt Settlements* (New York 1926), and the same authors' *Russian Debts and Russian Reconstruction* (New York 1924); a modern discussion is available in Dan P. Silverman, *Reconstructing Europe after the Great War* (Cambridge, Mass. 1982).

2 APPROACHING THE RUSSIAN PROBLEM

1 *H. C. Debs.*, 5th ser., vol. 152, col. 1900, 3 April 1922. Lenin's speech is in *PSS*, vol. 44, pp. 155–75; a typescript translation is in Lloyd George's papers (F149/2/12, 1 November 1921).

2 *Times*, 2 December 1921, p. 10, and 19 November 1921, p. 10; *Le Matin*, 2 December 1921, p. 1; *New York Times*, 5 October 1921, p. 19, and 7 October 1921, p. 1.

3 Lyubov Krassin, *Leonid Krassin: His Life and Work* (London 1929), p. 156.

4 *PSS*, vol. 44, pp. 75–6, 2 August 1921.

5 DVP, IV, no. 170, pp. 251–3.

6 Note of Interview, 5 August 1921, Lloyd George papers F 203/3/7.

7 E. F. Wise memorandum, 5 August 1921, ibid., F48/3/38.

8 Cabinet minutes 64(21)1, Cab 23/26, 5 August 1921.

9 Meeting at Board of Trade, 6 August 1921, Lloyd George papers F203/3/8.

10 Supreme Council minutes, 10 and 13 August 1921, ICP 205 and 207, Cab 29/93.

11 Note of Meeting, 4 September 1921, Cabinet paper CP 3283, Cab 24/127.

12 *Izvestiya*, 9 September 1921, p. 2.

13 *PSS*, vol. 44, p. 116, and p. 545 n. 59.

14 DVP, IV, no. 193, pp. 281–6, and nos. 201–2, pp. 294–8.

15 *Izvestiya*, 8 September 1921, p. 1.

16 Minutes of proceedings, 15–16 September 1921, FO 371/68924/N11122.

17 Minutes of proceedings, 6–8 October 1921, FO 371/6925/N11528.

18 *Izvestiya*, 29 October 1921, p. 1.

19 *H. C. Debs.*, 5th ser., vol. 147, cols. 1742 and 1943, 3 November 1921.

20 Memorandum, 9 September 1921, Lloyd George papers F58/2/25.

21 *Izvestiya*, 29 October 1921, p. 1.

22 Minutes, 31 October 1921, FO 371/6933/N12085.

23 Curzon to Chicherin, 1 November 1921, ibid.
24 *Times*, 1 November 1921, p. 10.
25 MAE to Hardinge, 8 November 1921, Millerand papers, vol. 69.
26 Hardinge to MAE, 16 November 1921, MAE: Europe: Russie, vol. 348.
27 MAE to Hardinge, 30 December 1921, MAE: Europe: Russie, vol. 157.
28 *Pravda*, 15 November 1921, p. 1.
29 Krasin to Lloyd George, 16 November 1921, Lloyd George papers F58/2/29.
30 Krasin to Chicherin, 17 December 1921, DVP, IV, no. 330, pp. 579–82.
31 Krasin to Chicherin, 28 December 1921, ibid., no. 339, pp. 605–6.
32 Wise to Jones, 29 December 1921, AJ 309, Cab 29/35.
33 DVP, IV, no. 330, pp. 579–82, 17 December 1921.
34 Central party archives cited in P. N. Pospelov et al., *Istoriya Kommunisticheskoi partii Sovetskogo soyuza*, vol. 4, part 1 (M. 1970), p. 250.
35 *Leninskii sbornik*, vol. 36 (M. 1959), pp. 338–9, 339 n. 1.
36 Ibid., p. 339 n. 2; Lenin's amendments are in *PSS*, vol. 44, pp. 185–8, 24 October 1921.
37 *Leninskii sbornik*, vol. 37 (M. 1970), pp. 331–2.
38 Ibid., pp. 332–3, 333–4.
39 Ibid., p. 334; for the note, see *Pravda*, 15 November 1921, p. 1.
40 Briand to Hardinge, 25 November 1920, in *L'Europe nouvelle*, 27 August 1921, pp. 1116–18.
41 Raymond Poincaré, *Histoire politique*, 4 vols. (Paris 1920–2), III, pp. 207–9, 15 July 1921. Krasin's discussions, particularly with Felix Deutsch of the electrical firm AEG, are documented from Soviet archival sources in V. A. Shiskin, *Sovetskoe gosudarstvo i strany zapada v 1917–1923 gg.* (Leningrad 1969), pp. 263–4.
42 D'Abernon to Curzon, 30 September 1921, D'Abernon papers Add. Mss. 48924A.
43 Harold Nicolson, *Curzon: The Last Phase* (London 1934), pp. 242–3.
44 *Times*, 5 October 1921, p. 12.
45 *Times*, 11 November 1921, p. 11.
46 *Le Temps*, 21 November 1921, p. 1; *Manchester Guardian*, 26 November 1921, p. 12.
47 Walter Rathenau, *Tagebuch 1907–1922* (Düsseldorf 1967), pp. 269–70.
48 See memoranda of 3, 10 and 24 December 1921, Millerand papers, vol. 69.
49 'Conversations avec M. Rathenau', n.d. (September 1921), MAE: Europe: Russie, vol. 476.
50 'Projets de coopération internationale', 29 October 1921, ibid.
51 Poincaré, *Histoire politique*, III, p. 209.
52 *Manchester Guardian*, 6 December 1921, p. 8.
53 Louis Loucheur, *Carnets secrets 1908–1932* (Brussels and Paris 1962), pp. 185–8.
54 Churchill papers 2/118, in Martin Gilbert, *Winston S. Churchill*, vol. 4, *Companion*, part 3 (London 1977), p. 1688.
55 Cabinet minutes 93(21)2, Cab 23/27, 16 December 1921.
56 Ibid.

57 Churchill to Curzon, 24 December 1921, Curzon papers F112/219.
58 Curzon to Churchill, 30 December 1921, ibid. F112/232.
59 Cabinet minutes 88(21)2, 22 November 1921, Cab 23/27.
60 Briand to Saint-Aulaire, 4 December 1921, in *Documents relatifs aux négociations concernant les guaranties de sécurité contre une aggression de l'Allemagne (10 janvier 1919–7 décembre 1923)* (Paris 1924), no. 17, p. 90.
61 Saint-Aulaire to Briand, 14 December 1921, ibid., no. 18, pp. 90–3.
62 British documentation is in ICP 209–13, Cab 29/94; a less complete French documentation is in 'Entretiens de Londres', MAE: Y Internationale, vol. 684, in R.C. vol. 102, and in AN: Conférence de Londres, AJ⁵ vol. 79.
63 ICP 209, 19 December 1921, Cab 29/94.
64 ICP 210, 20 December 1921, Cab 29/94.
65 Report by Horne, ICP 211, 21 December 1921, Cab 29/94.
66 Ibid.
67 ICP 212, 21 December 1921, Cab 29/94.
68 ICP 211A, 21 December 1921, Cab 29/94.
69 ICP 213, 22 December 1921, Cab 29/94; the memorandum in its original form is in App. I, as adopted in App. II and AJ 307, Cab 29/35.
70 ICP 215, 30 December 1921, Cab 29/94; a less complete French documentation is in 'Syndicat international', MAE: R.C., vol. 102.
71 ICP 216, 218 and 220, 30 and 31 December 1921, Cab 29/94; the memorandum as approved is in ICP 220, App. III and AJ 310, Cab 29/35.
72 Note for Prime Minister, 28 December 1921, Grigg papers, reel 9.
73 Briand to M. Bonin, 26 December 1921, in ASD: Ambasciata Parigi 1922, vol. 51/8.
74 Bonin to Rome, 31 December 1921, in ibid.
75 Bonin to Rome, 30 December 1921, in ibid.
76 Graham to Curzon, 29 December 1921, FO 371/7473/C107.
77 *Atti parlamentari della Camera dei Deputati*, sessione 1921–2, vol. 3, pp. 2872–5, 21–2 December 1921.
78 Belgian ambassador to Curzon, 26 December 1921, FO 371/6040/C23969.
79 Sir G. Grahame to Curzon, 29 December 1921, FO 371/6040/C24070.
80 *Times*, 28 December 1921, p. 8; *Byulleten' NKID*, 23 January 1922, p. 17.
81 *Le Temps*, 26 December 1921, p. 1; *Times*, 30 December 1921, p. 7.

3 FROM CANNES TO BOULOGNE

1 J. Laroche, *Au Quai d'Orsay avec Briand et Poincaré, 1913–1926* (Paris 1957), p. 147.
2 *Times*, 3 January 1922, p. 10, and 4 January 1922, p. 10.
3 *Le Temps*, 5 January 1922, p. 1.
4 *Le Temps*, 4 January 1922, p. 1.
5 Notes of Conversation, 4 January 1922, ICP 220A, Cab 29/94.
6 Ibid., ICP 220B, Cab 29/94.

7 Notes of Conversation, 5 January 1922, ICP 220D, Cab 29/94.
8 Notes of Conversation, 8 and 10 January 1922, ICP 225C and 229A, Cab 29/94. Further correspondence on the subject is contained in *Documents relatifs aux négociations concernant les guaranties de sécurité contre une aggression de l'Allemagne (10 janvier 1919–7 décembre 1923)* (Paris 1924) and *Papers respecting Negotiations for an Anglo-French Pact*, Cmd. 2169 (London 1924).
9 British documentation is contained in ICP 221–35, Cab 29/94 and 95; for French documentation, see MAE: Y Internationale, vol. 21 and R.C. vols. 79–84 and 102; for Italian documentation, see ASD: Archivio conferenze, vol. 86/2, Ambasciata Parigi 1922, vol. 51/8, and Ambasciata Londra 1922, vol. 539/1.
10 ICP 221, 6 January 1922, Cab 29/94.
11 ICP 222, 6 January 1922, Cab 29/94.
12 ICP 228, 10 January 1922, Cab 29/94.
13 *Izvestiya*, 11 January 1922, p. 1.
14 Wise to Krasin, 6 January 1922, Lloyd George papers F149/1.
15 Krasin to Wise, 9 January 1922, ibid., and Crowe to Curzon, 9 January 1922, FO 371/7417/C459. Similar views were expressed in a telegram from Chicherin to the Supreme Council (*Izvestiya*, 11 January 1922, p. 1).
16 ICP 230, 10 January 1922, Cab 29/95; the text of the invitation as agreed is in AJ 330, Cab 29/35.
17 ICP 231 and 232, 11 January 1922, Cab 29/94; the agenda is in AJ 335, Cab 29/35.
18 ICP 233 and 234, 12 January 1922, Cab 29/95.
19 ICP 234, 12 January 1922, and 235, 13 January 1922, Cab 39/95.
20 Millerand to Briand, 7 January 1922, Millerand papers, vol. 81.
21 Briand to Millerand, 8 January 1922, quoted in G. Saurez, *Briand: sa vie, son oeuvre*, 6 vols. (Paris 1941–52), v, pp. 367–8.
22 Millerand to Briand, 10 January 1922, Millerand papers, vol. 81.
23 Briand to Millerand, 10 January 1922, ibid.
24 Text in ibid.; also in CP 3623, Cab 24/132, and in *Le Temps*, 14 January 1922, p. 1.
25 *Le Temps*, 13 January 1922, p. 1.
26 Cabinet minutes 1(22)1, 10 January 1922, Cab 23/29.
27 Millerand to Briand, 11 January 1922, Millerand papers, vol. 81.
28 P. Miquel, *Poincaré* (Paris 1961), p. 440.
29 *Le Matin*, 11 January 1922, p. 1, and 12 January 1922, p. 1.
30 *Débats parlementaires: Chambre des Députés*, 1922, vol. 1, pp. 18–22.
31 *Le Matin*, 13 January 1922, p. 1; *Le Temps*, 14 January 1922, p. 1.
32 *Le Temps*, 16 January 1922, p. 1.
33 Laroche, *Au Quai d'Orsay*, p. 156.
34 Notes of Conversation, 14 January 1922, FO 371/8249/W528.
35 *Times*, 18 January 1922, p. 10; Cabinet minutes 2(22)2, 18 January 1922, Cab 23/29.
36 *Débats parlementaires: Chambre des Députés*, 1922, vol. 1, pp. 37–51.
37 *Le Matin*, 20 January 1922, p. 1; Hardinge to Curzon, 20 January 1922, FO 371/7473/C990.
38 Graham to Curzon, 11 January 1922, FO 371/7417/C542.

39 Graham to Curzon, 13 January 1922, FO 371/7417/C1065.

40 Grahame to Curzon, 25 January 1922, FO 371/8236/W927.

41 See for instance d'Abernon to Curzon, 6 January 1922, FO 371/7473/C311; Charles Laurent to MAE, 7 January 1922, Millerand papers, vol. 81.

42 Laurent to Poincaré, 27 January 1922, Poincaré papers, NAF 16006.

43 Saint-Aulaire to Millerand, 17 January 1922, Millerand papers, vol. 67; see also Saint-Aulaire to Millerand, 24 January 1922, ibid., vol. 69.

44 Hardinge to Curzon, 20 January 1922, Curzon papers F112/200.

45 Hardinge to Curzon, 27 January 1922, ibid.

46 Text in FO 371/7418/C1830, 6 February 1922.

47 Cheetham to Curzon, 10 January 1922, FO 371/7418/C2020.

48 Memorandum, 7 February 1922, FO 371/7418/C2024. The committee had been set up by the Chancellor of the Exchequer on his return from Cannes; Foreign Office representatives were later added (see FO 371/7417/C1143, 21 January 1922).

49 Minutes, 9 and 10 February 1922, FO 371/7418/C2041.

50 See Curzon to Hardinge, 9 February 1922, FO 371/7418/C2000, and Saint-Aulaire to MAE, 10 February 1922, Millerand papers, vol. 73.

51 The Bonomi government resigned on 2 February; the Facta government was not formed until 26 February 1922.

52 Conference of Ministers, 10 February 1922, Cab 23/29.

53 Memorandum of Conversation, 10 February 1922, S-39, Cab 23/35.

54 Curzon to Hardinge, 11 February 1922, FO 371/7418/C2041.

55 Minutes of this meeting are in MAE: R.C., vol. 112; minutes of further meetings are in ibid., vols. 106, 107, 113 (which contains the committee's final report, 8 March 1922).

56 Memorandum, 13 February 1922, FO 371/7419/C2243; see also Saint-Aulaire to Poincaré, 13 February 1922, MAE: R.C., vol. 86.

57 Memorandum, 13 February 1922, FO 371/7419/C2243.

58 Curzon to Saint-Aulaire, 14 February 1922, FO 371/7419/C2243; Saint-Aulaire to Poincaré, 15 February 1922, MAE: R.C., vol. 86.

59 Curzon to Hardinge, 16 February 1922, FO 371/7419/C2392; Saint-Aulaire to Poincaré, 16 February 1922, MAE: R.C., vol. 86.

60 Memorandum by Sir Eyre Crowe, 18 February 1922, FO 371/7420/C2598.

61 Saint-Aulaire to Crowe, 19 February 1922, FO 371/7420/C2599; Poincaré to Saint-Aulaire, 18 February 1922, MAE: R.C., vol. 87.

62 Minute, 19 February 1922, in FO 371/7420/C2598.

63 Memorandum, 17 February 1922, S-43, Cab 23/36; see also S-43, 16 February 1922, ibid.

64 Memorandum of meeting, 20 February 1922, S-45, FO 371/7420/C2674.

65 Memorandum of meeting, 20 February 1922, S-46, Cab 23/36. Beneš reported on his meeting to Prague on 21 February 1922 (*Dokumenty i materialy po istorii sovetsko-chekhoslovatskikh otnoshenii*, vol. 1 (M. 1973), no. 426, p. 477); his memorandum to Poincaré is in MAE: R.C., vol. 87, 21 February 1922.

66 Curzon to Hardinge, 20 February 1922, FO 371/7420/C2598.

67 Hardinge to Curzon, 21 February 1922, FO 371/7420/C2621.
68 Curzon to Hardinge, 21 February 1922, ibid.
69 *Le Temps*, 20 February 1922, p. 1.
70 Notes of Meeting, 25 February 1922, ICP 236, Cab 29/95; French minutes are in MAE: R.C., vol. 88, and Millerand papers, vol. 73.
71 *Manchester Guardian*, 28 February 1922, p. 8. A report and minutes of the meeting are in MAE: R.C., vol. 103, and ASD: Conferenza di Genova, vol. 108/7.
72 Notes of Interview, 28 February 1922, MAE: R.C., vol. 102.

4 DIPLOMATIC PRELIMINARIES

1 *Times*, 27 February 1922, p. 9.
2 *Le Temps*, 27 February 1922, p. 1.
3 Saint-Aulaire to Poincaré, 2 March 1922, in *Documents relatifs aux négociations concernant les guaranties de sécurité centre une aggression de l'Allemagne (19 janvier 1919–7 décembre 1923)* (Paris 1924), no. 29, p. 137.
4 Hardinge to Curzon, 1 March 1922, Hardinge papers, vol. 45.
5 Bonin to Rome, 27 February 1922, ASD: Ambasciata Parigi 1922, vol. 52/1.
6 Lord d'Abernon, *An Ambassador of Peace*, 3 vols. (London 1929–30), I, p. 263; A. J. Sylvester, *The Real Lloyd George* (London 1947), p. 77.
7 *Times*, 27 January 1922, p. 9; Graham to Curzon, 27 January 1922, Lloyd George papers F56/2/41.
8 *Times*, 18 February 1922, p. 10, and 3 March 1922, p. 11.
9 *Times*, 22 February 1922, p. 11; telegram to foreign governments, 23 February 1922, ASD: Conferenza di Genova, vol. 109–10.
10 Torretta to Bonin, 22 February 1922, ASD: Ambasciata Parigi 1922, vol. 52/1.
11 Graham and Barrère to Torretta, 26 and 27 February 1922, ASD: Conferenza di Genova, vol. 109/10.
12 Schanzer to London, 9 March 1922, Schanzer papers, vol. 11; similarly Schanzer to Paris, 11 March 1922, ASD: Ambasciata di Parigi 1922, vol. 52/1.
13 Graham to Curzon, 3 March 1922, FO 371/7421/C3321.
14 Chicherin to Torretta, 22 February 1922, ASD: Conferenza di Genova, vol. 109/10.
15 Torretta to Chicherin, 23 February 1922, ibid.; also in *Izvestiya*, 26 February 1922, p. 1.
16 Chicherin to Torretta, 25 February 1922, ASD: Ambasciata Parigi 1922, vol. 52/1; also in *Pravda*, 28 February 1922, p. 2.
17 Chicherin to Allied governments, 15 March 1922, ASD: Conferenza di Genova, vol. 122/37.
18 Ricci to Hughes, 16 January 1922, USNA: 550 E1/9, and US Consul, London, to Hughes, 20 January 1922, USNA: 861.01/367.
19 Child to Hughes, 30 January 1922, and 1 March 1922, USNA: 550 E1/23 and 62.

20 Hughes to Ricci, 8 March 1922, USNA: 550 E1/78A.
21 Hughes to Child, 24 March 1922, USNA: 550 E1/119.
22 Child's reports from Genoa are in USNA: 550 E1/183–295.
23 See for instance Radek in *Le Matin*, 1 February 1922, p. 1; Note of Interview, 23 February 1922, MAE: R.C., vol. 107; 'Affaires russes d'après la presse quotidienne', 13 February 1922, MAE: Europe: Russie, vol. 476; Chicherin in *Izvestiya*, 7 November 1922, p. 2.
24 D'Abernon to Curzon, 27 January 1922, FO 371/7353/C1597.
25 Saint-Quentin to Poincaré, 2 April 1922,MAE: Europe: Russie, vol. 476; Charles Laurent to Poincaré, 23 and 25 February 1922, MAE: R.C., vol. 106.
26 Economic Department, Dutch Foreign Ministry, 3 April 1922, Ministerie van Buitenlandse Zaken archives A81.
27 Belgian embassy to Poincaré, 2 March 1922, MAE: R.C., vol. 102.
28 Finance Ministry to MAE, 30 March 1922, MAE: R.C., vol. 102; President, Finance Commission of the Senate, to Poincaré, 24 February 1922, ibid.; Poincaré memo., ibid., vol. 115.
29 *Le Matin*, 9 February 1922, p. 1. The interview was accounted a serious diplomatic mistake by Lenin and Chicherin (*PSS*, vol. 54, pp. 176–7 and 615–16): more cautious interviews with Rakovsky and Krasin appeared in *Le Matin* on 10 and 15 February respectively (both p. 1).
30 *Daily Herald*, 14 March 1922, p. 3; *Débats parlementaires: Chambre des Députés*, 31 March 1922, p. 1323 (Poincaré), and 1 April 1922, pp. 1346–7.
31 Charles Laurent to Paris, 15 February 1922, MAE: Europe: Russie, vol. 349; Laurent to Paris, 6 March 1922, ibid.
32 Poincaré to Saint-Aulaire, 9 February 1922, Millerand papers, vol. 73; *Débats parlementaires: Chambre des Députés*, 31 March 1922, p. 1323.
33 On business particularly, see ibid., 24 March 1922, pp. 1083–90.
34 See for instance French minister, Riga, to Paris, 21 February 1922,MAE: Europe: Russie, vol. 349; Report from the Conference of the Three Internationals, n.d., ibid., vol. 158; Note of Conversation with Radek, 23 February 1922, MAE: R.C., vol. 107.
35 Kilmarnock to Curzon, 27 February 1922, FO 371/8184/N1955. Chicherin privately confirmed these discussions at a meeting with Baltic ministers at the end of March (Wilton (Riga) to Curzon, 5 April 1922, FO 371/8105/N3414).
36 Tirard to Poincaré, 10 April 1922, MAE: R.C., vol. 91; French minister, Prague, to Poincaré, 11 and 13 April 1922, ibid.; Saint-Aulaire to Paris, 30 March 1922, ibid., vol. 90.
37 Saint-Aulaire to Sir W. Tyrrell, 15 March 1922, ibid., vol. 90.
38 Curzon to Hardinge, 19 February 1922, FO 371/7423/W2488.
39 Cabinet Paper CP 3702, 8 February 1922, Cab 24/133; see also above, pp. 63–4.
40 Cabinet Paper CP 3762, 20 February 1922, Cab 24/133.
41 Chapman memorandum, 10 March 1922, FO 371/7422/C3684.
42 Notes by Seydoux, 10 and 14 March 1922, MAE: R.C., vol. 89.
43 Poincaré to Seydoux, 18 March 1922, ibid., vol. 115.
44 Chapman report, 26 March 1922, Grigg papers, reel 9.

45 Seydoux to Poincaré, 21 March 1922, MAE: R.C., vol. 115; Grigg memorandum, 23 March 1922, Grigg papers, reel 9.
46 Hankey to Lloyd George, 24 March 1922, Lloyd George papers F26/1/23.
47 Chapman report, 26 March 1922, Grigg papers, reel 9.
48 A British report on the Allied experts' meetings is in FO 371/8187/N3075, 28 March 1922; French minutes and documents are in MAE: R.C., vol. 115; Italian reports and telegrams are in ASD: Amba-sciata Londra 1922, vol. 538/3; and the Belgian delegates' report is in BFM 10.991, B 366/6, 28 March 1922.
49 Cabinet Paper CP 3902, Cab 24/136; also in ASD: Conferenza di Genova, vol. 109/8, and MAE: R.C., vols, 90 and 115.
50 Maxse minute, 29 March 1922, FO 371/8187/N3075.
51 Churchill to his wife, 7 February 1922, in Martin Gilbert, *Winston S. Churchill*, vol. 4: *Companion*, part 3 (London 1977), p. 1757.
52 Churchill to Chamberlain, 18 March 1922, Chamberlain papers AC 23/6/17.
53 Churchill to Lloyd George, 18 March 1922, in Gilbert, *Companion*, part 3, pp. 1810–11.
54 Chamberlain to Lloyd George, 21 March 1922, Lloyd George papers F7/5/20.
55 Lloyd George to Chamberlain, 22 March 1922, Chamberlain papers AC 23/6/19.
56 Lloyd George to Horne, 22 March 1922, Lloyd George papers F27/6/57.
57 Chamberlain to Lloyd George, 23 March 1922, ibid., F7/5/22.
58 Horne to Lloyd George, 23 March 1922, ibid., F27/6/58.
59 Chamberlain to Curzon, 24 March 1922, Curzon papers F112/223.
60 Horne to Lloyd George, 24 March 1922, Lloyd George papers F27/6/59.
61 Chamberlain to Lloyd George, 25 March 1922, ibid., F7/5/24.
62 Cabinet paper CP 3890, 25 March 1922, Cab 24/134.
63 The text of the speech is in *PSS*, vol. 45, pp. 1–16.
64 Conference of Ministers, 27 March 1922, Cab 23/29.
65 Ibid., 28 March 1922, Cab. 23/29.
66 The reference is apparently to an interview with Vanderlip in *The Times*, 20 March 1922, p. 11.
67 Cabinet minutes 21(22)2, 28 March 1922, Cab 23/29.
68 Conference of Ministers, 2 April 1922, Cab 23/29.
69 Lenin's speech, in fact delivered on 17 October 1921, is in *PSS*, vol. 44, pp. 155–75; the prime minister, Lloyd Greame later recalled, 'placed an exaggerated faith' in it (Lord Swinton, *I Remember* (London 1948), p. 17). See also above p. 30.
70 *H.C. Debs.*, 5th series, vol. 152, cols. 1885–92, 3 April 1922.

5 SOVIET RUSSIA AND GENOA

1 See above, p. 30.
2 See for instance David Lloyd George, *The Truth about the Peace Treaties*, vol. 2 (London 1938), pp. 328, 383.

3 See above, Chapters 2–4.
4 Grove to Curzon, 20 January 1922, FO 371/8182/N944.
5 Ibid., 21 February 1922, FO 371/8182/N1904.
6 Ibid., 14 and 20 February 1922, FO 371/8182/N1892 and N1901.
7 Ibid., 3 February 1922, FO 371/8182/N1478.
8 Notes of Conversation, 20 February 1922, S–46, Cab 23/36; see also above, p. 67.
9 Hodgson to Foreign Office, 3 February 1922, FO 371/8185/N1372.
10 See above, pp. 30, 95–6.
11 Notes of Interview, 23 February 1922, Lloyd George papers F149/2/13.
12 DVP, v, no. 88, pp. 157–62; also in Berzin to Curzon, 1 April 1922, FO 371/8187/N3172.
13 Hodgson to Curzon, 31 March 1922, BED 225, Cab 31/1.
14 Minute in FO 371/187/N3236, about 3 April 1922.
15 Grove to Curzon, 17 March 1922, FO 371/8178/N2599; similarly ibid., 21 March 1922, FO 371/8182/N2924.
16 Wilton (Riga) to Gregory, 29 March 1922, FO 371/8187/N3130.
17 *Le Matin*, 16 February 1922, p. 1.
18 French chargé d'affaires, Reval, to Paris, 27 March 1922, MAE: R.C., vol. 90.
19 Saint-Aulaire to Millerand, 17 January 1922, Millerand papers, vol. 67.
20 Secret report no. 9606, 30 March 1922, MAE: R.C., vol. 89.
21 Martel to Poincaré, 1 April 1922, ibid., vol. 109.
22 Poincaré to Millerand, 12 April 1922, Millerand papers, vol. 81.
23 Soviet archives, cited in R. F. Karpova, *L. B. Krasin – sovetskii diplomat* (M. 1962), pp. 121–2.
24 Ibid., p. 122.
25 Soviet archives, cited in V. A. Shishkin, *Sovetskoe gosudarstvo i strany zapada v 1917–1923 gg.* (Leningrad 1969), p. 295.
26 N. N. Lyubimov, 'Vospominaniya uchastnika Genuezskoi konferentsii', in *Po zavetam V. I. Lenina*, vyp. 3 (M. 1973), pp. 94–103, at p. 97.
27 M. I. Trush, *Vneshnepolitischeskaya deyatel'nost' V. I. Lenina 1921–1923 den' za dnem* (M. 1973), p. 33.
28 Alexandre Barmine, *Memoirs of a Soviet Diplomat* (London 1938), p. 156.
29 *Manchester Guardian*, 13 March 1922, p. 6.
30 See for instance *Daily Herald*, 23 January 1922, p. 4.
31 *PSS*, vol. 54, pp. 133–5, at p. 134, 22 January 1922.
32 Ibid., p. 164, 14 February 1922.
33 FO 371/8186/N2350, 11 March 1922; also ASD: Conferenza di Genova, vol. 122/37 item 12.
34 Karpova, *Krasin*, p. 125; *PSS*, vol. 54, pp. 133–4, 22 January 1922.
35 Report of Second Meeting, 10 February 1922, in Hodgson to Curzon, FO 371/8187/N3610, 4 April 1922.
36 See N. I. Rogovsky et al., eds., *Protokoly Prezidiuma Gosplana za 1921–1922 gody*, 2 vols. (M. 1979), II, part 1, pp. 58–60, 72 and ff.
37 Trush, *Vneshnepoliticheskaya deyatel'nost'*, pp. 30–1.
38 G. V. Chicherin, *Stat'i i rechi po voprosam mezhdunarodnoi politiki* (M. 1961), p. 284.

39 *Izvestiya*, 21 January 1922, p. 1; see also above, pp. 56–7.
40 *PSS*, vol. 54, p. 596 n. 201.
41 *Pervaya i vtoraya sessii Vserossiiskogo TsIK IX sozyva (29 dek. 1921 g., 27 yan. 1922 g.): Stenograficheskii otchet* (M. 1923), pp. 25–6; Graham to Curzon, 2 February 1922, FO 371/8185/N1149.
42 Trush, *Vneshnepolitcheskaya deyatel'nost'*, p. 47; DVP, v, no. 66, pp. 110–12.
43 *Leninskii sbornik*, vol. 36 (M. 1959), p. 409.
44 Ibid., p. 410.
45 See DVP, v, pp. 58 and 716 n. 14.
46 See the texts of the invitations as communicated by the Italian ambassadors in London (FO 371/7417/C912, 16 January 1922), The Hague (Ministerie van Buitenlandse Zaken archives A81 dossier 175, 17 January 1922), Paris (ASD: Ambasciata Parigi 1922, vol. 52/11, 16 January 1922) and Berlin (PAAA: Sonderreferat Wirtschaft, vol. 1, 16 January 1922). The Italian invitation was evidently based on the text adopted at 11.00, not as finally adopted at 15.30 on 6 January; see ASD: Conference de Cannes, Notes du sécretaire français, P.V. nos. 1 and 2, vol. 96/3, and Torretta's circular telegram to ambassadors of 15 January, ASD: Conferenza di Genova, vol. 111/13. The Cannes resolution was correctly reproduced in *Pravda*, 10 January 1922, pp. 2–3.
47 *PSS*, vol. 44, pp. 374–6, at p. 376, 1 February 1922.
48 *PSS*, vol. 54, pp. 118 and 596 nn. 202–3 (Chicherin spent some time in Europe recuperating after the conference had ended).
49 Ibid., pp. 136–7 and 601 n. 229. (A copy of Lenin's letter is in the Trotsky papers, T725).
50 Lenin to Chicherin, 7 February 1922, *PSS*, vol. 44, pp. 385–6.
51 Ibid., vol. 54, pp. 133–5, 22 January 1922.
52 Ibid., vol. 44, pp. 374–6, 1 February 1922.
53 Ibid., pp. 382–4, 6 February 1922, and 587 n. 167.
54 Ibid., pp. 406–9, 24 February 1922, and 590 n. 179.
55 Ibid., vol. 54, pp. 614–15 n. 285, 15 February 1922.
56 Ibid., pp. 170–1, 16 February 1922.
57 Ibid., vol. 45, pp. 34–40, 10 and 14 March 1922.
58 Ibid., pp. 63–4, 23 March 1922.
59 Ibid., pp. 69–71, 27 March 1922.
60 *Izvestiya*, 11 January 1922, p. 1, and 28 January 1922, p. 1.
61 *Pravda*, 10 January 1922, p. 2.
62 *Trud*, 11 January 1922, p. 1; *Pravda*, 12 January 1922, p. 1.
63 *Izvestiya*, 5 January 1922, p. 1.
64 French minister, Warsaw to Paris, 26 February 1922, MAE: R.C., vol. 88.
65 *Pervaya i vtoraya sessii*, pp. 19, 20.
66 A. O. Chubar'yan, *V.I. Lenin i formirovanie sovetskoi vneshnei politiki* (M. 1972), pp. 240–1.
67 *Odinnadtsatyi s"ezd RKP (b) 27 marta–2 aprelya 1922 g. Stenograficheskii otchet* (M. 1922), pp. 91, 90.
68 Grove to Curzon, 9 March 1922, FO 371/8186/N2276; Lenin's speech is in *PSS*, vol. 46, pp. 1–16.

69 *Odinnadtsatyi s"ezd*, pp. 66–9.
70 Ibid., pp. 93–7.
71 Ibid., pp. 71–2.
72 Ibid., pp. 280–1; *XI vserossiiskaya partiinaya konferentsiya RKP (b) (19–22 dekabrya 1921 g.): Stenograficheskii otchet* (Samara 1922), pp. 197–200.
73 See above, pp. 39, 106.
74 Soviet archives, cited in V. A. Shishkin, *V. I. Lenin i vneshne-ekonomicheskaya politika sovetskogo gosudarstva (1917–1923 gg.)* (Leningrad 1977), p. 233.
75 *Dvenadtsatyi s"ezd RKP(b) 17–25 aprelya: Stenograficheskii otchet* (M. 1923), pp. 118, 352–5.
76 Report, 16 January 1922, in Millerand papers, vol. 67.
77 *Russkaya mysl'*, March 1922, p. 203; *L'Humanité*, 7 March 1922, p. 1.
78 *Pravda*, 7 February 1922, p. 1.
79 *PSS*, vol. 45, p. 161, 18 April 1922.
80 *Byulleten' NKID*, no. 116, 27 February 1922, p. 5.
81 *Obshchee delo*, 15 December 1921, p. 1, and 22 December 1922, p. 1.
82 Ibid., 11 January 1922, p. 1, and 20 January 1922, p. 1.
83 Kartachov to MAE, 18 February 1922, MAE: R.C., vol. 106.
84 'Declaration', March 1922, MAE: Europe: Russie, vol. 476; Guchkov to MAE, 20 March 1922, ibid.; Council to Dutch Ministry of Foreign Affairs, 13 April 1922, Ministerie van Buitenlandse Zaken archives A81 dossier 173. Several related appeals are in MAE: Europe: Russie, vol. 476, and elsewhere.
85 *Golos rodiny*, 24 December 1921, p. 1, and 1 January 1922, p. 1.
86 *Poslednye novosti*, 6 January 1922, p. 1, and 7 December 1921, p. 1.
87 Memorandum, 16 January 1922, in Committee to Seydoux, 25 March 1922, MAE: R.C., vol. 109.
88 *Smena vekh*, 7 January 1922, pp. 1, 3, and 21 January 1922, p. 8.
89 *Nakanune*, 26 March 1922, p. 1, and 11 April 1922, p. 1.
90 *Novyi mir*, 10 March 1922, p. 1.
91 *PSS*, vol. 44, pp. 380, 628n; *L'Humanité*, 22 April 1922, p. 1.
92 *Izvestiya*, 7 May 1922, p. 1.
93 N. N. Lyubimov and A. N. Erlikh, *Genuezskaya konferentsiya* (M. 1963), pp. 129–30.
94 *Izvestiya*, 6 May 1922, p. 2.
95 *Le Matin*, 10 March 1922, p. 1.
96 Dem'yan Bednyi, *Sobranie sochinenii*, vol. 4 (M. 1965), pp. 281–313.
97 *Izvestiya*, 12 April 1922, p. 1.
98 *Pravda*, 25 January 1922, p. 1.
99 *L'Europe nouvelle*, 27 May 1922, p. 647.
100 *Pervaya i vtoraya sessii*, pp. 21, 24.
101 *Le Matin*, 25 February 1922, p. 1; *Pravda*, 27 January 1972, p. 1.
102 *Poslednye novosti*, 30 March 1922, p. 1.
103 Barrère to Poincaré, 8 March 1922, MAE: R.C., vol. 89.
104 French police archives: Russie: dossier général, F^7 13,491, 5 February 1922.
105 *Daily Herald*, 26 April 1922, p. 1; *Trud*, 23 April 1922, p. 1.

106 Krasin to Chicherin, 7 January 1922, Trotsky papers T722.
107 *PSS*, vol. 45, p. 453. Lenin had already advised the Politburo that, in view of the warnings that had been received from Krasin and others, neither he, Trotsky nor Zinoviev should attend the conference wherever it was held (Lenin to Molotov, 12 January 1922, Trotsky papers T722).
108 *Pravda*, 10 March 1922, p. 1.
109 *Izvestiya*, 29 March 1922, p. 1.
110 Ibid., 9 April 1922, p. 2.
111 *Pravda*, 26 March 1922, p.1; *Izvestiya*, 26 March 1922, p. 1.
112 *Izvestiya*, 1 April 1922, p. 1.
113 *Izvestiya*, 29 March 1922, p. 1; Martel (Riga) to Paris, 29 March 1922, MAE: R.C., vol. 90.
114 DVP, v, no. 96, pp. 173–5.
115 Wilton (Riga) to Curzon, 5 April 1922, FO 371/8105/N3414.
116 See above, Chapter 7.
117 *Daily Herald*, 7 April 1922, pp. 1, 3.

6 THE CONFERENCE OPENS

1 A full British documentation of the conference proceedings is in Cab 31; a less complete French documentation is in MAE: Y Internationale, vols. 29–36, and R.C., vols. 85–128; and an Italian documentation is in ASD: Archivio Conferenze: Conferenza di Genova, classe 52, vols. 1–44. The fullest Soviet source is *Materialy Genueszkoi konferentsii* (M. 1922).
2 *Nation and Athenaeum*, 22 April 1922, p. 110.
3 *Elenco dei membri delle Delegazioni*, 2nd ed. (Genoa n.d.), in ASD: Ambasciata Londra, vol. 538/3.
4 See above, Chapter 3.
5 Elenco dei giornalisti, in ASD: Conferenza di Genova, vol. 109/9; *Le Temps*, 10 April 1922, p. 1; Max Eastman, *Love and Revolution* (New York 1965), p. 286.
6 Richard W. Child, *A Diplomat Looks at Europe* (New York 1925), p. 27.
7 Typescript of speech, 26 April 1922, in Lloyd George papers F149/3/1.
8 *Manchester Guardian*, 8 April 1922, p. 11.
9 *La Stampa*, 6 April 1922, p. 4; *Giornale d'Italia*, 7 April 1922, p. 1; *Corriere della sera*, 7 April 1922, p. 1.
10 *Avanti*, 7 April 1922, p. 1.
11 N. N. Lyubimov and A. N. Erlikh, *Genuezskaya konferentsiya* (M. 1963), pp. 34–5; Pierre Pascal, *Mon état d'âme: mon journal de Russie*, vol. 3 (Lausanne 1982), p. 50.
12 *Corriere della sera*, 8 April 1922, p. 1; *Avanti*, 8 April 1922, p. 1.
13 *Corriere della sera*, 7 April 1922, p. 5.
14 *Izvestiya*, 11 May 1922, p. 1; Lyubimov and Erlikh, *Genuezskaya konferentsiya*, p. 31.
15 'Organizzazione materiale della conferenza', n.d., in Schanzer papers, vol. 3.
16 *Manchester Guardian*, 30 March 1922, p. 7; see also above, p. 118.

17 Ibid., 5 April 1922, p. 8; *Trud*, 9 April 1922, p. 2.

18 *Times*, 7 April 1922, p. 11, and 8 April 1922, p. 11.

19 Ibid., 7 April 1922, p. 11, and 8 April 1922, p. 11.

20 *Manchester Guardian*, 8 April 1922, p. 11.

21 *L'Humanité*, 15 April 1922, p. 1.

22 *Revue des Deux Mondes*, 1 May 1922, pp. 200–1; *New York Times*, 6 April 1922, p. 3.

23 Martel to Poincaré, 25 March and 3 April 1922, MAE: R.C., vol. 109; *Giornale d'Italia*, 7, 13 and 28 April 1922, p. 1; *Izvestiya*, 23 April 1922, p. 1.

24 *Corriere della sera*, 8 April 1922, p. 1.

25 Lyubimov and Erlikh, *Genuezskaya konferentsiya*, pp. 33–4.

26 French ambassador, Copenhagen, to Paris, 11 April 1922, MAE: Y Internationale, vol. 29.

27 *Izvestiya*, 23 April 1922, p. 1.

28 Litvinov to NKID, 9 April 1922, DVP, v, no. 107, p. 191.

29 *H.C. Debs.*, 5th ser., vol. 151, col. 2353, and vol. 152, col. 232.

30 Curzon minute, 1 February 1922, in FO 371/7419/C2251.

31 Curzon to Hardinge, 1 April 1922, Hardinge papers, vol. 45.

32 Curzon to Lloyd George, 6 April 1922, Lloyd George papers F13/3/15.

33 *Sovetskaya istoricheskaya entsiklopediya*, 16 vols. (M. 1961–76), v, p. 213.

34 *Elenco dei membri delle Delegazioni*, pp. 8–10.

35 Bonin to Rome, 25 March 1922, ASD: Ambasciata Parigi 1922, vol. 52/1; Hardinge to Curzon, 29 March 1922, Hardinge papers, vol. 45.

36 Poincaré to Facta, 11 April 1922, in FO 371/7426/C5389.

37 *Débats parlementaires: Chambre des Députés*, 1 April 1922, pp. 1355–9.

38 ICP 236B, 7 April 1922, Cab 29/95.

39 *Times*, 8 April 1922, p. 12.

40 Ibid., 29 March 1922, p. 11, and 3 April 1922, p. 11.

41 Ibid., 3 April 1922, p. 11.

42 Poincaré to Barthou, 6 April 1922, MAE: R.C., vol. 92.

43 SG 1A, 8 April 1922, Cab 31/5.

44 ICP 237, 9 April 1922, Cab 29/95.

45 ICP 238, 9 April 1922, Cab 29/95.

46 *Il comune di Genova*, 15 April 1922, p. 1, in ASD: Conferenza di Genova, vol. 117/29; Kenneth O. Morgan, *Consensus and Disunity: The Lloyd George Coalition Government 1918–1922* (Oxford 1979), p. 312.

47 *Times*, 3 April 1922, p. 12, and 5 April 1922, p. 11.

48 *Manchester Guardian*, 6 February 1922, p. 8.

49 *Toronto Daily Star*, 13 April 1922, p. 17.

50 Child, *A Diplomat*, p. 27.

51 *Times*, 3 April 1922, p. 12, and 5 April 1922, p. 11.

52 *La Conferenza di Genova: Come fù organizzata* (Napoli 1922), in Schanzer papers, vol. 3.

53 'Promemoria', 7 June 1922, in ACS: Presidenza del Consiglio dei Ministri: I Guerra Mondiale, vol. 184/11.

54 *Pravda*, 13 April 1922, p. 2.

55 *Nakanune*, 12 April 1922, p. 1; *Le Matin*, 11 April 1922, p. 1.

56 Lloyd-Greame to his wife, 10 April 1922, Swinton (Cunliffe-Lister) papers, vol. 2/3.

57 *Le Matin*, 11 April 1922, p. 1; *Pravda*, 13 April 1922, p. 2; Gregory to Foreign Office, 14 April 1922, FO 371/8187/N3704.

58 Minutes of the First Plenary Session, 10 April 1922, Cab 31/4.

59 *Pravda*, 13 April 1922, p. 2; similarly Pascal, *Mon état d'âme*, pp. 52, 62.

60 Child, *A Diplomat*, p. 30; Graf Harry von Kessler, *Tagebücher 1918–1937* (Frankfurt 1961), pp. 288–9.

61 Minutes of the First Plenary Session, 10 April 1922, Cab 31/4.

62 Lloyd-Greame to his wife, 10 April 1922, Swinton (Cunliffe-Lister) papers, vol. 2/3.

63 Hankey to Chamberlain, 12 April 1922, Hankey papers, vol. 8/23.

64 Kesler, *Tagebücher*, pp. 290–1.

65 Siegfried to Gout, 12 April 1922, Millerand papers, vol. 76.

66 Jean Roger to Charles-Roux, 14 April 1922, Charles-Roux papers, vol. 10.

67 PC 1, 11 April 1922, Cab 31/6.

68 PCS 1, 11 April 1922, ibid.

69 ICP 238A, 13 April 1922, Cab 29/95.

70 Lyubimov and Erlikh, *Genuezskaya konferentsiya*, p. 59.

71 ICP 238B, 14 April 1922, Cab 29/95.

72 ICP 238G, 15 April 1922, ibid. The Soviet counterclaims were fully set out in a published memorandum: see DVP, v, no. 150, pp. 293–359.

73 ICP 238C, 15 April 1922, Cab 29/95.

74 ICP 238D, 15 April 1922, ibid.; French notes of these negotiations are contained in Seydoux, 'Négociations avec les russes', 2 May 1922, Millerand papers, vol. 80.

75 Chicherin to NKID, 15 April 1922, DVP, v, no. 119, pp. 217–20.

76 Hankey to Chamberlain, 16 April 1922, Hankey papers, vol. 8/23.

77 Gregory to Foreign Office, 13 April 1922, FO 371/7426/C5473.

78 Hankey to his wife, 15 April 1922, Hankey papers, vol. 3/30.

79 Grigg to Chamberlain, 18 April 1922, Grigg papers, reel 1.

80 Barthou to Poincaré, 16 April 1922, MAE: Y Internationale, vol. 29.

81 Charles-Roux to Poincaré, 18 April 1922, ibid., vol. 30.

82 François Charles-Roux, *Souvenirs diplomatiques* (Paris 1961), pp. 166–7.

83 Ibid., p. 167.

84 Ibid., pp. 169–70.

85 Roger to Charles-Roux, 16, 19 and 21 April 1922, Charles-Roux papers, vol. 10.

86 Barthou to Poincaré, 14 April 1922, and Poincaré to Barthou, 15 and 16 April 1922, MAE: Y Internationale, vol. 29.

87 Barthou to Poincaré, 16 April 1922, ibid.

88 Barthou to Ministère des Finances, 17 April 1922, ibid.

89 Poincaré to Barthou, 18 and 19 April 1922, ibid., vol. 30.

90 Hankey to his wife, 12 April 1922, Hankey papers, vol. 3/30.

91 Chamberlain to Lloyd George, 12 April 1922, Lloyd George papers F150.

7 RAPALLO

1 The best modern studies of Soviet–German relations during this period are Renata Bournazel, *Rapallo: naissance d'un mythe* (Paris 1974), and Hartmut Pogge von Strandmann, 'Rapallo-strategy in preventive diplomacy: new sources and new interpretations', in Volker R. Berghahn and Martin Kitchen, eds., *Germany in the Age of Total War* (London 1981); see also Gerald Freund, *Unholy Alliance* (London 1957), Lionel Kochan, *Russia and the Weimar Republic* (Cambridge 1954), and, for Soviet interpretations, A. A. Akhtamzyan, *Rapall'skaya politika* (M. 1974), and G. M. Trukhnov, *Iz istorii sovetsko-germanskikh otnoshenii (1920–1922 gg.)* (Minsk 1974).

2 Text in SGO, II, no. 187, pp. 318–23.

3 Ministerstvo vneshnei torgovli SSSR, *Vneshnyaya torgovlya SSSR za 1918–1940 gg.: Statisticheskii obzor* (M. 1960), pp. 21, 23.

4 Pogge von Strandmann, 'Rapallo-strategy', pp. 124–6; Freund, *Unholy Alliance*, pp. 100–2.

5 On this last point, see for instance SGO, II, pp. 304–6, 341–3, 359–60.

6 See Hans W. Gatzke, 'Russo-German military collaboration during the Weimar republic', *American Historical Review*, 63, no. 3 (April 1958), pp. 565–97, and F. L. Carsten, *The Reichswehr and Politics 1918–1933* (London 1966), pp. 135–47.

7 Hans von Seeckt, *Aus seinem Leben 1918–1936* (Leipzig 1940), p. 309.

8 *Izvestiya*, 9 November 1921, p. 1.

9 D'Abernon to London, 19 November 1921, FO 371/6880/N13011.

10 SGO, II, no. 190, pp. 330–5, 13 May 1921.

11 DVP, v, p. 724 nn. 38, 39; *Berliner Tageblatt*, 9 December 1921, in FO 371/6880/N14161.

12 Chicherin to Lenin, 14 June 1921, SGO, II, no. 201, p. 347.

13 Ibid., no. 237, pp. 396–405, 10 December 1921.

14 Lenin to Trotsky, 30 November 1921, in *PSS*, vol. 54, p. 41.

15 See Freund, *Unholy Alliance*, pp. 49–50, 91.

16 See V. A. Shishkin, *Sovetskoe gosudarstvo i strany zapada v 1917–1923 gg.* (Leningrad 1969), pp. 321–3, an account partly based on Soviet archival sources.

17 'Aufzeichnung', 27 January 1922, in PA: Politische Abteilung IV: Deutsch-russischer Vertrag, vol. 1.

18 Ibid., 30 January and 11 February 1922.

19 Text in SGO, II, pp. 459–61.

20 Soviet archives, cited in I. K. Koblyakov, 'Vydayushchiisya uspekh leninskoi politiki mira', *Istoriya SSSR*, 1972, no. 2, pp. 46–7.

21 Ibid., p. 47.

22 Charles Laurent to Poincaré, 21 January 1922, MAE: R.C., vol. 85.

23 D'Abernon to Curzon, 20 January 1922, Curzon papers F112/204.

24 D'Abernon to Curzon, 28 January 1922, D'Abernon papers Add. Mss. 48924A.

25 Charles Laurent to Poincaré, 20 February 1922, MAE: R.C., vol. 81.

26 SGO, II, no. 248, pp. 427–31, 21 February 1922.

27 D'Abernon to Curzon, 1 and 6 February 1922, D'Abernon papers Add. Mss. 48924A.
28 Lord d'Abernon, *An Ambassador of Peace*, 3 vols. (London 1929–30), I, p. 258.
29 Chicherin to NKID, 4 April 1922, DVP, v, no. 101, p. 181.
30 Pashukanis to NKID, 8 April 1922, DVP, v, no. 106, pp. 188–90.
31 Ibid., pp. 189–90; similarly Chicherin to NKID, 10 April 1922, ibid., p. 205. The German draft agreement of early April is in SGO, II, no. 255, p. 455.
32 Secret service message, Stockholm, 2 April 1922, MAE: R.C., vol. 91.
33 Saint-Quentin to Paris, 4 April 1922, ibid., vol. 92.
34 Saint-Quentin to Poincaré, 11 April 1922, ibid., vol. 93.
35 Frassati to Rome, 7 April 1922, ASD: Conferenza di Genova, vol. 52/20.
36 Belgian minister, Berlin, to Brussels, 12 April 1922, BFM: 10.991.
37 'Letzte Vorgänge vor der Unterzeichnung des deutsch-russischen Vertrages', PA: Büro Reichsminister: Genua, vol. 1/1, 17 April 1922.
38 Müller to Berlin, 15 April 1922, ibid., vol. 2.
39 'Letze Vorgänge', ibid., vol. 1/1, 17 April 1922.
40 Ibid.
41 According to Lyubimov and Erlikh, it was in fact the legal adviser Andrei Sabanin who had telephoned on Chicherin's behalf (*Genuezskaya konferentsiya* (M. 1963), p. 70).
42 'Letzte Vorgänge', vol. 1/1, 17 April 1922.
43 Louis Fischer, *The Soviets in World Affairs*, 2 vols. (London 1930), I, pp. 339–40.
44 D'Abernon, *Ambassador of Peace*, I, pp. 319–22.
45 Lyubimov and Erlikh, *Genuezskaya konferentsiya*, pp. 65–6.
46 Chicherin to Rathenau and Rathenau to Chicherin, 16 April 1922, SGO, II, no. 269, pp. 481–2.
47 Text in ibid., no. 268, pp. 479–81; and in *Izvestiya*, 10 May 1922, p. 1.
48 Maltzan to Litvinov, 17 April 1922, SGO, II, no. 271, p. 483.
49 ICP 239, 17 April 1922, Cab 29/95.
50 ICP 240, 18 April 1922, ibid.
51 Lloyd George et al. to Wirth, 18 April 1922, PA: Delegationen: Konferenz Genua: Vertrag mit Russland, vol. 1.
52 Notes of a Meeting, 19 April 1922, SG 8, Cab 31/5; see also 'Aufzeichung über eine Unterredung', 19 April 1922, PA: Büro Reichsminister: Genua, vol. 2/2.
53 'Pamyatnaya zapiska', 19 April 1922, SGO, I, no. 4, pp. 33–4.
54 ICP 243, 20 April 1922, Cab 29/96.
55 Hankey to his wife, 18 April 1922, Hankey papers, vol. 3/30.
56 Hankey to Chamberlain, 18 April 1922, ibid., vol. 8/23.
57 Hankey to Chamberlain, 20 April 1922, ibid.
58 Grigg to Chamberlain, 18 April 1922, Grigg papers, reel 1.
59 Gregory to Curzon, 17 April 1922, FO 371/8187/N3583.
60 Minutes, 18 April 1922, in FO 371/8187/N3583.
61 Gregory to Curzon, 20 April 1922, FO 371/8187/N3723.

62 SIS report, 21 April 1922, FO 371/8188/N3778; *Daily Mail*, 22 April 1922, p. 7.

63 Curzon to d'Abernon, 26 April 1922, FO 371/8188/N3869.

64 Hodgson to London, 24 April 1922, FO 371/8188/N3918.

65 D'Abernon to Curzon, 26 April 1922, d'Abernon Papers Add. Mss. 48924B.

66 D'Abernon to London, 23 April 1922, FO 371/8188/N3869.

67 D'Abernon to Curzon, 24 April 1922, Curzon papers F112/204.

68 D'Abernon to Curzon, 24 April 1922, d'Abernon Papers Add. Mss. 48924B.

69 Tyrrell to Curzon, 24 April 1922, Curzon papers F112/227.

70 Minutes, 24 and 29 April 1922, in FO 371/8188/N3869.

71 Comte de Saint-Aulaire, *Confessions d'un vieux diplomate* (Paris 1960), p. 620.

72 *Times*, 18 April 1922, p. 13, and 19 April 1922, p. 13.

73 *Manchester Guardian*, 21 April 1922, p. 11.

74 Poincaré to Barthou, 18 April 1922, MAE: Y Internationale, vol. 30.

75 Poincaré to Barthou, 19 April 1922, in Poincaré to Millerand, 22 April 1922, Millerand papers vol. 82.

76 Barthou to Poincaré, 18 April 1922, MAE: R.C., vol. 116.

77 Poincaré to Barthou, 19 April 1922, MAE: Y Internationale, vol. 30.

78 Bonin to Rome, 20 April 1922, ASD: Conferenza di Genova, vol. 52/20.

79 Charles Laurent to Poincaré, 21 and 29 April 1922, MAE: Y Internationale, vols. 30 and 31.

80 Martel to Poincaré, 24 April 1922, MAE: R.C., vol. 116.

81 Saint-Aulaire to Poincaré, 3 May 1922, MAE: Y Internationale, vol. 32.

82 For instance in German ambassador to FO, 6 May 1922, PA: Politische Abteilung IV: Deutsch-russischer Vertrag, vol. 2; see also SGO, I, no. 9, p. 39, 1 May 1922.

83 See for instance Belgian ambassador, Berlin, to Brussels, 13 May 1922, BFM: 10.991; Martel to Poincaré, 8 May 1922, MAE: R.C., vol. 117; *Times*, 22 April 1922, 11 and 20.

84 Lloyd George papers F149/3, 20 April 1922.

85 Poincaré to Millerand, 20 April 1922, Millerand papers vol. 82.

86 Barthou to Facta, 21 April 1922, ASD: Conferenza di Genova, vol. 52/20.

87 Wirth to Lloyd George et al., 21 April 1922, ibid.

88 Meeting of Members of the Sub-Committee, 22 April 1922, PCS 2A, Cab 31/7. For the subsequent meeting on 23 April, see PCS 2B, ibid.

89 Lloyd George et al. to Wirth, 23 April 1922, PA: Delegationen: Konferenz Genua: Vertrag mit Russland, vol. 1.

90 See for instance H. Graml, 'Die Rapallo-Politik im Urteil der westdeutschen Forschung', *Vierteljahrshefte für Zeitgeschichte*, 18, no. 4 (1970), pp. 369–91, and A. E. Ioffe, 'Sovetskaya istoriografiya Genuezskoi konferentsii', in P. N. Pospelov, ed., *Istoricheskii opyt velikogo Oktyabrya* (M. 1975), pp. 393–400.

91 Note, 7 August 1922, MAE: R.C., vol. 117; d'Abernon to Curzon, 27 October 1922, FO 371/8209/N9937. The further development of German–Soviet economic relations is surveyed in Werner Beitel and

Jürgen Nötzold, *Deutsch-sowjetische Wirtschaftsbeziehungen in der Zeit der Weimarer Republik* (Baden-Baden 1979); the relevant statistics are contained in *Vneshnyaya torgovlya SSSR za 1918–1940 gg.*, p. 23.

8 CLOSING STAGES

1 E. F. Wise, Memorandum of Meeting, 20 April 1922, Grigg papers, reel 9.
2 Note of Conversation, 20 April 1922, SG11, Cab 31/5; the letter, as amended, is in ibid.
3 Chicherin to Lloyd George, 20 April 1922, DVP, v, no. 127, pp. 259–60.
4 Notes of an Informal Meeting, 21 April 1922, ICP 244, Cab 29/96.
5 Notes of Meeting, 21 April 1922, PCS 2, Cab 31/7.
6 Notes of Meeting, 22 April 1922, PCSE 1, Cab 31/6.
7 Notes of Meeting, 11 April 1922, PCSE 2, ibid.
8 *Izvestiya*, 7, 8 and 10 May 1922, pp. 1–2, 1 and 1; also DVP, v, no. 126, pp. 232–45.
9 Rakovsky to Worthington-Evans, 22 April 1922, DVP, v, no. 132, pp. 254–6; Notes of Meeting, 23 April 1922, ICP 247, Cab 29/96.
10 Notes of Meeting, 23 April 1922, PCSE 3, Cab 31/6.
11 Notes of Meeting, 24 April 1922, PCSE 4, ibid.
12 Statement of the Soviet Delegation, 24 April 1922, DVP, v, no. 135, pp. 268–9.
13 Notes of Meeting, 24 and 25 April 1922, PCSE 5 and 6, Cab 31/6.
14 Hankey to Chamberlain, 23 April 1922, Hankey papers 8/23.
15 Poincaré to Barthou, 21 April 1922, MAE: Europe: Russie, vol. 158.
16 Cited in Poincaré to Millerand, 23 April 1922, Millerand papers, vol. 82.
17 Ibid.
18 Barthou to Poincaré, 23 April 1922, MAE: R.C., vol. 94.
19 Poincaré to Millerand, 23 April 1922, Millerand papers, vol. 82.
20 Belgian ambassador, Paris, to Brussels, 24 April 1922, BFM: 10.991.
21 Text in Poincaré papers, NAF vol. 16042; and in *Le Temps*, 25 April 1922, p. 4.
22 Cheetham to Curzon, 24 April 1922, FO 371/7427/C5986.
23 Ibid., FO 371/7427/C5985.
24 Notes of Meeting, 25 April 1922, PCSE 6, Cab 31/6.
25 Cited in Poincaré to Millerand, 26 April 1922, Millerand papers, vol. 82.
26 Notes of Conversation, 26 April 1922, SG 18, Cab 31/5.
27 Hankey to Chamberlain, 23 April 1922, Hankey papers 8/23.
28 Ibid., 25 and 27 April 1922, ibid.
29 Notes of Conversation, 26 April 1922, SG 18, Cab 31/5.
30 Notes of an Informal Meeting, 26 April 1922, ICP 247C, Cab 29/96.
31 Notes of Conversation, 27 April 1922, ICP 247E and 247F, Cab 29/96.
32 Notes of Meeting, 28 April 1922, PCS 3, Cab 31/7; both drafts are in ibid.
33 Notes of Meeting, 29 April 1922, PCS 4, Cab 31/7.
34 Notes of Meeting, 29 April 1922, PCS 5, ibid.
35 Notes of Meeting, 1 May 1922, PCS 6, ibid.

36 Notes of Meeting, 1 May 1922, PCS 7, ibid.
37 Notes of Meeting, 2 May 1922, PCS 8, ibid.
38 Text in ibid., Annex II; and in DVP, v, pp. 373–8.
39 Hankey to Curzon, 2 May 1922, Curzon papers F112/225; Hankey to Chamberlain, 4 May 1922, Hankey papers 8/23.
40 Tyrrell to Curzon, 26 April 1922, Curzon papers F112/227.
41 Bolletino no. 18, 5 May 1922, in ASD: Conferenza di Genova, vol. 118/31.
42 Chateauneuf (Copenhagen) to Paris, 4 May 1922, MAE: R.C., vol. 110.
43 Bolletino nos. 17 and 22, 4 and 10 May 1922, in ASD: Conferenza di Genova, vol. 118/31.
44 Note, 26 April 1922, PA: Delegationen: Konferenz Genua: Vertrag mit Russland, vol. 1.
45 Lenin to Chicherin and Sosnovsky, 19 April 1922, *Leninskii sbornik*, vol. 36 (M. 1959), p. 474. (A copy of Lenin's letter is in the Trotsky papers, T748).
46 Lenin to Chicherin, 21 April 1922, ibid.
47 *PSS*, vol. 45, p. 538 n. 103. The Politburo's directives of 17 April 1922 are in ibid., p. 537 n. 100; they provided *inter alia* for the cancellation of Russian war debts and interest in return for the abandonment of counter-claims, and absolutely ruled out the restitution of private property.
48 Lenin to Stalin, 24 April 1922, *Leninskii sbornik*, vol. 36, p. 475.
49 Ibid., pp. 475–6.
50 *PSS*, vol. 45, pp. 540–1 n. 108.
51 Lenin to Chicherin, 30 April 1922, ibid., p. 171.
52 Litvinov to NKID, 30 April and 2 May 1922, ibid., p. 541 n. 109.
53 Ioffe to Politburo, 1 and 2 May 1922, ibid., pp. 541–2 n. 109.
54 Note for Politburo, 2 May 1922, ibid., p. 172 (emphasis in original).
55 Draft telegram to Chicherin, 2 May 1922, ibid., pp. 172, 542 n. 110.
56 Draft telegram to Chicherin, 5 or 6 May 1922, ibid., p. 183.
57 Telegram to Litvinov, 8 May 1922, ibid., p. 184.
58 Telegram to Chicherin, 9 May 1922, ibid., p. 185.
59 Chicherin to Facta, 28 April 1922, DVP, v, no. 139, pp. 176–7.
60 Facta to Chicherin, 29 April 1922, ibid., p. 278.
61 *Izvestiya*, 23, 24 and 25 May 1922, pp. 2, 1–2 and 1; and DVP, v, no. 153, pp. 361–72.
62 Barthou to Paris, 1 May 1922, MAE: R.C., vol. 96; and Hardinge to Genoa, 4 May 1922, Cab 31/13. The rumours were categorically denied by Lloyd George (to Hardinge, 4 May 1922, Grigg papers, reel 10), and Poincaré was informed accordingly (Hardinge to Genoa, 5 May 1922, Cab 31/13). The oil diplomacy of this period is considered in Louis Fischer, *Oil Imperialism* (New York 1926); the American ambassador, Richard W. Child, suggests that the importance of such matters was greatly exaggerated (*A Diplomat Looks at Europe* (New York 1925), pp. 15–16).
63 Barrère to Poincaré, 4 May 1922, MAE: Y Internationale, vol. 32.
64 Poincaré to Barrère, 3 May 1922, ibid.
65 Poincaré to French ambassador, Brussels, 3 May 1922, ibid.

66 Poincaré to Barrère, 3 May 1922, ibid.
67 Hardinge to Genoa, 4 May 1922, FO 371/7431/C6594; Poincaré to Barrère, 5 May 1922, MAE: Europe: Russie, vol. 349.
68 Poincaré to Barthou, 5 May 1922, MAE: Y Internationale, vol. 32.
69 Hardinge to Curzon, 5 May 1922, and Curzon to Hardinge, 8 May 1922, Hardinge papers, vol. 45.
70 Notes of Conversation, 6 May 1922, SG 29, Cab 31/5.
71 Grigg to Chamberlain, 7 May 1922, Grigg papers, reel 1; Hankey to Chamberlain, 7 May 1922, Hankey papers, vol. 8/23.
72 Barthou to Ministère de Finances, 30 April 1922, MAE: R.C., vol. 102.
73 Inverforth to Horne, 29 April 1922, Cab 31/13.
74 Ministère des Finances to M. Sergent, 22 June 1922, MAE: R.C., vol. 102.
75 Binder to Sergent, 3 July 1922 and 16 January 1923, ibid.
76 Horne to Worthington-Evans, 23 April 1922, Worthington-Evans papers, vol. c. 930.
77 Sassoon to Lloyd George, 28 1 1922, Lloyd George papers F45/1/13.
78 Sassoon to Lloyd George, 28 April 1922, ibid. F45/1/12.
79 Chamberlain to Hankey, 1 May 1922, Curzon papers FO 800/157.
80 Curzon to Hardinge, 2 May 1922, Hardinge papers, vol. 45.
81 Chamberlain to Worthington-Evans, 3 May 1922, Worthington-Evans papers, vol. c. 930.
82 Chamberlain to British ministers at Genoa, 4 May 1922, Grigg papers, reel 10.
83 Lloyd-Greame to wife, between 4 and 8 May 1922, Swinton (Cunliffe-Lister) papers, vol. 2/3.
84 Lloyd-Greame to Baldwin, 6 May 1922, ibid.
85 Lloyd George to Chamberlain, 5 May 1922, Grigg papers, reel 10.
86 Chamberlain to Lloyd George, 9 May 1922, FO 371/8190/N4498.
87 Chamberlain to Lloyd George, 10 May 1922, FO 371/8190/N4552.
88 Notes of Meeting, 10 May 1922, Cab 31/1.
89 Notes of Conversation, 11 May 1922, SG 30B, Cab 31/5.
90 Notes of Conversation, 11 May 1922, ICP 247J, Cab 29/96.
91 Notes of Conversation, 12 May 1922, ICP 247K, Cab 29/96; Notes of Conversation, 12 May 1922, SG 30E, Cab 31/5.
92 Poincaré to Barthou, 14 May 1922, MAE: R.C., vol. 98.
93 Notes of Meeting, 13 May 1922, PCS 9, Cab 31/7.
94 Notes of Meetings, 13 May 1922, PCS 10, Cab 31/7; 14 May 1922, ICP 248, Cab 29/96; 14 May 1922, ICP 249, Cab 29/96; and 15 May 1922, PCS 11, Cab 31/7.
95 Notes of Meeting, 16 and 17 May 1922, PCS 12 and 13, Cab 31/7.
96 Notes of Meeting, 17 May 1922, PCS 14, ibid.
97 Minutes of Third Plenary Session, 19 May 1922, Cab 31/4.

9 GENOA AND AFTER

1 *H.C. Debs.*, 5th ser., vol. 154, cols. 1449–68, 25 May 1922.
2 Ibid., cols. 1469, 1471.

3 Ibid., col. 1474.
4 *Times*, 20 May 1922, p. 17.
5 *Economist*, 20 May 1922, p. 941.
6 *Glasgow Herald*, 20 May 1922, p. 8.
7 *Débats parlementaires: Chambre des Députés*, cols. 1608–46, 1 June 1922.
8 See for instance ibid. and *Le Temps*, 20 May 1922, p. 1.
9 French ambassador, Brussels, to Paris, 24 May 1922, Millerand papers, vol. 80.
10 Graham to London, 24 May 1922, FO 371/7433/C7910.
11 Marling to London, 19 May 1922, FO 371/7433/C7895.
12 *Exposé de M. Beneš au sujet de la Conférence de Gênes* (Prague 1922), pp. 27–8.
13 *Atti parlamentari della Camera dei Deputati*, pp. 5796–80, 7 June 1922.
14 Ibid., p. 5845; Graham to Balfour, 9 June 1922, FO 371/7658/C8413.
15 *Corriere della sera*, 21 May 1922, p. 1.
16 Graham to Curzon, 26 May 1922, FO 371/7433/C7797.
17 Note of interview, PA: Büro Reichsminister: Genua, vol. 4.
18 Text in ibid., 28 May 1922.
19 *Verhandlungen des Reichstags*, vol. 355, pp. 7678ff, 29 May 1922.
20 Ibid., vol. 356, col. 8271, 4 July 1922; SGO, II, no. 320, pp. 563–6, 5 November 1922.
21 'Doklad Ya. E. Rudzutaka o Genueszkoi konferentsii', *Istoricheskii arkhiv*, 1961, no. 2, pp. 80–92, at p. 87.
22 *Pravda*, 13 May 1922, p. 1.
23 A. A. Ioffe, *Genuezskaya konferentsiya* (M. 1922), p. 25.
24 *Toronto Daily Star*, 24 April 1922, pp. 1–2.
25 Jacques Bardoux, *Lloyd George et la France* (Paris 1923), p. 418.
26 E. A. Preobrazhensky, *Itogi Genuezskoi konferentsii i khozyaistvennye perspektivy Evropy* (M. 1922), p. 27.
27 'Doklad Rudzutaka', p. 92.
28 *Pravda*, 17 May 1922, p. 1; *Izvestiya*, 18 May 1922, p. 2
29 Text in DVP, v, no. 159, 17 May 1922, pp. 383–6.
30 Quoted in *Pravda*, 23 May 1922, p. 1.
31 *Izvestiya*, 30 May 1922, p. 1.
32 *Pravda*, 7 June 1922, p. 1.
33 Ibid., 1 June 1922, p. 1.
34 *Times*, 22 June 1922, p. 9.
35 *Mezhdunarodnaya politika RSFSR v 1922 g. Otchet NKID* (M. 1923), p. 3.
36 A Soviet documentation on the Hague congress is contained in *Gaagskaya konferentsiya, iyun'-iyul' 1922 g. (Sobranie dokumentov)* (M. 1922). Dutch documentation is in Ministerie van Buitenlandse Zaken archives A81 dossier 174; Italian documentation is in ASD: Archivio Conferenze, classe 54; French documentation is in MAE: R.C., vols. 129–35, and Y Internationale, vol. 37; and a British documentation is in Confidential Print 11966 (1922).
37 Text in CP 4016, 2 June 1922, Cab 24/137.
38 See for instance *Izvestiya*, 17 June 1922, p. 1.
39 See ASD: Conferenza di Genova, vol. 52/37.
40 Text in Schanzer papers, vol. 13; not in DVP.

41 *Mezhdunarodnaya politika*, p. 28; DVP, v, no. 185, 17 June 1922, p. 453; and exchange of notes, 7 and 11 February 1924, DVP, vii, no. 41, pp. 91–2. The Soviet–British exchange of notes is in ibid., no. 30, 1 and 8 February 1924, pp. 53–5.
42 *Izvestiya*, 8 June 1922, p. 1.
43 Text in DVP, v, no. 180, 5 June 1922, pp. 441–4.
44 Curzon to Hardinge, 13 October 1922, FO 371/8184/N9208.
45 Exchange of notes, 28 October 1924, DVP, vii, no. 246, pp. 514–17.
46 Texts in DVP, viii, no. 342, 12 October 1925, pp. 582–617, and ix, no. 141, 24 April 1926, pp. 250–4; see also above, Chapter 7.
47 See DVP, xvi, nos. 362 and 364–6, 16 November 1933, pp. 641, 644–54.
48 DVP, iii, no. 344, 16 March 1921, p. 608, and vii, no. 246, p. 515.
49 Exchange of notes, 16 November 1933, DVP, xvi, no. 363, pp. 642–3.
50 Dagboek betreffende Conferentie van Genua, entries for 28 April and 10 and 13 May 1922, Ministerie van Buitenlandse Zaken archives.
51 *L'Europe nouvelle*, 29 April 1922, p. 517; see also above, pp. 124–5.
52 F. Charles-Roux, *Souvenirs diplomatiques* (Paris 1961), pp. 163, 164.
53 P. Cambon, *Correspondance 1870–1924*, vol. 3 (Paris 1946), p. 408.
54 PCS 9, 13 May 1922, Cab 31/7.
55 Notes of Conversation, 7 May 1922, SG 30, Cab 31/5.
56 'Some memories and reflections', p. 180, Chapman papers.
57 *The Collected Writings of J. M. Keynes*, ed. Elizabeth Johnson, vol. 17 (London 1977), p. 119; see also ibid., p. 326, 5 January 1922.
58 *Manchester Guardian*, 6 April 1922, pp. 9–10.
59 Ibid., 10 April 1922, p. 6.
60 Keynes to Ransome, 19 April 1922, in Keynes, *Collected Writings*, xvii, p. 378.
61 *Manchester Guardian*, 19 April 1922, p. 6.
62 Ibid., 4 May 1922, p. 6.
63 Ibid., 18 April 1922, p. 6; *Manchester Guardian Commercial*, 15 June 1922, pp. 132–3.
64 The literature on this subject is conveniently surveyed in Martin McCauley, *The Origins of the Cold War* (London 1983), esp. chap. 6.
65 A survey of recent Soviet–Western relations is available in Adam Ulam, *Dangerous Relations: The Soviet Union in World Politics, 1970–1982* (New York 1983); on the general background, see particularly Gordon A. Craig and Alexander L. George, *Force and Statecraft: Diplomatic Problems of our Time* (New York 1983), esp. chaps. 9, 10 and 17.
66 The *locus classicus* of this approach is President Reagan's 'evil empire' speech; text in *Coexistence*, 21, no. 1 (April 1984), pp. 51–8.

Select bibliography

A. MANUSCRIPT SOURCES

PUBLIC ARCHIVES

Belgium

Ministère des Affaires Étrangères: Correspondance politique

France

Archives Nationales, Paris: Ministère de l'Intérieur: Administration générale: Police générale
    Delegation française à la Commission des Réparations
Ministère des Affaires Étrangères, Paris
    Série B Relations Commerciales 1920–1939: Délibérations internationales
    Série Europe 1918–1929: Russie
    Série Y Internationale 1918–1940: Conférences politiques
Ministère des Finances, Paris: Russie: Affaires générales, 1918–1916

Germany

Bundesarchiv, Koblenz: Akten der Reichskanzlei
Politisches Archiv des Auswärtiges Amtes, Bonn
    Büro des Reichsministers
    Politische Abteilung II (Frankreich, Italien)
    Politische Abteilung III (England)
    Politische Abteilung IV (Russland)
    Abteilung II F–M (Militäre und Marine)
    Geheimakten 1920–1936
    Sonderreferat Wirtschaft
    Delegationen: Konferenz Cannes; Konferenz Genua

Italy

Archivio Centrale dello Stato, Rome
    Atti del Consiglio dei Ministri

I Guerra Mondiale: Conferenza dell'Aja; Conferenza di Genova
Verbali del Consiglio dei Ministri
Archivo Storico Diplomatico del Ministero degli Affari Esteri, Rome
Affari Politici: Russia
Archivo Conferenze: Conferenza di Cannes; Conferenza di Genova
Rapprezentanze Diplomatiche: Berlin; Parigi; Londra; Russia

Netherlands

Ministerie van Buitenlandse Zaken, The Hague
Directory of Economic Affairs: Konferentie Genua en Den Haag
Kabinets-archief: Rusland 1918–1924
Konferentie van Genua

United Kingdom

Public Record Office, London
Cabinet papers
Cabinet minutes (Cab 23)
Cabinet minutes: AJ and ICP series (Cab 29)
Cabinet memoranda (Cab 24)
Genoa (International Economic) Conference (Cab 31)
Registered Files (Cab 21)
Foreign Office papers
Confidential Print (FO 408, 418, 421, 425)
Green Papers (1921–22)
Political Correspondence (FO 371)

United States

United States National Archives, Washington, DC: Diplomatic Branch
records

PRIVATE ARCHIVES

France

Archives Nationales, Paris: Alexandre Millerand papers
Bibliothèque de l'Institut de l'histoire des relations internationales contem-
poraines, Paris: Louis Loucheur papers (microfilm)
Bibliothèque Nationale, Paris: Poincaré papers
Ministère des Affaires Étrangères, Paris
Charles Alphand papers
François Charles-Roux papers
Albert-Jules Defrance papers
Marcel Plaisant papers
Alexandre Millerand papers

Germany

Bundesarchiv, Koblenz: Walter Rathenau papers

Italy

Archivo Centrale dello Stato, Rome
  Carlo Schanzer papers
  Carlo Sforza papers
  Pietro Tomasi della Torretta papers

Netherlands

International Instituut voor Sociale Geschiedenis, Amsterdam: Krasin
  papers
Ministerie van Buitenlandse Zaken, The Hague: Collectie van Karnebeek

United Kingdom

Birmingham University: Austen Chamberlain papers
Bodleian Library, Oxford
  Grigg papers (microfilm)
  Worthington-Evans papers
British Library, London: d'Abernon papers
Cambridge University Library
  Kennet papers
  Hardinge papers
Churchill College, Cambridge
  Swinton (Cunliffe-Lister) papers
  Hankey papers
House of Lords Record Office, London: Lloyd George papers
India Office Library, London: Curzon papers
Manchester University Library: Chapman papers
National Library of Wales, Aberystwyth: Thomas Jones papers
Public Record Office, London
  Curzon papers
  Hankey papers

United States

Houghton Library, Harvard University: Trotsky papers
Yale University Library: Louis Fischer papers

B. PRINTED SOURCES

OFFICIAL AND DOCUMENTARY PUBLICATIONS

Belgium

C. de Vischener and F. Vanlangenhove, eds., *Documents diplomatiques belges
  1920–1940*, 5 vols. (Brussels 1964–6)

France

Journal Officiel de la République Française. *Débats parlementaires: Chambre des Députés*
Journal Officiel de la République Française. *Débats parlementaires: Sénat*
Ministère des Affaires Étrangères. *Conférence économique internationale de Gênes, 9 avril–19 mai 1922. (Documents diplomatiques)* (Paris 1922)
Ministère des Affaires Étrangères. *Documents diplomatiques. Documents relatifs aux négociations concernant les guaranties de sécurité contre une aggression de l'Allemagne (10 janvier 1919–17 décembre 1923)* (Paris 1924)

Germany

Akten der Reichskanzlei Weimarer Republic. Die Kabinette Wirth I und II, ed. Ingrid Schulze-Bidlingmeier, 2 vols. (Boppard am Rhein 1973)
Auswärtiges Amt. *Material über die Konferenz von Genua* (Berlin 1922)
Deutsch-sowjetische Beziehungen von den Verhandlungen in Brest-Litovsk bis zum Abschluss des Rapallovertrages. Dokumentensammlung, ed. V. M. Khvostov et al., 2 vols. (East Berlin, 1967–71)
Reichstag. *Verhandlungen des Reichstags. Stenografische Berichte*

Italy

Camera dei Deputati. *Atti parlamentari della Camera dei Deputati. Discuzzioni*
Senato. *Atti parlamentari della Camera dei Senatori. Discuzzioni*
Les documents de la Conférence de Gênes, ed. A. Giannini (Rome 1922)
La Conferenza di Genova. Cronache e documenti, ed. P. Bernasconi and G. Zanelli (Bologna 1922)

Netherlands

Documenten betreffende de buitenlandse politiek van Nederland 1919–1945: periode A 1919–1930: deel III, 1 september 1921–31 juli 1922, ed. J. Woltring (The Hague 1980)

United Kingdom

Documents on British Foreign Policy 1919–1939, ed. E. L. Woodward and Rohan Butler, 1st ser., vols. 1–23 (London 1947–81; in progress)
Parliamentary Debates: Official Report, Fifth Series. House of Commons
Parliamentary Debates: Official Report, Fifth Series. House of Lords
Parliamentary Papers (Cmd. 1621, 1637, 1667, 1742 (1922) and 2169 (1924))

United States

Papers relating to the Foreign Relations of the United States, 1918–1922 (Washington DC 1931–38)
The Paris Peace Conference, 1919, 13 vols. (Washington DC 1942–7)

USSR

Gosudarstvennyi planovoi komitet SSSR etc. *Protokoly Prezidiuma Gosplana za 1921–1922 gody*, ed. N. I. Rogovsky et al., 2 vols. (Moscow 1979)

Ministerstvo inostrannykh del SSSR. *Dokumenty i materialy po istorii sovetsko-chekhoslovatskikh otnoshenii*, ed. P. N. Pospelov et al., tom 1: *Noyabr' 1917 g. – avgust 1922 g.* (Moscow 1973; in progress)

Dokumenty i materialy po istorii sovetsko-pol'skikh otnoshenii, ed. I. A. Khrenov et al., tom 4: *Aprel' 1921 g. – mai 1926 g.* (Moscow 1966; in progress)

Dokumenty vneshnei politiki SSSR, ed. A. A. Gromyko et al., 21 vols. (Moscow 1957–77)

Sovetsko-germanskie otnosheniya ot peregovorov v Brest-Litovske do podpisaniya Rapall'skogo dogovara. Sbornik dokumentov, ed. S. Dërnberg et al., 2 vols. (Moscow 1968–71)

Sovetsko-germanskie otnosheniya 1922–1925 gg. Dokumenty i materialy, ed. S. Dërnberg et al., 2 vols (Moscow 1977)

Narodnyi komissariat po inostrannym delam RSFSR. *Gaagskaya konferentsiya, iyun'–iyul' 1922 g. (Sobranie dokumentov)* (Moscow 1922)

Genuezskaya konferentsiya. Materialy i dokumenty, vyp. 1 (Moscow 1922)

Godovoi otchet NKID k IX s"ezdu sovetov (1920–1921) (Moscow 1921)

Instruktsiya konsulam RSFSR (Moscow 1921)

Materialy Genuezskoi konferentsii (Moscow 1922)

Mezhdunarodaya politika RSFSR v 1922 g. Otchet NKID (Moscow 1923)

Mezhdunarodnaya politika noveishego vremeni v dogovorakh, notakh i deklaratsiyakh, ed. Yu. V. Klyuchnikov and A. Sabanin, 3 parts (Moscow 1926–9)

Sbornik deistvuyushchikh dogovorov, soglashenii i konventsii, zaklyuchennykh RSFSR s inostrannymi gosudarstvami, vyp. 1–3 (Moscow 1921–2)

Rossiiskaya kommunisticheskaya partiya (bol'shevikov). *XI vserossiiskaya partiinaya konferentsiya RKP(b) (19–22 dekabrya 1921 g.) Stenograficheskii otchet* (Samara 1922)

Vserossiiskaya [XI] konferentsiya RKP(b). Byulleten', nos. 1–5 (Moscow 1924)

Odinnadtsatyi s"ezd RKP(b) 27 marta–2 aprelya 1922 g. Stenograficheskii otchet (Moscow 1922)

Dvenadtsatyi s"ezd RKP(b) 17–25 aprelya. Stenograficheskii otchet (Moscow 1923)

RSFSR. Vserossiiskie s"ezdy sovetov. *Devyatyi Vserossiiskii s"ezd sovetov, 22–27 dekabrya 1921 g. Stenograficheskii otchet* (Moscow 1922)

RSFSR. Vserossiiskii tsentral'nyi ispolnitel'nyi komitet (VTsIK). *Pervaya-chetvertaya sessii VTsIK Vserossiiskogo TsIK VIII sozyva (31 dek. 1920 g. – 7 okt. 1921 g.). Stenograficheskii otchet* (Moscow 1922)

Pervaya i vtoraya sessii Vserossiiskogo TsIK IX sozyva (29 dek. 1921 g., 27 yan. 1922 g.). Stenograficheskii otchet (Moscow 1923)

Tret'ya sessiya Vserossiiskogo TsIK IX sozyva (14–28 maya 1922). Stenografichskii otchet, nos. 1–12 (Moscow 1922)

[Other] *Resheniya partii i pravitel'stva po khozyaistvennym voprosam*, ed. K. U. Chernenko and M. S. Smirtyukov, tom 1: 1917–1928 (Moscow 1967; in progress).

PERIODICAL PUBLICATIONS

Avanti! (Rome and Milan, daily)
Byulleten' NKID (Moscow, weekly)
Corriere della sera (Milan, daily)
Daily Chronicle (London, daily)
Daily Herald (London, daily)
Ekonomicheskaya zhizn' (Moscow, daily)
L'Europe nouvelle (Paris, weekly)
Le Figaro (Paris, daily)
Giornale d'Italia (Rome, daily)
Golos Rossii (Berlin, daily)
L'Humanité (Paris, daily)
Izvestiya (Moscow, daily)
Kommunisticheskii international (Moscow, monthly)
Krasnaya nov' (Moscow, bimonthly)
Manchester Guardian (Manchester, daily)
Le Matin (Paris, daily)
Mezhdunarodnaya zhizn' (Moscow, fortnightly)
Nakanune (Berlin, daily)
New York Times (New York, daily)
Novyi mir (Berlin, daily)
Obshchee delo (Paris, daily)
Il Popolo d'Italia (Rome, daily)
Poslednye novosti (Paris, daily)
Pravda (Moscow, daily)
Revue des deux mondes (Paris, monthly)
Rul' (Berlin, daily)
Russkaya mysl' (Prague, quarterly)
Smena vekh (Paris, weekly)
La Stampa (Turin, daily)
The Times (London, daily)
Trud (Moscow, daily)
Vestnik NKID (Moscow, monthly)

SELECTED WRITINGS, MEMOIRS AND SECONDARY WORKS

Adamoli, Gerasio et al., *La Conferenza di Genova e il trattato di Rapallo* (Rome 1974)
Akhtamzyan, A. A., *Rapall'skaya politika* (Moscow 1974)
Aldcroft, Derek, *From Versailles to Wall Street 1919–1929* (London 1977)
Bardoux, Jacques, *Lloyd George et la France* (Paris 1923)
Bariéty, Jacques, *Les relations franco-allemandes après la première guerre mondiale* (Paris 1977)
Barmine, Alexandre, *Memoirs of a Soviet Diplomat* (London 1938)
[Beneš, Édouard] *Exposé de M. Beneš au sujet de la Conférence de Gênes* (Prague 1922)
Besedovsky, G. Z., *Na putyakh k termidoru*, 2 vols. (Paris, 1930–1)

Bonnefous, Édouard, *Histoire politique de la IIIe République*, 2nd ed., tome III: *L'Après-guerre (1919–1924)* (Paris 1968)

Bonnet, Georges, *Le Quai d'Orsay sous trois républiques (1870–1961)* (Paris 1961)

Bonomi, Ivanoe, *Dieci anni di politica italiana*, ed. Feruccio Rubbiani (Milan 1923)
   From Socialism to Fascism (London 1924)
   Discorsi politici di Ivanoe Bonomi (Rome 1954)

Bournazel, Renata, *Rapallo: naissance d'un mythe* (Paris 1974)

[Briand, Aristide] *Aristide Briand: discours et écrits de politique étrangère*, ed. Achille Elisha (Paris 1965)

Cambon, Paul, *Correspondance 1870–1924*, tome III: *1912–1924* (Paris 1946)

Carr, E. H., *German–Soviet Relations between the Two World Wars 1919–1939* (London 1951)
   A History of Soviet Russia, 14 vols. (London 1950–78)

Carsten, F. L., *The Reichswehr and Politics 1918–1933* (London 1966)

Catellani, Enrico, *Sulle vie della pace: la Conferenza di Genova* (Venice 1929)

Celtus (pseud.), *La France a Gênes: un programme français de reconstruction économique de l'Europe* (Paris 1922)

Charles-Roux, François, *Souvenirs diplomatiques: une grande ambassade à Rome, 1919–1925* (Paris 1961)

Chastenet, Jacques, *Histoire de la Troisième République*, new ed., tome III (Paris 1974)

Chicherin, G. V., *Motsart: issledovatel'skii etyud* (Leningrad 1970)
   Stat'i i rechi po voprosam mezhdunarodnoi politiki (Moscow 1961)

Child, Richard W., *A Diplomat Looks at Europe* (New York 1925)

Chossudovsky, E. M., 'Genoa revisited: Russia and coexistence', *Foreign Affairs*, 50, no. 3 (April 1972), pp. 554–77.
   G. V. Chicherin and the Evolution of Soviet Foreign Policy and Diplomacy (Geneva 1973)

Chubar'yan, A. O., *V. I. Lenin i formirovanie sovetskoi vneshnei politiki* (Moscow 1972)

Chubar'yan, A. O., et al., *Evropa v mezhdunarodnykh otnosheniyakh 1917–1939* (Moscow 1979)

Conte, Francis, *Christian Rakovski (1873–1941): essai de biographie politique* (Lille and Paris, 1975)

Craig, Gordon A. and Gilbert, Felix, eds., *The Diplomats, 1919–1939* (Princeton 1953)

d'Abernon, Lord, *An Ambassador of Peace*, 3 vols. (London 1929–30)

Le Débâcle des Soviets et la restauration économique de la Russie: mémoires présentés à la Conférence de Gênes par l'Association Financière, Industrielle et Commerciale Russe et le Comité des Représentants des Banques Russes à Paris (Paris 1922)
   Aperçu général des mémoires (Paris 1922); *Supplément aux mémoires* (Paris 1922)

Desyat' let sovetskoi diplomatii. (Akty i dokumenty) (Moscow 1927)

Eastman, Max, *Love and Revolution* (New York 1964)

Eyck, Erich, *A History of the Weimar Republic*, 2 vols. (London 1962–4)

Felice, Renzo de, ed., *Storia d'Italia contemporanea*, vol. III: *Guerra e fascismo 1915–1929* (Naples 1978)

Fischer, Louis, *Oil Imperialism: The International Struggle for Petroleum* (New York 1926)
   The Soviets in World Affairs, 2 vols. (London 1930)
[Frassati, Alfredo] *Un uomo, un giornale: Alfredo Frassati*, ed. Luciana Frassati, 2 vols. (Rome 1978–9)
Freund, Gerald, *Unholy Alliance: Russo-German Relations from the Treaty of Brest-Litovsk to the Treaty of Berlin* (London 1957)
Gilbert, Martin, *Winston S. Churchill*, vol. iv: *Companion*, part 3 (London 1977)
Gladkov, I. A. et al., *Istoriya sotsialisticheskoi ekonomiki SSSR*, vols. 1–2 (Moscow 1976)
Goldbach, Marie Louise, *Karl Radek und die deutsch-sowjetischen Beziehungen 1918–1923* (Bonn and Bad Godesberg 1973)
Gorokhov, I. M. et al., *G. V. Chicherin: diplomat leninskoi shkoly*, 2nd ed. (Moscow 1974)
Gromyko, A. A. et al., eds., *Istoriya diplomatii*, 2nd ed., vol. iii (Moscow 1965)
Gromyko, A. A. and Ponomarev, B. N., eds. *Istoriya vneshnei politiki SSSR*, 4th ed., 2 vols. (Moscow 1980)
Gurevich, M., *V Genue* (Khar'kov n.d. [1922])
Helbig, Herbert, *Die Träger der Rapallo-Politik* (Göttingen 1958)
Hemingway, Ernest, *By-line: Selected Articles and Despatches of Four Decades* (London 1968)
   Reportazhi, ed. T. S. Tikhmenevaya (Moscow 1969)
Hiden, John W., *Germany and Europe 1919–1939* (London 1977)
Hilger, Gustav and Meyer, Alfred G., *The Incompatible Allies: A Memoir History of German–Soviet Relations 1918–1941* (New York 1953)
Hogenhuis-Seliverstoff, Anne, *Les relations franco-soviétiques 1917–1924* (Paris 1981)
Ioffe, A. A., *Genuezskaya konferentsiya* (Moscow 1922)
   Ot genui do Gaagi: sbornik statei (Moscow 1923)
Ishii, Viscount Kikujiro, *Diplomatic Commentaries*, ed. William R. Langdon (Baltimore 1936)
Karpova, R. F., *L. B. Krasin – sovetskii diplomat* (Moscow 1962)
Kessler, Graf Harry von, *Tagebücher 1918–1937* (Frankfurt 1961)
   Walter Rathenau: sein Leben und sein Werk (Berlin 1928)
[Keynes, J. M.] *The Collected Writings of John Maynard Keynes*, vol. xvii: *Activities 1920–1922: Treaty Revision and Reconstruction*, ed. Elizabeth Johnson (London 1977)
Khovratovich, I. M., *Georgii Vasil'evich Chicherin* (Moscow 1980)
Kochan, Lionel, *Russia and the Weimar Republic* (Cambridge 1954)
Krasin, L. B., *Voprosy vneshnei torgovli* (Moscow and Leningrad 1928)
Krasin, Lyubov, *Leonid Krasin: His Life and Work* (London 1929)
Laroche, Jules, *Au Quai d'Orsay avec Briand et Poincaré, 1913–1927* (Paris 1957)
[Lenin, V. I.] *Leninskii sbornik*, vyp. 36–9 (Moscow 1959–80; in progress)
Lenin, V. I., *Polnoe sobranie sochinenii*, 55 vols. (Moscow 1958–65)
Lensen, George, A., *Japanese Recognition of the USSR: Soviet–Japanese Relations, 1921–1930* (Tokyo 1970)
Linke, Horst Günther, *Deutsch-sowjetische Beziehungen bis Rapallo* (Cologne 1970)

Lloyd George, David, *The Truth about Reparations and War Debts* (London 1932)

Lloyd George, Frances, *The Years That Are Past* (London 1967)

Loucheur, Louis, *Carnets secrets 1908–1932* (Brussels and Paris 1962)

Lowe, Cedric J. and Dockrill, M. L., *The Mirage of Power: British Foreign Policy 1902–1922*, 3 vols. (London 1972)

Lowe, Cedric J. and Marzari, F., *Italian Foreign Policy 1870–1940* (London 1975)

Lyubimov, N. N., *Balans vzaimnykh trebovanii SSSR i derzhav soglasiya* (Moscow and Leningrad 1924)

'Vospominaniya uchastnika Genuezskoi konferentsii', in *Po zavetam V. I. Lenina*, vyp. 3 (Moscow 1973), pp. 94–103.

Lyubimov, N. M. and Erlikh, A. N., *Genuezskaya konferentsiya: vospominaniya uchastnikov* (Moscow 1963)

Maisky, I. M., *Lyudi, sobytiya, fakty* (Moscow 1973)

Vneshnyaya politika RSFSR 1917–1922 (Moscow 1922)

Millet, Philippe, *Les conférences de Washington et de Cannes et les perspectives de Gênes* (Paris 1922)

Mills, J. Saxon, *The Genoa Conference* (London 1922)

Miquel, Pierre, *Poincaré* (Paris 1961)

Morgan, Kenneth O., *Consensus and Disunity: The Lloyd George Coalition Government 1918–1922* (Oxford 1979)

Morgan, Kenneth O., ed., *Lloyd George Family Letters, 1885–1936* (Cardiff and London 1973)

Moulton, Harold G. and Pasvolsky, Leo, *Russian Debts and Russian Reconstruction* (New York 1924)

War Debts and World Prosperity (Washington 1932)

Mourin, Maxine, *Les relations franco-soviétiques 1917–1967* (Paris 1967)

Le Vatican et l'URSS (Paris 1965)

Mowat, Charles Loch, *Britain between the Wars 1918–1940* (London 1955)

Néré, Jacques, *The Foreign Policy of France from 1914 to 1945* (London 1975)

Nicolson, Harold, *Curzon: The last phase 1919–1925* (London 1934)

Nish, Ian, *Japanese Foreign Policy 1869–1942* (London 1977)

Ol'shansky, P. M., *Rizhskii mir i razvitie sovetsko-pol'skikh otnoshenii (1921–1924)* (Moscow 1974)

Pascal, Pierre, *Mon état d'âme: mon journal de Russie*, vol. III: *1922–1926* (Lausanne 1982)

Pavlovich, M. N., *RSFSR v kapitalisticheskom okruzhenii*, vyp. 1–2 (Moscow 1922)

Pavlovich, M. N., et al., *Ot Vashingtona do Genui* (Moscow 1922)

Petracchi, Giorgio, *La Russia revoluzionaria nella politica italiana 1917–1925* (Bari 1982)

Pierrefeu, Jean de, *La saison diplomatique: Gênes (avril à mai 1922)* (Paris 1928)

Pizzigallo, Matteo, *Mediterraneo e Russia nella politica italiana (1922–1924)* (Milan 1983)

Pogge von Strandmann, Hartmut, 'Rapallo-strategy in preventive diplomacy: new sources and new interpretations', in Volker R. Berghahn and

Martin Kitchen, eds., *Germany in the Age of Total War* (London 1981), pp. 123–46

Poincaré, Raymond, *Histoire politique: chronique de quinzaine*, vols. 3–4 (Paris 1921–2)

Preobrazhensky, Evgeny, *Itogi Genuezskoi konferentsii i khozyaistvennye perspektivy Evropy* (Moscow 1922)

Radek, Karl, *Vneshnyaya politika Sovietskoi Rossii* (Moscow and Petrograd 1923)

Rakovsky, Christian, *Nakanune Genui* (Moscow 1922)

Rathenau, Walter, *Cannes und Genua* (Berlin 1922)
  Politische Briefe (Dresden 1929)
  Tagebuch 1907–1922 (Düsseldorf 1967)

Ronaldshay, Earl of, *The Life of Lord Curzon*, vol. III (London 1928)

Rosenko, I. A., *Sovetsko-germanskie otnosheniya 1921–22 gg.* (Leningrad 1965)

Russian Liberation Committee, *Genoa and the Ruin of Russia* (London 1922)

Saint-Aulaire, Comte de, *Confessions d'un vieux diplomate* (Paris 1960)

Saurez, Georges, *Briand: sa vie, son oeuvre, avec son journal*, vol. V (Paris 1941)

Schanzer, Carlo, *Sulla società della nazioni: discorsi, studi i noti* (Rome 1925)
  Sulla Conferenza di Genova e sulla politica estera dell'Italia: discorsi, ed. A. Giannini (Rome n.d. [1922])

Seeckt, Hans von, *Aus seinem Leben 1918–1936* (Leipzig 1940)

Seton-Watson, Christopher, *Italy from Liberalism to Fascism 1870–1925* (London 1967)

Sforza, Carlo, *L'Italia dal 1914 al 1944 quale io la vidi*, 2nd ed. (Rome 1944)
  Diplomatic Europe since the Treaty of Versailles (New Haven 1928)

Shishkin, V. A., *Sovetskoe gosudarstvo i strany zapada v 1917–1923 gg.* (Leningrad 1969)
  V. I. Lenin i vneshne-ekonomicheskaya politika sovetskogo gosudarstva (1917–1923 gg.) (Leningrad 1977)

Shtein, B., *Genuezskaya konferentsiya* (Moscow 1922)
  Torgovaya politika i torgovye dogovory Sovetskoi Rossii 1917–1922 gg. (Moscow 1923)

Silverman, Dan P., *Reconstructing Europe after the Great War* (Cambridge, Mass. 1982)

Stevenson, Frances, *Lloyd George: A Diary*, ed. A. J. P. Taylor (London 1971)

Swinton, Viscount, *I Remember* (London 1948)

Sylvester, A. J., *The Real Lloyd George* (London 1947)

Taylor A. J. P., ed., *My Darling Pussy: The Letters of Lloyd George and Frances Stevenson, 1913–1941* (London 1975)

Toynbee, A. J., *Survey of International Affairs 1920–1923* (London 1925)

Trachtenberg, Marc, *Reparation in World Politics: France and European Economic Diplomacy 1916–1923* (New York 1980)

Trotsky, L. D., *Kak vooruzhalas' revolyutsiya*, 3 vols. (Moscow 1923–5)
  Moya zhizn', 2 vols. (Berlin 1930)
  Sochineniya, 12 vols. [all published] (Moscow 1926–7)

[Trotsky, L. D.] *The Trotsky Papers*, ed. J. M. Meijer, 2 vols. (The Hague 1964–71)

Trukhnov, G. M., *Iz istorii sovetsko-germanskikh otnoshenii (1921–1922 gg.)* (Minsk 1974)

Trush, M. I., *Vneshnepoliticheskaya deyatel'nost' V. I. Lenina 1921–1923 den' za dnem* (Moscow 1967)

Uldricks, Teddy J., *Diplomacy and Ideology: The Origins of Soviet Foreign Relations 1917–1930* (Beverly Hills and London 1979)

Val'nitsky, K. M., *Ot Versalya do Genui* (L'vov 1923)

Vneshnyaya torgovlya SSSR za 1918–1940 gg.: statisticheskii obzor (Moscow 1960)

Vorovsky, V.V., *Stat'i i materialy po voprosam vneshnei politiki* (Moscow 1959)

Wandycz, Piotr, *France and her Eastern Allies 1919–1925* (Minneapolis 1962)

Weill-Raynall, Etienne, *Les réparations allemandes et la France*, 3 vols. (Paris 1947)

White, Stephen, *Britain and the Bolshevik Revolution: A Study in the Politics of Diplomacy, 1920–1924* (London 1980)

Zarnitsky, S. V. and Sergeev, A. V., *Chicherin*, 2nd ed. (Moscow 1975)

Zarnitsky, S. V. and Trofimova, L. I., *Sovetskoi strany diplomat* [Krasin] (Moscow 1962)

Zelikman, M., *Ot Vashingtona k Genue* (Moscow 1922).

Index